PLACE-NAMES OF ROSS AND CROMARTY

PLACE-NAMES

OF

ROSS AND CROMARTY

BY

W. J. WATSON

M.A., ABERD. ; B.A., OXON.

RECTOR OF INVERNESS ROYAL ACADEMY

1996

Published by
HIGHLAND HERITAGE BOOKS
Tir nan Oran, 8 Culcairn Road, Evanton IV16 9YT

Printed by
HIGHLAND PRINTERS LTD, INVERNESS

ACKNOWLEDGEMENT

This reprint of Professor Watson's valuable work has been arranged by Highland Heritage Educational Trust in association with Ross and Cromarty District Council from whom financial assistance was generously forthcoming. The submergence of the District Council on 1st April 1996 into the new Highland Council must not obscure the roots of our community.

Since the first reprint in 1976 arranged by Ross and Cromarty Heritage Society demand has continued to register for this benchmark in placename studies. Not only is it a model of scholarship, it is an inspiration to increase our understanding of the placenames in the Ross-shire landscape.

Our place names are an indelible part of our cultural heritage but their history and meaning, which had become suddenly less clear with the retreat of spoken Gaelic from east Ross-shire in this century, have been in large measure preserved for us by the scholarship and labours of W.J. Watson who was brought up at Delny not far from Invergordon and was a native speaker of the Gaelic of Easter Ross.

His classical education at Aberdeen and Oxford was a solid foundation to the later varied studies which he made, so notably in the field of Scottish place-names, as Professor of Celtic at Edinburgh University.

A CHUID DE PHARAS DHA

PREFACE.

THE uncertainty and lack of precision which have characterised so much of the work attempted in connection with the study of our Scottish names of places are due chiefly to defective or imperfectly ascertained data. In Lowland districts, where the sole data for names of Celtic origin consist of modern Anglicised forms and old spellings, this uncertainty is largely inevitable : the old Celtic pronunciation, the quantity of vowels, and the quality of consonants must often be matter of sheer conjecture. But wherever Gaelic is still vernacular, or when, as often, genuine Gaelic forms of names occurring in districts once Celtic but now English are procurable, these difficulties are immensely simplified. It will be found that modern Gaelic pronunciation as handed down by unbroken tradition is in the main intensely conservative, whether the names so transmitted are Pictish, Scandinavian, or purely Gaelic in origin. With the aid of these modern Gaelic forms, either alone or supplemented by old written forms, the investigator, given knowledge and experience, should in

most cases be able to arrive at a high degree of
accuracy in interpretation. The work is raised from
the sphere of conjecture to that of solid scientific
enquiry.

In the present work, dealing with the Place
Names of Ross and Cromarty, the method thus
indicated has been followed throughout. In every
case the genuine native Gaelic forms of names have
been ascertained with absolute accuracy. In
addition, the old spellings found in charters, etc.,
have been given wherever such were available.
The result is that the interpretations offered can be
criticised by Celtic scholars in the light of a full
knowledge of the data. Incidentally a large number
of new and important facts are offered for the con-
sideration of philologists, both in the shape of
obsolete Gaelic words rescued from oblivion, and in
the treatment in Gaelic of Norse and Pictish names.

An attempt has been made in the Introduction
to focus the general results obtained. The opening
historical sections, though necessarily much com-
pressed, will, it is hoped, serve to lend perspective.
The sections which deal with the formation of
Gaelic names and with the Pictish and Norse
elements, should afford some not unnecessary assistance to future investigators. The account given of
the treatment in Gaelic of the Old Norse vowels

and consonants is a pioneer piece of work which will, I hope, be found generally trustworthy, but may at least be amplified by further research. The collection of facts adduced with regard to traces of the old Celtic Church proves the strength of the hold which that Church took in the North, and indicates the wealth of material that awaits collection. As for the Pictish language, its remains in place names are only beginning to be scientifically considered. Everything so far goes to prove its close affinity to Cymric, but we still desiderate a thorough critical examination of the place names of Dalriada on the one hand and of the Central Highlands on the other, respectively the most Gaelic and the most Pictish of Scottish districts where Gaelic is still spoken.

In collecting materials for this work I have personally traversed all parts of the County except Lewis, and therefore the number of those to whom I am indebted runs to hundreds. But I am under special obligation to Mr Kenneth Mackenzie, Shader, Barvas, both for general information on Lewis names and in particular for permission to make use of a valuable paper on that subject contributed by him to the *Highland News*. To that distinguished Celtic authority, Dr A. Macbain of Inverness, I owe much in friendly criticism and suggestions, especially on the philological aspect of the names, and he has kindly read all my proofs. I have to acknowledge most valuable, and indeed indispensable assistance generously rendered by the Rev. Charles M. Robertson, who has freely placed at my disposal his unique knowledge of the Gaelic forms of Scottish names of places. The majority of the Gaelic forms contained in the following pages have been independently verified both by him and myself. Valuable assistance has also been received from Mr Donald Mackenzie, Inland Revenue, Bonar-Bridge ; Mr John Whyte, Inverness ; and from Mr J. Mathieson, H.M. Ordnance Survey, to whose painstaking diligence we shall soon owe a map of Scotland largely purged from those erroneous and misleading forms of names which render the existing O.S. maps useless to philologists.

The complete Alphabetical Index of about 3000 names has been prepared by my colleague, Mr H. F. Robson, with the help of our pupils, and revised by myself.

W. J. WATSON.

INVERNESS, *May, 1904.*

CONTENTS.

INTRODUCTION.

Section I.—Historical.

Section II.—Divisions.

Section III.—The Basis of Interpretation.

Section IV.—The Formation of Gaelic Names.

Section V.—The Pictish Element.

Section VI.—The Norse Element.

CONTENTS.

Section VII.—Church Names.

Section VIII.—General.

INTRODUCTION.

I.—HISTORICAL.

THE County of Ross and Cromarty, including Physical Lewis, the northern and larger part of the Long Features. Island, is the third largest in Scotland. Its mainland part extends from sea to sea, and falls naturally into three divisions, Easter, Wester, and Mid Ross, each of which possesses a character of its own. Much of Easter Ross, between the Dornoch and Cromarty Firths, is distinctly Lowland or even English in type. Its great alluvial plain, *Machair Rois*, the plain of Ross, comprises some of the richest agricultural land in Scotland; much of it stands only a few feet above the sea level, and the skeleton of a " cetaceous animal "[1] found at Fearn proves that it was actually covered by the sea at no very remote period as geological time is reckoned. With it goes the large peninsula known as the Black Isle, between the Firths of Cromarty and Inverness, not level like the *Machair*, but sloping gently to both firths, and nowhere particularly Highland in aspect. Mid-Ross may be said to extend from the western watershed to the uplands of

[1] New Statistical Account.

Alness and Rosskeen.   It is a region of glens, straths, and streams, dominated by the massive bulk of Ben Wyvis, and drains through the Conon and its tributaries Orrin, Meig, Blackwater into the head of the Cromarty Firth.   Wester Ross is the long strip to the west of the watershed, between the latter and the sea, deeply indented by sea lochs and seldom far from sea influence.   The great "hinterland" of Wester and Mid-Ross is wholly mountain and moor, with the exception of the beautiful valleys of the Kincardine Carron and its tributaries, and the Oykell and Kyleside Valley, the latter facing Sutherland.

Ptolemy's Account.   Our earliest information about the inhabitants of Ross comes from the geographer Ptolemy of Alexandria, who lived about 120 A.D., and wrote an account of Britain, in which he locates a number of places and tribes, the position of which can be determined with more or less confidence.   He states that from the Lemannonius Sinus (Loch Fyne) to the estuary of the Varar (Beauly Firth), and on the east side of Drumalban, lay the Caledonii ; westward of them were the Cerones or Creones.   These, then, lay on the southern border of Ross.   In the district corresponding to Ross were the Carnonacae on the west coast, the Decantae in Easter Ross from the Beauly to the neighbourhood of Edderton, and the Smertae, who may have occupied the valleys of the Carron, the Oykell, and the Shin.   Northwards of these lay three tribes, the Caereni and Cornavii in north-west Sutherland and Caithness, and in the east of Sutherland the Lugi. At a later period all The Picts. the tribes to the north of the Roman wall between the Firths of Forth and Clyde were included under the general name of Picts, those north of the Grampians being referred to as Northern Picts, and the others as Southern Picts. The headquarters of the King of the Northern Picts at the time of Columba's visit in 565 were near Inverness ; his authority extended at least as far as the Orkneys, probably to the Shetlands. With regard to the Northern Picts, two questions arise which have to be kept separate, the question of race, and the question of language. On the latter point the place-names should throw some light ; here it is enough to say that most authorities now agree that the Picts spoke a Celtic language not of the Gaelic but of the Welsh or Brittonic type. When this Celtic language was introduced into the North it is hard to say ; certainly it was there in the first century, for Ptolemy's names are Celtic. Good authorities place the coming of the Celts into Britain about 600 B.C., others much earlier. One thing is certain, that when they came they found in possession another people less highly civilised, of a different race, with different manners and customs. And, as Celtic influence would reach the north last, and would long be comparatively weak, it is reasonable to suppose that there these primitive people would survive longest and have most influence on the new-comers. In point of fact, the northern Picts show very distinct traces of non-Celtic

institutions and customs in respect of their family
relations and their mode of succession. It may be
concluded, therefore, that the Picts were a mixed
race, combining a Celtic strain with a strong dash
of non-Celtic and probably non-Aryan blood.   In
very remote places such as Lewis this non-Celtic
element would naturally be strongest, and, indeed,
is probably still recognisable.

The Scots,   In the early centuries of the Christian era Scots
from Ireland began to settle among the Picts of the
West Coast.   The first colony on record was led in
the second century by Cairbre Riada, whence the
name Dàl-Riada or Riada's lot.[1]   In 501 the coming
of the sons of Erc with a strong following marks
the establishment of Dalriada as a Scottish kingdom
roughly co-extensive with the modern Argyle.   The
influence of the Gaelic-speaking Dalriadic Scots
gradually spread northward along the coast and
among the islands.   When it reached the west
coast of Ross we cannot say exactly, but it is
significant that in 673 Malruba, an Irish priest and
noble, founded the monastery of Applecross, and it
is probably safe to assume that at that date Applecross was well within Dalriadic territory.   There
are at least two other indications of the rapid spread
of the Gaels on the west.   When the Norsemen came
in 793, they called the Minch Skotland-fjörðr, the
firth of the land of the Scots ; the province of

---

[1] "Scoti, duce Reuda de Hibernia egressi, amicitia vel ferro sibimet inter
Pictos sedes quas hactenus habent vindicaverunt." The Scots, led by Riada,
left Ireland, and by friendship or force won for themselves among the Picts
those territories which they still possess.—Bede. *Eccl. Hist.*, L. i., c. 1.

Argyle extended from the Clyde to Lochbroom, and
Argyle (Gael. Earra-Ghaidheal, older Airer Goedel),
means the bounds of the Gael or Scots from Ireland.
Not the least difficult of the problems in early
Scottish history is the manner in which the language
of the Gaels supplanted that of the Picts. For the
west coast the answer, as has been seen, is easy : it
was settled by Scots at an early date. In the east
various causes can be seen to have co-operated. In
the first place, Gaelic was the language of the more
highly civilised people, which made it *a priori*
unlikely that it should give way to Pictish.
Another factor, the importance of which can
hardly be over-estimated, was the influence
of the Celtic Church. Again, the advent of
the Norse on the West Coast must have had the
effect of driving the Gaelic-speaking settlers eastward. Lastly, we cannot tell how long Pictish
survived in Easter Ross. It is possible and even
probable that, just as on the West there was a
period when first Gaelic and Pictish, then Gaelic
and Norse, were spoken side by side, so on the East
Coast, Pictish, Gaelic, and Norse were spoken con-
currently. Pictish has, in any case, left very strong
traces in Easter Ross place-names.

The Norsemen began to make plundering expedi- The
tions on the coasts of Britain before the end of the Norsemen.
eighth century. In 793 they sacked Lindisfarne ;
in 798 they plundered part of Man and the Hebrides ;
in 802 they ravaged Iona, and in 806 they slew
sixty-eight of the monastic family there ; during

the same period they made incursions on the Irish
coasts also.   Monasteries, being rich and defenceless,
were special objects of attack, and there can be little
doubt, though record is silent on the subject, that to
them was due the destruction of Malruba's Monastery
of Applecross.

i. In the   By degrees they began to settle both in Ireland
Isles.   and in the Isles.   In 872 Harold Harfagr, King of
Norway, found it necessary to lead an expedition
against the western Vikings, when he subjugated
Orkney, Shetland, and the Sudreys (the Hebrides)
as far south as Man.   But as in Ireland settlement
began in the first quarter of the ninth century, it is
probable that the Hebrides, which lie on the way to
Ireland, were occupied long before King Harold's
expedition.   What is known of the subsequent
history of the Norse settlements in the Western
Isles has been related too often to need repetition.[1]
The Isles were finally ceded by Norway in 1266, in
consequence of the disastrous battle of Largs, having
been more or less under Norse influence for about
470 years.   For much of that time the Norse
language must have been predominant ; the Isles
were not felt to be part of Scotland ; mainland
Gaels referred to them as Innse Gall, the Isles of
the strangers.   And if Norse was spoken in Lewis
in 1266, as it doubtless was, it is not too much to
suppose that it was not wholly extinct at the time
of Bannockburn or even later.   Hence at once the

---

[1] Gregory's *History of the Western Highlands;* Dr A. Macbain in *Trans. of
Inverness Gael. Soc.*, vol. xix.

preponderance of Norse names and their remarkable freshness as preserved in common speech.

The Norse occupation of the western mainland ii. On the probably began later, ended earlier, and, to judge West Coast. from the place-names, was less continuous in extent. On the west of Ross they seem to have selected the parts most fertile and best adapted for grazing. Kintail and Glenshiel show very little Norse influence; it was strong in Gairloch and round the shores of Loch Maree. But in no part of Wester Ross did the old Celtic nomenclature wholly give way; from Loch Duich to Loch Broom not only old Gaelic but even Pictish names are well in evidence.

On the eastern mainland, according to the Sagas, iii. On the Thorstein the Red, together with Sigurd of Orkney, East Coast. conquered and ruled over Caithness and Sutherland, Ross and Moray, and more than half of Scotland.[1] Their exploits here referred to took place about 875, and the net result of them appears to have been that the Norsemen retained possession at least as far south as Dingwall. Over a hundred years later, circ. 980, Sigurd, Earl of Orkney, defeated Finlay, Mormaer of Moray, at Skida Myre in Caithness, and established his power over " dominions in Scotland, Ross and Moray, Sutherland and the Dales." Earl Sigurd fell at Clontarf, 1014. The Norse power on the mainland attained its highest point under his son Thorfinn, of whom the Sagas say that he held "nine Earldoms in Scotland, the whole of

[1] Islands Landnámabók.

the Sudreys, and a large territory in Ireland."[1] He
died in 1064, and after his time the Norse dominions
gradually contracted to Caithness. "Many rikis
which the Earl had subjected fell off, and the
inhabitants sought the protection of those native
chiefs who were territorially born to rule over
them."[2] At the beginning of the twelfth century
Norse may still have been spoken in Easter Ross,
but the power of the native chiefs was reviving, and
by the middle of it we find Malcolm MacHeth in
the position of Earl of Ross. The total duration of
the Norse supremacy in Easter Ross was rather less
than 200 years. The place-names are instructive.
No name of Norse origin appears south of the Beauly
valley. The centre of administration was Dingwall,
Thing-völlr, plain of the Thing, the Norse court of
justice. Some important valleys well inland bear
Norse names, Alladale, Dibidale, Strathrusdale,
Scatwell. The Black Isle shows only two or three;
elsewhere the proportion is about the same for the
area as on the West Coast. To Norse influence perhaps may be due the curious fact that none of the
larger streams that flow into the Cromarty Firth—
Uarie, Averon, Conon—show an Inver or an Aber.
Such Invers as exist belong to small streams, the
largest being the Peffery, which gives Inver-feoran
(Inbhir-pheofharain), the Gaelic name of Dingwall.
In the Dingwall Charters, the estuary of the Conon
appears as Stavek, plainly Norse, probably Staf-vík,

[1] Orkneyinga Saga.   [2] Orkneyinga Saga.

Staff-bay, a name which, it may be suggested, supplanted an old *Aberconon, to be in its turn forgotten.

In Wester Ross the Norsemen met the Gael ; on the eastern side they doubtless met both Gael and Pict.

The twelfth century saw the triumph of Gaelic English over Pictish and Norse ; and probably this period Influence. (circ. 1100-1200) was the only one since the coming of the Gaels, in which one language and only one was spoken throughout the mainland of Ross. Under Pictish rule, Ross was governed from Inverness ; in the time of Norse supremacy its over-lords hailed from Orkney. The twelfth century was a transition stage ; at its close Ross was fast coming into touch with the south of Scotland, and to some extent with the language of the Lowland Scots. That English is of long standing in the north is proved by the place-name Wardlaw, near Beauly, which appears on record in 1210 Wardelaue, the hillock where watch and ward was kept by the retainers of the Norman Lord of the Aird, John Byset. No Norman baron, however, obtained a grant of land in Ross ; English was introduced there through the Royal Castles and the Church. In 1179 William the Lion founded the Castles of Dunskaith in Nigg, and Eddirdover, now Redcastle. In the next century we find the Castles of Cromarty and Dingwall upheld by the Crown and the Castle of Avoch belonging to the De Moravia family. In all of these the garrison was, doubtless, composed chiefly of Lowlanders.   The seat of the Bishopric of Ross was at Rosemarkie ; in 1227 the Chapter of Ross consists wholly, with one exception,[1] of clerics bearing English names.   So with the Bishops of Ross, all except the first, Macbeth.   The other chief centre of ecclesiastical influence in Easter Ross at this period was the Abbey of Fearn, founded circ. 1225, whose Abbots as a rule came from Whithorn in Galloway, and may or may not have known Gaelic ; their names are usually English.   The fame of St Duthac's shrine at Tain was also a factor of some importance in attracting Lowland pilgrims. In 1306 we actually find Walter, son of the Earl of Ross, a scholar at Cambridge.   All this, of course, had little effect on the native Gaelic, but it shows that in the vicinity of Castle, Cathedral, and Abbey, as well as among the upper classes, there must have been some acquaintance with English.   And at the present day we find that it is precisely in these places—Tain, Cromarty, Rosemarkie, Avoch, and, to a less extent, Dingwall—that Gaelic, except for importations, has practically died out.   The Castles of the West Coast, Strome and Ellandonan, were garrisoned not by King's men, but by Gaelic-speaking clansmen of native chiefs, and were oftener held against the King than for him.

---

[1] The exception is Donald, Vicar of Locunethereth (Logie Wester).

II.—Divisions.

The ancient district of Ross,[1] which gives its Ross.
name to the modern county, originally extended from
the Stockford on the river Beauly to Tarbat Ness,
thus comprising Easter and Mid Ross, together with a
slice of Inverness-shire. The name has been explained
as from (1) Ir. and Gael. ros, a promontory; (2)
Ir. ros, a wood; (3) Welsh rhos, a moor; Breton
ros, a knoll, all equally possible phonetically. Ros,
a wood, does not seem to occur elsewhere in Scottish
topography; ros, a promontory, when it occurs, is
used with the article, e.g., an Ros Muileach, the
Ross of Mull, but the article never appears with
the county name; for these and other reasons a
Brythonic or Pictish origin seems most likely. The
meaning of "moor" would have been appropriate in
times antecedent to regular cultivation.

The Pictish kingdom was divided into provinces
—traditionally seven—ruled by petty kings called
Mormaers, who were subject to the head-king.
Whether Ross ever possessed a Mormaer of its own
does not appear; in the records it goes with Moray.

---

[1] Probably the earliest mention of Ross occurs in the Life of St Cadroe,
ascribed to the 11th century. "The Choerisci" (wandering Celts from Asia
Minor, according to the legend), crossed over from Ireland and peopled Iona.
Thereafter they coasted along the sea which adjoins Britain, and, through
the valley of the river Rosis, entered Rossia (per Rosim amnem, Rossiam
invaserunt). The river Rosis, according to Skene, is the Rasay, now called
the Blackwater. The legend may be based on an eastward movement of the
West Coast Gaels.

The first Earl of Ross was Malcolm MacHeth,[1]
circ. 1157, son of Ed, Earl of Moray, and Malcolm,
who succeeded his brother Angus slain in rebellion
in 1130, appears to have received the Earldom of
Ross on his reconciliation to King David I., as part
of his ancestral dominions.

The next Earl of Ross is the Count of Holland,
of whom nothing is recorded.   About 1220 the title
was conferred by Alexander II. on Ferchar Mac-in-
tagart (son of the priest), surnamed O'Beolan, who
appears to be rightly regarded as the then representative of the lay Abbots of Applecross.   The
accession of Ferchar was fraught with important
consequences, local and national.   As lord of the
Church lands of Applecross, he was already
practically chief of the district from Kintail to
Lochbroom, known then as North Argyle; when,
in addition, he became Earl of Ross, he was the
leading man in the north.   This power, loyally
exercised as it was by Ferchar and his descendants,
was largely instrumental in establishing the
authority of the Scottish Crown in the Highlands
at this critical period.   Locally he brought the
easter and the wester divisions together under one
strong hand, thus preparing the way for the modern
county.   Previous Earls were, of course, Earls of
Ross only, i.e., the district east of the central
watershed.

---

[1] Heth, Head, Eth, Ed all represented Gael. Aed, later Aodh, Hugh
(still used as a personal name in Sutherland).   MacHeth in modern Gaelic is
MacAoidh, Mackay.   Skene's *Highlanders of Scotland*, ed. Dr A. Macbain.

The western sea-board from Kintail to Lochbroom Ergadia
was, from the beginning of the Scottish Monarchy, Borealis.
known as North Argyle or Ergadia Borealis, a term
of which the significance has been explained above.
In 1292 William, Earl of Ross, grandson of Ferchar,
got his lands of " Skey, Lodoux, and North Argyle "
erected into the Sheriffdom of Skye by King John
Balliol. The West Coast continues to appear under
the name of North Argyll till the early part of the
fifteenth century.

The Sheriffdom of Cromarty, which appears to Cromarty.
have been originally connected with the Royal
Castle there, appears on record in 1266, when
William de Monte Alto was "vicecomes de Crumbauchtyn." It was of very small extent, apparently
not exceeding the bounds of the modern parish of
Cromarty, yet under its hereditary Sheriffs always
continued separate, and when in 1661 the Sheriffdom
of Ross was definitely disjoined from that of Inverness, Cromarty is specifically excepted. The first
Earl of Cromarty was Sir George Mackenzie of
Tarbat, grandson of the Tutor of Kintail (an
Taoitear Tàileach), who was made Earl in 1703,
and obtained the privilege of having his various
estates, large and small, throughout Ross erected
into the new County of Cromarty, an arrangement
extremely inconvenient, and now surviving only in
the county name Ross and Cromarty.

The Black Isle, Gael. an t-Eilean Dubh, a mis- The
nomer which can be easily paralleled, is the name of Black Isle.
the peninsula between the firths of Cromarty and Ardmeanach

Inverness. Peninsulas are frequently miscalled "islands ;" the classical instance is Peloponnesus, Pelops' Isle. The epithet " black " is sensibly explained by the writers of the Old Stat. Acc., from the fact that even in their time four-fifths of it was black moor, uncultivated. Its old official name is Ardmanache or Ardmeanach, meaning the " mid height," midway, that is to say, between the firths, surviving in the farm of Ardmeanach, near Fortrose. A still older name is Eddirdail, now obsolete, meaning apparently Eadar-da-dhail, Between two dales. The Lordship of Ardmanach went with the fortalice of Redcastle, and included all the Black Isle, except the Sheriffdom of Cromarty.

Ferindonald The district from the Averon or Alness River to the burn of Allt na Làthaid, to the east of Dingwall, was called of old Ferindonald, G. Fearainn Dòmhnuill, Donald's land, a name still in use. It comprises the parishes of Alness and Kiltearn, and is the land of the Clan Munro. The Donald in question is the traditional founder of the house of Fowlis, and is supposed to have received this grant of land from Malcolm II. (1005-1034) for services rendered against Danish invaders. Though this account cannot be verified—the origin of the Munros is one of the problems of Clan history—it may be substantially correct. The name Ferindonald is parallel to Dalriada and Ferintosh.

Ferintosh. The origin of the division of Ferintosh is explained at p. 114. It is expressly excluded from Ross in the

Act of Parliament of 1661, and till recent times continued to form part of the county of Nairn.

The "five quarters" of Ross appear in 1479 in connection with the confiscated estates of John, last Earl of Ross. They are (1) Delney, extending from Tarbat Ness to the Alness River; (2) Balkeny or Balcony, co-extensive with the bounds of Ferindonald as given above; (3) Kynnardy or Kinnairdie, including the valley of the Peffery, and the parts to the south and west of it, viz., Moy, Achilty, Scatwell Meikle, Brahan, Dunglust, Ussie; (4) Kynnellane, modern Kinnellan, which included "Coul, Rogy, cum le Ess, Litill Scathole cum le Ess, Foreste de Rannach, Meyn in Straquhonane, the two Eskatellis, Innermany, Innerquhonray, Kinlochbenquherane;" (5) Fyrnewer (a name now obsolete), from Fairburn round by the Beauly Firth to Kessock : " the Ferburnys, Auchansawle, Arcoyn, Balbrade, Urra, Kynculadrum, le Orde, Belblare, Balnagoun, Kynkell, Logyenreith, and the two Kessokis." Though this is the first appearance of the quarters as a whole, there appear on record the quarter of Petkenney in 1281 and the "maresium of Fernewyr" in 1350, from which it is a fair inference that the other "quarters" also existed long prior to 1479. They were evidently divisions of the Earldom of Ross, each under a "maor," or land steward, but they may have represented still older tribal divisions, or, possibly, the Norse organisation.

The Five
"Quarters."

Parishes.　The division into parishes must have been roughly contemporary with the organisation of the Bishopric of Ross, circ. 1128.　The Bishopric was co-extensive with the Earldom, and therefore it was only on the accession of Ferchar Mac-in-tagart, circ. 1220, that it came to include the churches of North Argyle. But little change seems to have taken place in the parochial organisation, the chief being the disjunction of Fearn from Tarbat in 1628, the union of Kiltearn and Lemlair, of Kinnettes and Fodderty, and of Urray and Gilchrist (date uncertain); of Kirkmichael and Cullicudden in 1662, of Urquhart and Logie Wester circ. 1669, and of Kilmuir Wester and Suddy in 1756, now Knockbain.　Glenshiel is a new parish carved out of Kintail.　Before the arrangement of 1661, the parish of Kilmorack belonged territorially to Ross, as it still does ecclesiastically.　In dealing with parish names, it is important to bear in mind that the name of a parish is regularly taken either from the old parish church, e.g. Kilmuir, or from the spot where the old church stood, e.g. Logie.

Hebrides.　The name Hebrides has arisen from a misreading of Pliny's Haebudes, which, he says were thirty in number.　Ptolemy gives only five Aebūdae.　The word must be Pictish, or pre-Pictish ; its meaning is quite obscure, but it has been suggested with some probability that its modern representative is Bute, Gael. Bód.　During the Norse occupation they were called by the Gaels Innse-Gall, by the Norse themselves Sudreys, the south isles.

III.—The Basis of Interpretation.

The study of names of places involves two pro-
cesses, collection of facts and interpretation, and if
the interpretation is to be sound, the facts on which
it is based must be accurate and adequate. It is
therefore proper at the outset to consider the nature
of the facts at our disposal in dealing with the
names encountered in Ross and Cromarty, names
which fall, in respect of language, into four
divisions — Pictish, Gaelic, Norse, and English.
These facts or data are, in the main, of three
kinds—

(1) The names as they are now pronounced.
(2) Old written forms.
(3) Physical characteristics of the places denoted by the
names.

(1) At the present day both Gaelic and English Modern
are spoken over the whole of the county, with this Pronuncia-
qualification, that in the eastern part English is tions.
predominant, while Gaelic still prevails on the West
Coast and in Lewis. The result is that to some
extent over the whole, but especially in Easter Ross,
we have a sort of double nomenclature; on the one
hand the names as they are pronounced by the
Gaelic-speaking natives, on the other the Anglified
forms used by English speakers, and by Gaelic
natives, too, when speaking English. These latter
are the "official" forms which appear in the
Valuation Roll, the Post-Office Directory, and on

the maps, and are often of considerable antiquity. The form Raddery, for instance, must have come into vogue at a period when the *d* of the modern G. *Radharaidh* was still audible as a consonant. Culbokie dates from a time when the *o* sound had not yet become *a*, as it has in modern G. *Cuil-bhàicidh*. Strathpeffer shows in an unaspirated form the *f* of modern G. *Srath-pheofhair*. Cromarty and Drumderfit show old teminations lost in the modern G. forms *Cromba'* and *Druima-diar*. Yet the practical value of modern English forms by themselves is small; at their best they fail to indicate the quantity or the quality of vowels, and often they have undergone changes that quite disguise the original. Modern Gaelic forms of Gaelic names which have been handed down by unbroken tradition have undergone only such changes as occur regularly within the language; they are, in fact, Gaelic words, conforming to the rules of Gaelic phonetics, and form as good a starting point for the philologist as any other Gaelic words. There remains the question of the value of Gaelic forms of names originally Pictish or Norse. In the case of Norse names, the answer is easy. Gaelic has been, on the whole, wonderfully consistent in its treatment of the old Norse vowels and consonants, and it possesses the great advantage of clearly indicating the quantity of the vowel in the first syllable of Norse names, which is usually the important part. In one small class of such names, indeed, it fails us badly, but it is safe to say that very slight authority can be attached to any investigation of Norse names that fails to take careful account of the modern Gaelic forms. These forms are imitations, but they are only one degree removed from the original; the English forms are imitations of an imitation. How Pictish names have fared in Gaelic mouths is the more difficult to determine, because practically no specimens of that language have come down to us. It may, however, be remarked that there is no reason to suppose that they were treated differently from the Norse names; Gaelic may be expected to preserve the vowel quantity of accented syllables, and to be tolerably consistent in its phonetics. In both cases there was a bilingual period, which gave the Gaels ample time to become familiar with the names which they adopted from Pict and Norseman. The changes undergone subsequently have, of course, been in accordance with those of Gaelic. Examples of Pictish and Norse names as they appear in the modern forms will appear later in treating of these elements; in the meantime some may be given to illustrate the comparative value of the modern Gaelic forms of Gaelic words as compared with their English equivalents—

Pitnellie(s)	Bail' an ianlaith.
Tenafield	Tigh na fidhle.
Kindeace	Cinn-déis.
Ardroil	Eadar dha fhaodhail.
Bogbain	am Bac Bàn.
Locheye	Loch na h-Uidhe.
Kilcoy	Cuil-challaidh.

Pookandraw	Bog an t-srath.
Fowlis	Fólais.
Kinrive	Ceanna-ruigh.
Fain	na Fèithean.
Dochcarty	Do'ach Gartaidh.

Other examples will be found *passim*.

Old Written Forms.

(2) The forms of names preserved in ancient documents have been utilised with much success by Dr Joyce in dealing with Irish names of places. In Irish writings, names have been transmitted with great care from very ancient times by scribes who were masters of the language, and from them the original forms can often be ascertained with immediate certainty. For Scotland, unfortunately, the case is different. The great bulk of our written forms date only from the period not earlier than the twelfth century, when charters came in under the sons of Margaret. Their authority, moreover, is largely discounted by the fact that they were written by scribes who knew no Gaelic, and consequently spelled at random. In the case of Highland names, it is obvious that charter forms must have been more or less phonetic attempts at reproducing Gaelic pronunciations, and their value is, therefore, greatest when they can be controlled and inter-preted by the modern Gaelic. This applies equally to all names not of English origin, whether they are Pictish, Norse, or Gaelic. Thus controlled, the charter forms are often helpful and suggestive ; as independent authorities, they are unreliable. A few examples are given in illustration ; others in abundance will be found elsewhere—

Pitnellies	Petnely 1512	Bail' an ianlaith.
Pitkerrie	Pitkeri 1529	Baile-chéiridh.
Strath of Pitcalnie	Culderare 1611	Cuilt-cararaidh.
Rhives	le Royis 1479	na Ruigheannan.
	Ruvis 1487	
Delny	Dalgeny 1356	Deilguidh.
Alness	Alenes 1227	Alanais.
Lemlair	Lemnelar 1227	Luim na' Làr.
Learnie	Larny 1576	Leatharnaidh.
Achterflow	Ochtercloy 1456	Uachdar-chlò.
	Achtirflo 1560	
Kilcoy	Culcolly 1294	Cuil-challaidh.
	Culcowy 1479	
Sanachan	Tannachtan 1548	Samhnachan.
	Saïnachan 1583	

Perhaps the best example in Ross of a really helpful old spelling, which must take precedence of the modern Gaelic, is Inverasdale, Inveraspidill 1566, &c. ; G. Inbhir-àsdal. The oldest record forms for Ross names belong to the first half of the 13th century, and come from the Register of Moray. Written forms antecedent to that date are very few. Ptolemy, the Alexandrian geographer, mentions two names of places which seem to be rightly located in Ross, Volsas Sinus, for which cf. Lochalsh, and High Bank, identified with Norse Ekkials-bakki, modern Oykell.[1] In addition, he mentions three tribal names. already referred to. The Carnonacae, somewhere on the West Coast, are, doubtless, the men of the Cairns, or of the Rough Bounds, and we may compare the modern Carranaich, the Lochcarron men. In Easter Ross were located the Decantae, but of their name no trace appears subsequently. So, too,

[1] This identification is due to the Rev. Charles M. Robertson.

with the Smertae, who may have dwelt from Kincardine northwards in the valleys of the Carron, Oykell, and Shin.   In the interval of over a thousand years between Ptolemy and the record forms, we find only the old forms of Applecross, Lewis, and Ross itself.

Physical Character-istics.
(3) As the names of places are usually descriptive, it is often useful, sometimes necessary, to see the place itself.   It is only by inspection and comparison that one learns, for instance, to differentiate between the numerous words for hill, or to distinguish between a strath, a glen, and a corry. Inspection is specially useful when names are applied in a metaphorical way, from likeness to some object, *e.g.*, *Meall an Tuirc*, Boar-hill, from its striking resemblance, as viewed from a certain point, to a boar.   *Na Rathanan*, the pulleys, require to be seen to be appreciated.   Places involving obsolete names such as *eirbhe*, *faithir*, *seòlaid*, *eileag*, have to be studied for confirmation of the meaning proposed.   This applies specially to Pictish names such as Allan, Alness, Contin, Aradie, Orrin.   But it is well to bear in mind that no amount of looking at a place can alter the phonetics of the name, and that inspirations derived from inspection must be received with caution.

In the discussions that follow, I have availed myself wherever it has been possible of the three-fold data above indicated.   In particular, the modern Gaelic forms, which, in the absence of reliable old spellings, must be regarded as by far

the most reliable basis of interpretation, have been
ascertained with accuracy from reliable native
sources. In addition, advantage has been taken
largely of the analogy of names occurring elsewhere Analogy.
which are wholly or partly the same as the names
under discussion, or which resemble them in assign-
able respects. This is, of course, merely the method
of comparative philology applied to place-names.
The field from which possible analogies may be
drawn is a wide one ; in practice it will be found
that for Gaelic names one has to compare names
occurring in Scotland and Ireland ; the pre-Gaelic
or Pictish element involves, in addition, an acquaintance with Welsh, Cornish, Old British, and Gaulish
names ; while for names of Norse origin the best
auxiliaries are the names that occur in the Sagas,
and especially the Landnáma-bók.

IV.—THE FORMATION OF GAELIC NAMES.

Gaelic place-names may be divided into four
classes according as they are—(1) simple or uncompounded words without extension ; (2) simple words
with extension ; (3) compounds ; (4) phrases.

(1) Simple words without extension, *e.g.*, crasg,
a crossing ; magh, a plain (Moy) ; sròn, a nose or
point (Strone). The names belonging to this class
are few, and present no difficulty.

(2) Simple words with extension or extensions.
This class is so important as to demand somewhat
extended treatment.

The following is a list of the extensions or terminations added on to primary Gaelic words in the names of Ross : -*ach*, -*adh*, -*ag*, -*an*, -*ar*, -*dan*, -*l*, -*lach*, -*lean*, -*t*(*d*) or -*id*.

Combinations of two of the above are ; -*ach* + *an*, -*ach* + *ar*, -*ag* + *an*, -*an* + *ach*, -*ar* + *ach*, -*ar* + *adh*, -*ar* + *an*.

Combinations of three are : -*ar* + *an* + *ach*, -*ach* + *ar* + *an*, -*an* + *ach* + *an*.

-*ach* (Gaulish -*ācus*, abounding in ; -*ācum*, place of) ; in the locative case it appears as -*aich* ; the most common of Gaelic terminations.

(*a*) With nouns : Crann-aich, place of trees ; Giuths-ach, place of fir ; Càrn-ach, place of stones or cairns ; Capl-aich, place of horses ; Mias-ach, place of platters ; Soc-ach, place of the snout ; Eilean-ach, place of islands ; Glaodh-aich, place of mire ; Av-och, place on the stream ; Sleagh-ach, ? spear-place ; Ceap-ach, tillage place.

(*b*) With adjectives, less common : Breac-ach, dappled place ; Ard-och, high place ; Dian-aich, steep place ; Liath-ach, grey place ; Leithe-ach, half place.

In old Gaelic, as is still the case in Irish, the dative or locative, and also the genitive case of nouns ending in -*ach* was formed in -*aigh* (pronounced nearly -*ie*), and this old formation survives in a considerable number of names. On the west coast we have Logie (twice), G. an Lagaidh ; Dornie (thrice), G. an Dòirnidh (cf. Dornoch, an accusative), both used with the article as nouns feminine, after the model of nouns in -ach; e.g., Dùn na Lagaidh, the fort of Logie; Ceannaiche na Dòirnidh, the merchant of Dornie, as compared with Ian Dubh na Càrnaich, &c. The other west coast instances are not found with the article, viz., Duchary (as against an Dubhch'roch in Lochbroom, for Dubh-chàtharach); Tolly (twice); Arriecheirie, G. Airigh-chéiridh; Ach-a-bhànaidh; Coire-bhànaidh. In Easter Ross names with this ending are more common, and they never have the article. The following occur here : Logie, Tolly (twice), Pitkerrie (G. Baile-chéiridh; cf. Airigh-chéiridh above); Delny; Muie-blairie (cf. Blairich in Sutherland; a locative); Kinn-airdie (cf. Ardoch); Drynie (cf. an Draighneach); Learnie (cf. Lernock in Stirlingshire); Comrie; Garty; Dounie; Tarvie; Càrn Sgolbaidh; Cambuscurrie (cf. Cambuschurrich on Lochtay-side), Raddery (cf. na Radharaichean in Perthshire); Cartomie (cf. Tomich); Culcraggie; Culbokie; Culvokie; Duchary; Balaldie; Cuil-challaidh (Kilcoy); Bealach Collaidh; Creag Iucharaidh; Balcony.

The above seem to be all tolerably certain cases of survival. In one or two instances the usage varies as between Gaelic and English : Pitglassie is in G. Bad a' ghlasaich; Glen Docharty is G. Gleann Dochartaich. Here the Gaelic forms may be due to a process of levelling up to the modern -aich formation.

In some other cases, especially in Easter Ross, this ending seems to have been introduced by analogy. It is difficult to account for otherwise in Pit-hoggarty, Fluchlady, Munlochy. Analogy may also account for Rhynie and Gany (now in plural Geanies), where the Gaelic is Ràthan and Gàan or Gàthan.

-*aidh*, diminutive : Indistinguishable in sound from the above is the diminutive ending -*aidh* found chiefly on the West Coast.[1] In Easter Ross there are Strathy in Rosskeen, Creagaidh-thòm in Knockbain, and perhaps Aldie near Tain. On the west we have Lochaidh, a small loch, thrice at least ; Badaidh, a little clump, is common ; Camasaidh, a little bay ; Coiridh, a little corry ; Strathy, a little strath. In the spoken language perhaps the best instance is *rudaidh beag*, " a wee bittie ;" in Sutherland one hears *beanaidh*, wifie ; and I have heard *eileanaidh beag*, a little islet. This is an ending which does not seem to occur in Irish names of places, and may be compared with the common Scots diminutive seen in " wifie," " lassie," " Jamie," &c.

-*adh* : this termination seems to occur only in conjunction with -*ar*, as -*aradh*.

-*ag* (Irish -*óc*), now the diminutive termination for nouns feminine, but in the old language added to nouns masculine also.

(*a*) With nouns : Breab-aig, a little start ; Glag-aig, a little noisy one ; Fearn-aig, the little place of alder.

(*b*) With adjectives : Leisg-eig, the little lazy one, a well ; Dubh-ag, the little black one, a

---

[1] It is also common in Sutherland.

common streamlet name ; Cas-aig, the little steep one, a rock.

-an (Ir. *-án* ; Proto-Celtic *-agnos*) now the diminutive ending for nouns masculine.

(*a*) With nouns : Creag-an, little rock ; Torran, little hillock ; Poll-an, little pool or hollow ; Loch-an, a little loch.

(*b*) With adjectives : Arc-an, the little black place ; Riabhach-an, the little brindled place ; Garbh-an, the little rough place.

(*c*) It is common in a collective sense : Còinneach-an, place of moss ; Dobhr-an, place of water ; Clach-an, place of stones (stone houses) ; Ràthan (Rhynie), place of raths, or, of the rath ; Poll a' Mhuc-ainn, pool, or hollow, of the place of swine ; Druineach-an, place of ? Druids.

-ar (cf. Gaulish *-aros*), rarely used alone. Croch-ar, place of the gallows ; Salach-ar, place of willows.

-dan, the diminutive or collective termination which Dr Joyce finds in Sailcheadain, &c., is probably seen in Ardoch-dainn ; possibly in Crumbauchtyn, the old form of Cromarty.

-l -ll (*-lo-*), probably in Srath-Chromb-ail, Poll-móral.

-lach (Gaul. Catu-slogi, war-folk ; G. sluagh) ; a noun, sunk to a termination.

(*a*) With nouns : Meagh-laich (mang-lach), place of fawns ; Muc-lach, place of pigs.

(*b*) With adjectives : Breac-lach, spotted place ; Garbh-lach, rough place ; Cuillich (cuing-laich), narrow place ; Fuara-lach, cold place.

-lean : Reidh-lean, a little plain ; Céis-lein, a little
sow (hill name). Very rare.

t, *d* (*-id*), found in Ireland by Dr Joyce, and not
uncommon with us. Seòl-aid, place of (careful)
sailing, or sailing mark ; Allt na Làth-aid, burn
of the miry place ; Ràth-t in Ratagan, from ràth,
a round fort ; Meith-eid, Meddat ; Blaad. In
Ireland this ending is specially common in stream
names : Duinn-id, the brown stream, is the only
example in Ross.

-ach + an : a combination in which *-an* usually seems
to have a collective force. Giùs-achan, place of
fir ; Duchan, for Dubh-ach-an, black place ;
Doire-achan, place of groves ; Càis-eachan, place
of cheese ; Achlorachan ; Fiacl-achan, place of
teeth. Na Bothachan (Boath) and na Peit'chan
are plural forms, though -an has in both the open
sound.

-ach + ar : Poll-ach-ar, place of pools, or hollows.

-ag + an : in form a double diminutive, seen in Irish
also. Coire Mhàil-eagan (twice), Ràt-agan.

-an + ach : a well-attested but rather uncommon
combination. Ràth-anaich, place of raths ; Cip-
eanoch, place of blocks ; Frianach for Friamh-
anach, place of roots ; cf. Bàid-eanach (Badenoch),
drowned place.

-ar + ach : with adjective ; Ruadh-ar-ach (Ruaroch),
the red place.

-ar + adh : Bog-aradh, soft place ; Fliuch-araidh,
wet place ; possibly Garbh-araidh, rough place ;
Loch a' Mhàgraidh, Loch of the place of pawing
(or, of toads).

The Gaelic pronunciation renders the first of these examples certain. The others, so far as sound goes, might come from a nominative in -*ach*, with the old genitive formation in -*aigh*.

-*ar+an* : Dos-muc-ar-an, clump of the place of swine ; Garbh-ar-an, rough place.

-*ar+an+ach* : Muc-ar-n-aich (Muckernich), place of pigs ; common ; Beith-ear-n-aich, place of birch : Ceap-ar-n-aich, place of blocks.

-*ach+ar+an* : Loch Beann-ach-ar-an ;

-*n-ach-an* : Samh-n-ach-an.

isidh, seen in Camaisidh, Caoilisidh, Lianisidh, Cruaidhsidh ; a difficult termination, possibly Pictish. It does not seem to occur in Ireland.

(3) Compounds :—

(*a*) Noun with noun ; an uncommon formation. Plucaird, lump promontory ; Càrnasgeir, Cairn-skerry ; Eigintol, difficulty hole ; Mor'oich, sea plain, are the only examples met in Ross.

(*b*) Adjective with noun : a much more common formation. Fionn-alltan, white burns ; Dùgaraidh, black den ; Cam-allt, bent burn ; Gearr-choille, short wood ; Crom-loch, bent loch ; Du-chary, black rough ground ; Dù-loch, black-loch ; Seann-bhaile, Oldtown, and others.

(*c*) Preposition with noun : Edderton, between duns : Eddracharran (New Kelso), between two Carrons ; Coneas, combined falls ; Contullich, combined hillocks ; Conchra, combined weirs ; Conachreig, combination of rocks ; Araird, fore-promontory ; Ach-eadarsain ; Urray for air-ràth or air-àth.

(4) Phrases, of which the component parts stand in grammatical relation :—

(a) Without the article ; these approximate to compounds, but have the principal accent on the second syllable. Beinn-damh, Stag-hill; Suil-bà, Cows' eye (a well) ; Acharn, field of the cairns, and others.

(b) With the article : Càrn a' Bhreabadair, the weaver's cairn ; Tobar a' Chlaidheimh dhuibh, well of the black sword ; Sgùrr nan Conbhairean, peak of the dog-men. This is a class too common and well known to need further illustration. There is, however, a variety, specially common on the West Coast, which deserves special notice, where, contrary to modern usage, the article is prefixed : an Lòn-roid, the meadow of bog-myrtle ; am Blàr-borraich, the moor of rough grass ; an t-Allt-giuthais, the fir-burn ; an Camas-raintich, the bracken bay. The modern Gaelic formation would be Lòn na roid, &c.; in the old formation Lòn-roid is treated as one word.

Periods represented. The different methods of formation indicated above may be taken roughly to represent different stages or periods. The second class of names, comprising those formed by extensions from a simple root, must have been given at a period when the language still retained its power of using those extensions and combinations of extensions to form fresh names, when, in other words, these were still living and active. When precisely or even approximately they ceased to be such is hard to say, but it

is significant that the Gaelic names of Lewis and of
Skye are almost wholly of the fourth class, phrase
names. Compounds like Ben Damh, Poll-cas-
gaibhre, Suil-bà, and names involving prefixed
adjectives, nouns, or prepositions, are also of an
antique cast. Phrase names are not necessarily
modern, for they are well in evidence in the Book of
Deer (circ. 1085-1150), but as a rule they belong to
the most recent stratum.

The formation of Gaelic names is closely connected with questions of accent, the position of
general and qualifying words, and the usage of the
article.

In modern Gaelic the adjective regularly follows
the noun, except in the case of the adjectives deagh,
good ; droch, bad ; sàr, excellent ; seann, old, which
always precede. The old language was freer in this *Prefixed*
respect, and in the place-names adjectives are prefixed *Adjectives*
which modern usage would place after their nouns. *and Accent.*
The number of such is small, and they are all adjectives of one syllable relating to colour or some
other physical feature. Among the adjectives thus
occasionally prefixed in the names of Ross are the
following :—dubh, black ; ? lòch, black ; fionn, white ;
ruadh, red ; liath, gray ; glas, green ; gorm, blue ;
gearr, short ; garbh, rough ; crom, bent ; cam,
crooked ; meirbh, slender ; geur, sharp ; cruinn,
round ; saobh, false (in saothair) ; mór, big.

In all such cases the principal accent falls on the
adjective, with the result that the noun following it
tends to be pronounced indistinctly, *e.g.*, Fuar-tholl

becomes Fuarthol ; Garbh-allt becomes Garbhalt. The effect is most apparent when the noun is of more than one syllable, in which case the first syllable of it is apt to be " jumped," *e.g.*, Dùgraidh for Dubh-garaidh ; or slurred, *e.g.*, Glaic nan Seann-innsean is pronounced Glaic na' Seannisean ; so also Bog na Seannan is probably for Bog nan Seann-àthan ; Seann-tulaich becomes Seannt'laich.

The adjective dubh, when placed first, is some-times lengthened to dù by the stress of the accent, as in Dùloch, Dùg(a)raidh.

Prefixed Nouns and Accent. Sometimes, though rarely, the prefixed part is a noun used as an adjective (see above 3 (*a*)), in which case the results are exactly the same in respect of accent and effect on the word following. A special instance of this formation is the very small class of names represented by Maoil Cheanndearg, a' Chlach Cheannli' for ceann-dearg and ceann-liath respectively, meaning " head-red " and " head-gray," or " red, gray in respect of the head." This was a favourite type of combination in Irish, and is seen in Gaelic in caisionn for cas-fhionn, foot-white, speckled; earrgheal, tail-white, etc., and in the common terrier name Busdubh, muzzle-black.

Prepositions and Accent. In compounds of which the first part is a pre-position the principal accent falls on the preposition, with consequent indistinctness or slurring of the second part. Thus Con-tulaich becomes Cunnt'laich, Con-chrà is Conachra; Far-braoin becomes Fara-braoin. When the preposition eadar, between, is compounded with a dissyllabic noun, there are two

principal accents, one on preposition, one on noun,
and eadar itself becomes ead'r, *e.g.*, Eadar-dha-
Charrann becomes Ead'ra-charrann ; Eadar-da-
chaolas becomes Ead'ra-chaolas. But if the second
part is a monosyllable the accent follows the usual
rule, *e.g.*, Ettridge in Badenoch, Gael. Eadrais for
Eadar-da-eas, between two falls ; cf. Edderton.

In phrase names the principal accent falls on the
qualifying part, whether adjective or noun, which
regularly comes after the generic part. In consequence, the first part sometimes suffers, while the
second part is preserved entire. Thus Achadh, a
field, appears as achd in Achd-a-chàrn, Achtercairn,
and many other names ; ach in Ach-na-seileach,
Achnashellach ; acha in Acha-mór, Achmore ; while
it retains its full form in Achadh-ghiùrain. Perhaps
the best example is afforded by the treatment of
neimhidh, church-land. Dalnavie is in Gaelic
Dal-neimhidh ; so also Cnoc-navie and Inch-navie ;
here the strong accent has preserved the second part
in full. But when neimhidh comes first, as the
generic part, it sinks to neo' as in Neo' na Cill,
Nonakiln ; an Neo-mhór, Newmore. This is,
fortunately, an extreme case.

Accent in Phrase-names

In uncompounded names the accent is always on
the first syllable, as in Deilgnidh, Delny ; a'
Mhucarnaich, Muckernich.

Accent in Simple Names.

The usage of the article is noteworthy. As a
rule it is used with Gaelic nouns wherever the
grammatical structure admits, and the presence of
the article is a sure sign that the word to which it

The Article.

is prefixed either is Gaelic or has been borrowed into Gaelic, and become naturalised as a Gaelic word.[1] In English we speak of Torran, Tullich, Boath ; in Gaelic these places are always an Torran, an Tulaich, na Bothachan.

The absence of the article, however, does not necessarily prove a name to be non-Gaelic, though it does raise that presumption. Pictish names never have the article ; Norse names very seldom, and then only in Lewis, never on the mainland. But we have already noted above an important class of names, chiefly found in Easter Ross, which almost consistently reject it, though they may be regarded as Gaelic. The exact explanation of this curious phenomenon is difficult ; these names were apparently regarded as in some way unfamiliar or foreign. Perhaps it was because of their retaining the old locative form, though this seems hardly an adequate reason. Another class seldom found with the article consists of names in -*achan*, e.g. Giusachan. The only exception met in Ross is *am Fiaclachan*. Apart from these the principal case of an apparently genuine Gaelic name without the article is Suddy, G. Suidhe, seat, see.

---

[1] This perhaps requires some qualification in view of the usage of the article with names of countries. Here it is sometimes capricious. Ireland is Eirin ; Scotland, Alba ; in Ireland is "Ann an Eirinn ;" in Scotland, "Ann an Alba ;" yet the article appears with the genitive ; "Cóig cóigimh na h-Eirinn ;" "Righreau na h-Alba ;" yet Braghad Albainn, Breadalbane. Rome, Italy, Spain, Germany, Holland, Greece, Egypt, Europe, Asia have the article in Gaelic—an Ròimh, an Eadailt, &c. But Scandinavia is Lochlann.

Finally in this connexion we may note that Case. place-names seldom (if ever) appear in the nominative case. They are usually in the dative or locative, the reason being that this was the case in most common use after a preposition; there was seldom occasion to use the nominative, for a place-name rarely forms the subject of a sentence. Thus we get Tullich, Cill-duinn (Kildun), Cinn-déis, where Cill-duinn,[1] is dative of Ceall-dhonn, Cinn of Ceann, and so on. Not unfrequently a name appears in the accusative, as would arise in cases where the custom was to speak of " *to* such a place."[2] Thus we have Tulloch, Dornoch, Ardoch, a' Chipeanoch, Ceann-a-ruigh (Kinrive), and others, all accusative.

V.—THE PICTISH ELEMENT.

The Picts of Alba[3] are sometimes called by the Terms used Irish writers Cruithnig and Cruithne, genitive pl. to denote Cruithnech, dative Cruithniu, and their land "Pict." appears as Cruithen-tuaith. From this form probably come such names of places as an Càrnan Cruithneachd in Kintail, Airigh nan Cruithneachd in Applecross and near Scourie (Sutherland), and Cruithneachan in Lochaber.

More often they are called in the Irish Chronicles Picti, Pictores, Pictones, rendered into Irish by Piccardai or Picardaig, genitive pl. Piccardach, dative Picardachaib. Their country is Pictavia. In Latin also they are Picti. There were Pictones,

---

[1] Cf. An Candidam Casam, the old Latin form of Whithorn.

[2] Cf. Stamboul for εἰς τὴν πόλιν.

[3] The Picts of Erin (immigrants thither) are always *Cruithne.*

later Pictavi, in Aquitanian Gaul, whose capital was Pictava.

The old Norse word for a Pict is Péttr, and the Norsemen called the channel between Caithness and Orkney (in G. an Caol Arcach) Péttlands-fjörðr, now corrupted into Pentland Firth. In Shetland there still survive names such as Pettawater, Pettidale, Pettasmog, Pettigarthsfell.[1]

In a charter of Alexander II. granted to the Monastery of Kinloss in 1221 appears the phrase " ad Rune Pictorum," glossed " Rune Pictorum, the carne of the Pethis or the Pechts feildis" (rune = G. raon). This gloss shows the old Scottish form of the name.

Modern philologists derive *Cruithne* from the root seen in G. cruth, a shape, "the pictured, tattoed men." The Welsh equivalent of *cruth* is *pryd*, and as the Welsh name for Britain and for Pict is Prydain,[2] this makes it probable that the name Britain is derived from the Brittonic form of Cruithne, and means the land of the Picts.[3] The name Pict itself, in view of the Gaulish Pictones or Pictavi, cannot be connected with the Latin *pictus*, painted. It was evidently the name by which the northern Picts were known to the Norsemen, and by which they doubtless called themselves. The initial p indicates Cymric affinities, and the word has been equated with Ir. *cicht*, engraver, carver, thus again leading to the notion of tattooing.

---

[1] J. Jakobsen *Dialect and Place-names of Shetland.*

[2] The best and oldest forms of Britain show *p*, Gr. Πρεττανοί, Πρεττανική ; our form is from the Latin Britannia.

[3] See further A. Macbain's *Etym. Gael. Dict.*, p. 353.

Linguistic evidence goes to show that the Pictish P and Q
language was Celtic, and belonged to the Cymric Celts.
branch represented now by Welsh and Breton, and
until recent times by Cornish. One outstanding
difference between the Brittonic and Gadelic
branches of Celtic is their treatment of the
primitive Indo-Germanic *qu* sound. In Gaelic and
Irish this primitive *qu* invariably becomes *c* hard ;
in Welsh, Breton, and Cornish it is represented by
p. Thus a primitive maquo-s, son, becomes Gael.
mac, Old Welsh *map*. As for the primitive *p*
sound, it never appears in Gaelic. Initially and
between vowels it has dropped entirely, *e.g.*, Lat.
pater, piscis as against G. athair, iasg. Elsewhere
it is not wholly lost, but leaves some trace either by
way of compensatory lengthening or by a new combination.[1] It follows that no genuine Gaelic word
contains a *p*, except as the result of some late combination of consonants.

Initial *p* is seen in the names involving *Pit*,[2] to Non-Gaelic
be compared with Welsh *peth*, a part, Gael. *cuid*, Names.
a share portion, O. Ir. *cuit*, English *piece* ; in Book i. P-names.
of Deer *pett*. For the usage we may compare dàl,
a share, lot, in Dàl-riada. The Pictish *pett* was
borrowed by Gaelic, and treated as a Gaelic word,
e.g., na Peit'chan, the places of Pits ; Petty, G.
Peitidh, a locative of Peiteach, place of Pits. For
reasons that will occur to Gaelic scholars, Gaels have
usually translated it, most frequently into *baile*, a

[1] For examples, cf. A. Macbain's *Etym. Gael. Dict.*, xxxv.
[2] *v.* Index.

stead, *e.g.*, Pitkerrie, G. Baile-chéiridh ; sometimes into *innis*, a meadow, *e.g.*, Innis-fiùr, formerly Pit-fuir, or *bad*, a clump, *e.g.*, Pitglassie, G. Bad a' ghlasaich. Sometimes it is left untranslated, as in the Black Isle Pitfuir, G. Pit-ùir ; Pitmaduthy, G. Pit-'ic Dhuibh, also Baile-'ic-Dhuibh. The Pits are mostly confined to Easter Ross, where Pictish influence was most lasting, but Peitneane appears on record in Lochcarron, and Pitalmit in Glenelg. Other names with initial *p* are Peffer, Porin, Loch Prille, Peallaig, and those involving *preas*.

ii. Various. In addition to these *p* names, which are obviously non-Gaelic, the following are non-Gaelic either in whole or in part :—

Achilty (2)	Drumderfit	Monar
Achterneed	Fannich	Navity
Allan (4)	Fodderty	Oykell
Alness	Kinnettes	Pitcalnie
Balkeith	Kincardine	Tarlogie
Blairwhyte	Lochalsh	Udais
Contin	Lundy (3)	Urquhart
Dallas	Multovy	

With the exception of Lochalsh and that Lundy and perhaps Achilty are repeated on the West Coast, all the above occur in Easter and Mid Ross. The explanation of Multovy offered in the text requires qualification ; the termination is better compared with the Old Welsh suffix -*ma*[1] (Ir. mag, a plain), the whole representing a primitive *Moltomagos*, Wedder-plain. So with Mucovie, Migovie, Inver-

[1] Zeuss *Gramm. Celt.* 4, 890.

ness, and probably Rinavie, G. Roinnibhidh in Sutherland.

It will be observed that Balkeith, Blairwhyte, Kinnettes, and Kincardine are hybrids, *i.e.*, part Gaelic, part Pictish. The change from Pit into Baile has been already noted. That Pictish *pen*, head, has been translated into Gael. *cinn* is proved by names such as Kinneil and Kirkintilloch of old Pen-fahel and Caer Pen-taloch respectively. On this analogy we should have had also at one time Pencardine, Penettes. Blairwhyte is different; it means the Blair (moor) of Whyte, just as we say the Moor of Rannoch. Picto-Gaelic Hybrids.

The non-Gaelic termination *-ais* (open *a*), found only on Pictish ground, and referred to a proto-Celtic *vostis*, a dwelling, appears in Alness, G. Alanais; Dallas, G. Dalais; Farness, G. Fearnais; Kinnettes, G. Cinn-it-'ais or Cinn-iteais; Cnoc-ùdais. The most northerly instance known to me is Altas, G. Alltais, in Sutherland; elsewhere it appears in Forres, G. Farais; Geddes, G. Geadais. Termina-tion. *-ais.*

Another termination occurring only in Pictland is seen in Navity, G. Neamhaitidh or Neamhaididh (from neimhidh, Gaulish nemeton), Fodderty, Buchanty (as against Buchan) and others. *-tidh.*

Stream names are usually old, and probably most Ross-shire streams of any consequence possess names imposed in Pictish times. This, of course, applies only to the mainland; the names of Lewis streams, when they are not Norse, are unmistakably Gaelic and modern. The majority of the mainland streams iii. Stream Names.

—apart from mere burns, which are usually pure
Gaelic—admit of being classified by terminations,
one class, numerically small but comprising the
most important rivers, ending in -*n*, the other much
larger, consisting of relatively secondary streams,
ending in -*ie*.

(*a*) in -*n*.   The -*n* group includes the two Carrons, Conon,
Gaul. -*ona*. Orrin, Crossan, all of which in the text have been
treated as showing the Gaulish river ending -*ona*,
-*onna*, -*ana*, as in Matrona, Saogonna, Sequana.
To them should probably be added Averon and
Daan.[1] With these may be compared the Don,
G. Dian, proto-Celtic Divona ; Almond from Ambona
(Gaulish *ambis*, river) ; Spean, Spesona, from root
as in Spey cognate with Ir. scéim, vomo.

(*b*) in -*idh*.   To the -*ie* group belong the following :—
-*ios.*
-*ia.*
-*ēta.*

Allt Gowrie	Grudie (2)
Allt Rapaidh	Inver-breakie
Aradie	Inver-many
Ard-essie	Inver-markie
Balgaidh	Inver-riavenie
Coire-bhacaidh	Loch-calvie
Coire-chrùbaidh	Polly
Coire Lìridh	Raonaidh
Eathie (2)	Rogie
Glen-calvie	Uarie (Strathrory)
Glen-marxie	Ussie

One or two of these, *e.g.*, Breakie and perhaps
Bacaidh, may be regarded as diminutives of Gaelic
origin ; cf. p. xxxvi. sup. The majority, however,

[1] At p. 26 Daan is treated as a place-name. I have since found that the
little glen through which the stream passes near its source is called Gleann
Da'an, thus suggesting Daan to be a stream name.

seem to be of very old type, showing the termination
-*ios* seen in Ptolemy's Libn-ios, Tob-ios, Nov-ios,
or perhaps rather -*iā*, common in Gaulish rivers.
The Gaulish ending -*ēta* is also possible.[1] The
geographical distribution of these -*ie* stream names
points to a Pictish origin or strong Pictish influence.
Few or none are found in Dalriada, the oldest
Gaelic settlement. Of the above list nine are in
Wester Ross as against fifteen in the eastern parts.
In Sutherland, where Norse influence was strong,
fewer are found; there are, however, two Grudies.
But their great habitat is east of Drumalban in the
central Highlands, where Gaelic came latest; *e.g.*,
Feshie, Tromie, Mashie, Markie, Geldie, Nethy.

There remain some stream names which fall (c) Various.
under neither of the above categories, viz., Coran,
G. Còrainn, older Conrainn; Meig, G. Mìg; Sheil,
G. Seile, Adamnan's Sale; Dourag, G. Dobhrag,
from *dobur*, water. The first two are difficult
names, of which the explanations given must be
regarded as tentative; in any case they are obviously
pre-Gaelic. The river Ewe, G. Iù, I have taken,
with hesitation, from Ir. eó, yew tree; the fact that
Tobar na h-Iù in Nigg shows the article is practically
decisive in favour of *iù* being there at least a Gaelic
word. No Pictish name is accompanied by the
Gaelic article. But the river Ewe may be a Pictish
name from the same root, or from a totally different
one.

[1] Gaulish Albēta, White river; Gabrēta, Goat-wood; cf. Gowrie;
"flumen Gobriat in Pictavia."

foter.   Of prefixes usually regarded as Pictish, there
uachdar. occur in Ross *foter*, in Fodderty ; and *uachdar*, in
Achterneed, Achterflo, Achtertyre. The former is
undoubtedly Pictish ; the latter is good Irish,
though in point of fact in Scotland it is confined to
Pictish ground, and may therefore be of Pictish
origin. To these may probably be added the pre-
air. positions *ur*, Gaelic *air*, Gaulish *are*, as seen in
ur. Urray, G. Urra', on the Ford *(àth)*, or possibly near
the Fort *(ràth)*. The *ur* of Urquhart is certainly
Pictish.

In view of the number of Ross-shire rivers of
fair size, it is remarkable that we can show only one
abair. Aber, and that in a corrupt form, Apple-cross.
This may be ascribed partly to strong Norse
influence on the coast, partly to the Gaelic habit of
translating *abair* into *inbhir*. To Norse influence
may be due the singular circumstance that no
important stream flowing into the Cromarty Firth
has either *abair* or *inbhir* at its mouth ; translation
accounts for Invercarron, Inveraithie.

In dealing with the Pictish element in detail, the
following Welsh words have been compared in the
text :—

> *araf*, slow : Aradie, Inver-arity ; Gaul. Arar, Arabus.
> *cardden*, brake or thicket : Kin-cardine, Ur-quhart.
> *dol*, plateau : Dallas, Dal-keith ; dol-men.
> *gwaneg*, a wave : Loch Fannich.
> *gwydd*, wood : Bal-keith.
> *nant*, valley : Achter-need.
> *pawr*, pasture : Porin ; Inch-fuir ; Pit-fuir ; Bal-four ; Doch-
> four.

pefr, bright : Strath-peffer.
peth, portion : Pit-calnie, Pit-kerrie, &c.
prill, streamlet : Loch Prill.
rhos, moor : Ross.
tal, forehead : Tarlogie.
uchel, high : Achilty, Oykel ; Ochil ; Ochil-tree.
ud, a yell, blast : Cnoc-ùdais.

To these should be added the word *preas*, borrowed from Pictish into Gaelic ; cf. W. *prys*. In modern Gaelic *preas* means "bush ;" in place-names, however, it has rather the meaning of "clump" or "thicket," which echoes the Welsh *prys*, brushwood, covert.

In the above there is a distinct Brittonic element, which cannot be referred to Gaelic. Many other names show roots common to both branches, and are therefore difficult to classify. Thus Delny, G. Deilgnidh, might be referred to G. *dealg* or Cornish *delc ;* Lainn a' Choirc, Oat-flat, may show the rare G. *lann* or the common Welsh *llan*.

VI. The Norse Element.

While the list of Norse names given in the text may be regarded as exhaustive for the mainland part of the county, it is not so in respect of Lewis.

Lewis and Harris are more Norse in nomenclature than any other part of Scotland, and it would be possible from Lewis alone to add a thousand names, more or less. The great majority of Lewis names are wonderfully well preserved, and once the Gaelic pronunciation is heard, present little difficulty. But there also, as on the mainland, there is a residue difficult of explanation, to some extent no doubt involving old Norse words current in common speech, but not preserved in Icelandic literature.

Bólstaðr.   On the mainland the distribution of the term *bólstaðr* is analogous to that of G. *baile*. No name involving *bólstaðr* is found on the West Coast; on the east there are Arboll, Cadboll, Carbisdell, and Culbo. On the other hand, we have a parallel to erg. the distribution of G. *achadh* in the Norse *erg* shieling (borrowed at an early stage from G. àirigh; O. Ir. áirge), which appears on the west in Smirsary, Kernsary, Blaghasary, Aundrary, but is not found in the east.

Composition of Norse Names.   The composition of Norse names differs from that of Gaelic names, in that the specific or qualifying part, which in Gaelic comes after the generic term, is in Norse invariably prefixed to it. Thus N. *dalr*, a dale, comes at the end of names, after the descriptive epithet, *e.g.*, Slattadale, Attadale, Scamadale. G. *dal*, a dale, regularly stands first, *e.g.*, Dalmore, Dalbreck, Dalnacloich. In this respect Norse resembles English; Gaelic resembles Latin. The accent in Norse names, as in Gaelic names, falls on the qualifying part, that is, in this case, on the first syllable.

Quantity of first syllable.   In Norse names transmitted through Gaelic the quantity of the first syllable—which is the important one—can always be ascertained from native Gaelic pronunciation. The quantity of the following unaccented syllable or syllables (*i.e.*, of the generic part) is lost ; long vowels are shortened, *e.g.*, vík, bay, terminally becomes -*aig*. Further, in the case of polysyllabic names, or in the case of compounds consisting of three words—triple-barrelled—there is, unaer certain circumstances, a tendency to "telescope," *i.e.*, to slur or even wholly jump the Crasis. middle part of the name. Thus Askary in Caithness is historically known to represent *Asgrimsergin*, Asgrim's Shielings ; the old spelling of Inver-asdale is *Inver-aspedell*, G. Inbhir-àsdal. This affects only a small number of names, but where it has taken place there must, in the absence of record forms, be considerable uncertainty in restoring the part suppressed. Apart from this, the modern Gaelic pronunciation is extremely conservative in resisting corruption. A good example is Skibberscross in Sutherland, G. Slobarscaig ; in 1360, Sibyrs(k)oc ; 1562, Syborskeg, Schiberskek.

The hybrids that occur between Norse and Norse-Gaelic Gaelic are of a nature easily intelligible. Examples Hybrids. are Inver-kirkaig, Glen-dibidale, Strath-rusdale, Ard-shieldaig, Eilean Thannara. Here the Gaels accepted the legacy of the Norsemen, and finding such names as Kirkaig, Dibidale, &c., added on further Gaelic descriptive terms as they found occasion. The result is frequently unconscious tautology, as in Glen-dibidale, Glen-deepdale ; Strathrusdale, Strath-ram's-dale ; Ard-shilldinish, Cape of herring-cape, and so on. What is not found is the conscious blending of Gaelic and Norse, *e.g.*, it would be wholly impossible to find Norse *à*, river, *bólstaðr*, stead, *dalr*, dale, *ey*, island, *vik*, bay, qualified by a Gaelic adjective or noun. What we do find is the full-fledged Norse name further described by a Gaelic epithet or generic term, often unconsciously pleonastic. This is exactly parallel to the usage as between English and Celtic, *e.g.*, the River Avon, the Moor of Rannoch, the Strathpeffer Valley. There is, however, a very small class of names where the Norse *fjall*, hill, has been translated into Gaelic *beinn;* the instances known being Goatfell, G. Gaota-bheinn, Goathill; Blaven, G. Blàbheinn, Blue-fell; Sulven, G. Sùil-bheinn, Pillar-fell, and Badhais-bheinn in Gairloch. These must be regarded as the exceptions that prove the rule. Many Norse terms, of course, have been borrowed by Gaelic, the outward and visible sign of annexation being the prefixing of the definite article. On the mainland one of the names so borrowed was apparently *taða*, an in-field, of which we have a plural diminutive in Taagan, G. *na Tathagan;* the singular nominative is shewn in *Fear nan Tathag* (the genitive plural being in Gaelic identical with the nominative singular). In Lewis ordinary Norse names are sometimes found with the article, *e.g.*, *Cnoc a' Mhiasaid:* the inference is that there the meaning of these Norse names continued to be understood down to a late date.

Reliable interpretation of Norse names as preserved in Gaelic depends on an investigation of
Norse-Gaelic phonetics. A complete account of the
interchanges between Norse and Gaelic has never
so far been attempted, and that subjoined must be
regarded as subject to amplification and alteration
on subsequent enquiry. In the main I hope it is
correct.

Vowels.

Norse.	Gaelic.	
a	a	bakki, *bac* ; staðr, *stadh* ; stafr, *Staffa.*
á	à	á, *àmat* ; már, *Màsgeir* ; skári, *Scàrista* ; gás, *Gàsacleit* ; grár, *Gràdail* ; gjá, geòdh, geodha.
e	e, ea	klettr, *cleit* ; hesl, *Ard-heslaig* ; hestr, *Hestaval* ; melr, *Mealabhaig* ; gerði, *gearraidh* ; hellir, *Thealasvaigh.*
é	è	sléttr, *Slèiteadal.*
i	i	gil, *gil* ; fit, *fid* ; skip, *sgioba* ; rif, *Riof* ; timbr, *Teamradal.* Final *i* is dropped : bakki, skiki.
í	ì	hris, *Rìsadal* ; síld, *Sìldeag* ; íss, *ìslivig* ; lìn, *Lìnish* ; gnípa, *Gnìba* ; gríss, *Grìsamal.*
o	o	hross, *Rosay* ; kollr, *Colabol* ; ormr, *Ormiscaig.*
ó	ò	hóll, *tòll* ; hóp, *ob* ; óss, *òs* ; stjórn, *Steòrnabhadh* ; hólmr, *Tolm (-tuilm).*
u	u	kuml, *Tràigh Chumil* ; hund, *Hundagro* ; tunga, *Tungavat* ; hlunnr, *lunn.*
ú	ù	hrútr, *Srath-rùsdail* ; hús, *Hùsabost* ; súli, *Sùlbheinn* ; múli, *mùl* (also *maoil*).
y	i	myrkr, *Mircabat* ; kyrr, *Kirivick* ; hryssa, *Riseil* ; byrðingr, *birlinn.*
ý	iù	dýr, *Diùrinish.* ýr, *Uadal.*
æ	éi	græn, *Gréinatot.*
ö	o	möl, *mol* ; stöð, *stoth* ; örfiris-ey, *Orasay.*

Norse.	Gaelic.	
au	ò	straumr, *Stròm* ; haugr, *Tògh* ; sauðr, *Sòay* ; hraun, *Ròna.*
ei	ao	geit, *Gaota-bheinn* ; eið, *uidh(aoidh).*
	ei	breiðr, *Breidhvat* ; beit, *beid* ; steinn, *Steinn.*
ey	ao	reynis-á, *Raonasa* (Ranza) ; dreyr-vík, *Draoraig.*
	éi	reyrr, *Réireig.*
	eu	ey-fjörðr, *Euord* ; ey-fjall, *Euval* ; ey-fjörðr, *Euport.*
		but, eyland, *eilean.*
ja		tjörn gen. tjarnar, (Loch an) *tighearna* ; hjörtr gen. hjartar, *Thartabhat.*
já		gjá, *geòdh, geodha.*
jó	eò	Ljótr, *Mac-Leòid* ; fljót, *Srath-Fleòid* (Strath Fleet) ; but, grjót-à, *Grìde.*
kv	cu	kví, *Cuidhshader* ; svörðr, *Suardal* ; sveinn,
sv	su	*Suainabost.*
		Kvaran, *Cuaran.*
hv	f	hvar es, *far-as* [1] (where is ?); hvitr, *fiuit.* [2]
	bh, v	hvalr, *Valasay.*
	ch	hvammr, *Chamasord.*

Consonants (Non-Initial).

k	g	skip, *sgioba* ; thorskr, *trosg* ; vík, *-aig* ; skiki, *-sgaig (-scaig)* ; skata, *sgat, sgait*; sker, *sgeir.* After a consonant remains c : myrkr, *Mirckabat* ; but Arkból, *Arbol.*
kk	c	stokkr, *Stocanish* ; bakki, *bac* ; stakkr, *stac* ; bekkr, *Becamir.*
g	gh	haugr, *Tògh* ; hagi, *Tao'udal (Taghadal)* ; vágr, *-bhaigh* ; Sigurð-haugr = *Siwardhoch* 1160 ; fugl, *Fulasgeir.* But *ng* stands : *Tungavat, Stangarey.*
gg	g	Skeggi, *Sgiogarsta* ; egg, *Aignish, eig.*

---

[1] *War of the Gael and the Gall,* p. 174.
[2] Book of Leinster, 172a 7 ; 205b 48. To these may be added Hvitern (Whithorn), *Futerne,* evidently a Gaelic form.

Norse.	Gaelic.	
t	d, t	fit, *fid*; beit, *beid*; grjót, *Grìde*; setr, *Siadar* (Shader); flatr, *Plaid*; holt, *Nead-alt*; hrùtr, *rùta*. *tn* final becomes *t*: -vatn, -*bhat*; *t* before *s* is dropped; hrútsdalr, *Rùsdal*; after a consonant remains *t*.
tt	t	klettr, *cleit*; sléttr, *Sléit*; skattr, *Scatail* (Sgatail); brattr, *Brataig, Bratanish*.
p	b	gnípa, *Grìba*; hóp, *òb*, *Oban*; Pap-ey, *Paba*. But *pt* becomes *bht*, topt, *tobhta*.
pp	p	kleppr, *Cleipisgeir*; kappi, *Capadal*.
ð	th, dh	breiðr, *Breidhvat*; hlaða, *Lathamur*; taða, *Tathag*; sauða-ey, *Sòa*; staðr, -*sta(th)*; stöð, *Stoth*. For -*rð*- in the body of a word, cf. gerði, gearraidh; -*rð* final becomes -*rd*, -*rt*, fjörðr, *Siphort, Chamasord*.
d	d	hund, *Hundagro*; -*nd* final becomes -*id* in *Miasaid* for mjó-sund; remains in *Assynt* for áss-endi; elsewhere remains; sandr, *Sandabhaig*.
dd	d	oddi, *Toddin* (*the* point).
l	l	melr, *Mealabhaig*; but *ls* becomes *s*; háls, *Thàis*.
m	n	hamarr, *Puthar-hamar*; timbr, *Teamradail*. ormr, *Ormiscaig*.
n	n	always except in terminal -*nd*, which is sometimes -*id*; *gn* initial becomes *gr* in *Grìba* from gnípa.
f	f, bh	klif, *cliof*; rif, *riof*; scarf, *scarbh*; rof, *Robhanis*; gljúfr, *Globhur* (also ?*Gleadhair*); örfiris-ey becomes *Orasay*; *f* before *s* is dropped: klifsgro, *Clisgro*. Initial *f* is apt to become *p*; flatr, *Plaid* (being mistaken for *ph*); *fn* becomes *mn*, *nn*; höfn, gen. hafnar, *Thamnabhaigh, Tannara*.
th (initial)	t	throskr, *trosg*; thari, *Tarigeo*; Thórir, *Tòrasdal*.
b (initial)	b	regularly; but, búð, genitive búðar, *Putharol, Putharhamar*.

Initial *h* frequently developes *t* in Gaelic, being naturally mistaken for *th*, i.e., aspirated *t*; thus hafnar-ey becomes *Tannara*;

haga-dair, *Taghadal*; *hólmr*, *Tolm* and *-tuilm*; hjalli-dalr, *Tealladal*; hóll, *Tòll*.   In one important name at least *hj* becomes *se*: Hjaltland, *Sealtainn* (Shetland), or, in Reay, *Seoltain*.

VII. CHURCH NAMES.

Columba, the great Apostle of the Northern Picts, arrived in Iona from Ireland in 563, and two years later visited the Pictish King Brude at his palace near Inverness.   The Irish monks were full of missionary zeal.   On the occasion of Columba's visit to King Brude, incidental mention is made of a proposal by one of his brethren to seek "a desert in the sea" somewhere about the Orkneys.   By the end of the eighth century, as we know on the reliable authority of the Irish monk Dicuil, as also from other sources, the missionaries of the Celtic Church had reached even Iceland, which, however, they abandoned before the arrival of the Pagan Norsemen in 875. There is therefore no reason to doubt that before the year 800 the Christian religion had spread to Lewis also, though about that time it must have received a severe check from the influx of the invaders.   The direct proofs of Celtic Church influence are three :—
(1) records, (2) sculptured stones, (3) dedications and ecclesiastical terms preserved in place-names.

i. **Records.**   Of records we have only those relating to the Monastery of Applecross, as follows :—

A.D.
671 Maelruba in Britanniam navigavit (Tig. Ann.)
673 Maelruba fundavit ecclesiam Aporcrossan (ib.).

A.D.

722 Maelruba in Apercrossan, anno LXXX. aetatis suae et
tribus mensibus et XIX. diebus peractis in XI. kl. Mai,
tertiae feriae die, pausat (ib.).

737 Failbe mc Guaire, Maelrubai eiris .i. Apuorcrosain .i.
profundo Pelagi dimersus est cum suis nautis numero
XXII. (ib.).[1]

From other sources we learn that Malruba before
he left Ireland was Abbot of Bangor, and that, like
Columba, he was of noble birth.[2] His name has
been derived from *mael*, tonsured, and *ruba*, peace
or patience ; another quite feasible explanation is
from *ruba* (now *rudha*), a promontory ; Mal-ruba =
Gille an Rudha, the Lad of the Point. Names
were often given from the accident of place or time
of birth.[3] Dedications to him are extremely common,
and his name assumes a variety of forms. In Ross
we have *Combrich Mulruy*, *i.e.*, Comraich Maol-
ruibh, Malruba's sanctuary, to wit, Applecross. On
Eilean Ma-Ruibh, Isle Maree, is a burying-ground
and sacred well, whose waters used to cure insanity.
In honour of him the finest of our northern lakes
has changed its name from Loch Ewe to Loch
Maree. Near Jamestown in Contin is *Preas Ma-*

A.D.

[1] 671 Malruba sailed to Britain.

673 Malruba founded the Church of Aporcrossan.

722 Malruba died at Apercrossan at the age of eighty years three months
and nineteen days, on the 21st day of April, being a Tuesday.

737 Failbe, son of Guaire, successor of Malruba in Apuorcrosain, was
drowned in the open sea with his sailors to the number of twenty-
two.

[2] Practically all that can be gathered about St Malruba is to be found in
Dr Reeves' article (Proc. Soc. Scott. Antiq. vol. III.)

[3] Cf. Mael-Mocheirigh, Slave of Early-rising ; Lat. Manius.

Ruibh, Malruba's Grove, long a place of sanctity, and now the burial-place of the family of Coul. An autumn fair, *Féill Ma-Ruibh*, was long held at Contin, later at Dingwall, where it died out within living memory. Two or three places are said to be called *Suidh Ma-Ruibh*, Malruba's seat, where he was wont to rest on his journeys, but I have been so far unable to verify them. One is said to be marked by a low pillar stone in a field at *Bad a' Mhanaich*, Monk's Clump, at the west end of Loch Rosque.

ii. Sculptured Stones. Sculptured stones belonging to the Celtic Church have been found at Applecross, Rosemarkie, Nigg, Tarbat, Edderton, and Kincardine. The presence of such, most of them indicating a very high degree of skill in workmanship, is in itself a conclusive proof of strong Church influence.

iii. Ecclesiastical Terms. For convenience, it will be well to include all the ecclesiastical terms found, distinguishing those peculiar to the early Church from later ones.

Neimhidh. The word *neimhidh*, church-land ; O. Ir. *nemed*, sacellum, chapel ; Gaulish nemĕton or nemēton, a shrine in a grove, is a pagan term grafted on to Christian usage. It is a common element in Gaulish names, *e.g.*, *Nemetomarus*, great shrine ; *Augustonemeton*, shrine of Augustus ; *Vernemetis*, fanum ingens, very great shrine. Zeuss quotes " de sacris silvarum quae nimidas vocant," concerning shrines in woods which they call *nimidae;* " silva quae vocatur nemet," the wood which is called *nemet*. The root is seen in Latin *nem-us*, a grove ; Gael.

nèamh, heaven. It is quite possible that the places in which the word occurs with us were originally sacred to the pagan deities of the Picts ; later they were church-land. In Rosskeen are *Dalnavie, Cnocnavie*, and *Inchnavie*, Dale, Hill, and Haugh of the Church-land ; all adjacent to *Nonakiln*, G. Neo' na Cille, in 1563 Newnakle, Glebe of the Church, viz., the ancient chapel whose ruins still exist.[1] The N. Stat. Acc. mentions that in Rosskeen there were at the time of writing two glebes, one " at Noinikil, the cell or chapel of St Ninian," a derivation obviously impossible, for it would require Cill-Ninian. With this goes also the assumed dedication to Ninian, who is nowhere commemorated in Ross. Eastwards of Nonakiln is *Newmore*, G. Neo'-mhór, of old Nevyn Meikle, Great-glebe, the exact representative of Nemetomarus above. It was church-land before the Reformation. All these names occur together. The only other instance in Ross is Navity, near Cromarty, also church-land, G. Neamhaitidh, the formation of which makes it very doubtful whether it was ever given by the Celtic Church, and strongly suggests Pictish origin.[2] It recurs in Fife as *Navaty*, in 1477 Nevody. *Rosneath*, G. Ros-neo'idh, in 1199 Neveth, 1477 Rosneveth may mean Promontory of the Nemet. *Nevay* occurs as a parish name in W. Forfar.

---

[1] In 1275 we have "Nevoth et Roskevene" (Theiner, *Vet. Mon.*), *i.e.*, Navie and Rosskeen. It is probable that at this date "Nevoth" included both Nonakiln and Newmore.

[2] The well-known legend that the final Judgment is to take place on the moor of Navity may have its root in some pagan superstition.

Annat.
Annaid. *Annat*, G. annaid or annait, Ir. annóid, O. Ir. andóid, is a very old term, peculiarly and decisively characteristic of the Celtic Church. It appears to come from late Lat. *antas, antat-is*, glossed *senatus*, council of the ancients or elders. In Irish usage the *annóid* was the church in which the patron saint of the monastery or monastic district was educated, or in which his relics were kept. The Book of Armagh (c. 800) relates that St Patrick left Iserninus or Iarnan at a certain place to found his monastery *(manche)* and his patron saint's church *(andoóit)*. The exact position of the Scottish Annats is not so clear ; they are at anyrate of great antiquity, indi-cating doubtless the earliest Christian settlements in their particular districts. We have *Ach-na-h-Annaid* in Kincardine ; *Annat* and *Loch na h-Annaid* in Nigg ; *Annat* and *Clach na h-Annaid* beyond Clachuil on the way to Strathconon ; *Annat* opposite Invermany ; *Annat* at Torridon ; and *Annat* at Kildonan, Lochbroom—six in all, on the main-land of Ross. In the Island of Crowlin, off Apple-cross, is *Port na h-Annaid*. In Lewis there is *na h-Annaidean*, the Annats at Shader ; there is also an *Annat* in the Shiant Isles, G. na h-Eileanan Sianta, the Charmed Isles. These names must have survived through the Norse occupation from the time of the early missionaries.

Cill. *Cill* is the locative case of O.I. *cell*, a church, from Lat. *cella*, a cell. In place-names it always means church, in modern G. churchyard. As a rule *cill* stands first in compounds, followed by the name

of the saint commemorated by the dedication.
Sometimes, but rarely, the specific part of the compound is not a saint's name, *e.g.*, *Kildun*, G. Cillduinn, appears to be the locative of Cell-dhonn,
Brown Church. The Cill's of the Celtic Church
may be distinguished by their dedications to Celtic
saints, *e.g.*, Kilmachalmag ; names such as *Kilmuir*
and *Kilchrist* are of Roman Catholic origin. In
English spelling and pronunciation, but not in
Gaelic, *cill* is apt to be confused with *cùil*, corner,
e.g., Kilcoy ; *caol*, narrow, *e.g.*, Kildary ; *coille*,
wood, *e.g.*, Kinkell, G. Ceann na Coille, Woodhead.
For the Ross Cill's see index under Kil-, Cill-.

Clachan, a stone church, Ir. clochán, a stone Clachan.
bee-hive monastic hut. On the mainland of Ross
clachan is practically confined to the West Coast :
on the east the only instance known to me is *Beinn
a' Chlachain*, not far from the Parish Church of
Kincardine. On the west, as a reference to the
index will show, it is common.

Teampull, a church, borrowed from Lat. *templum*, Teampull.
a temple, occurs only twice on the mainland, and in
both cases it seems likely that the term applied not
to a "temple made with hands," but to places
naturally adapted to shelter a few worshippers.
In the Isles it means simply church, and is regularly
followed by a saint's name.

Eaglais, from Lat. *ecclesia*, the modern G. for Eaglais.
church, occurs seldom in place-names. *Beinn na
h-Eaglaise* above Annat, Torridon, is one of the few
examples with us.

Seipeil.   *Seipeil* is a late word from Eng. *chapel*, as is shown by initial *s;* a direct loan from Lat. *capella* would give *caibeal.*

Manachainn   *Manachainn*, a monastery, abbey, priory, from *manach*, a monk. From the Abbey of Fearn the parish is in G. Sgir na Manachainn. The other northern example is Beauly Priory, G. Manachainn 'ic Shimidh, *v.* Fearn.

Comraich.   There were in Ross two girths or sanctuaries, that of St Malruba in Applecross, and of St Duthac at Tain. The memory of the former is preserved in the G. name for Applecross, *a' Chomraich*, and of the latter by *Clais na Comraich*, on the Scotsburn road, two miles from Tain. The limits of both were marked by stone crosses. Reference to the Tain girth-crosses is made in the text; in Applecross one was to be seen just opposite the U.F. Church Manse till recent times, when the zeal of a Protestant mason smashed it. The most notable personages who sought to the sanctuary of St Duthac were the queen and daughter of King Robert Bruce (1306); "but that travele they mad in vane," for the influence of the English King was sufficient to induce William, then Earl of Ross, to violate the girth and surrender the fugitives. The last occasion of public importance in this connection was in 1483, when William, Lord Crichton, on a charge of treason, took refuge in the girth of Tain.

Celtair.   *Celtair*, an Irish word for church, is perhaps seen in *Kildermorie*, Alness, though in the absence of the Gaelic form we can have no certainty. Natives

speak only of *Gleanna-Mhoire*, Mary's Glen. Perhaps Kildermorie is to be regarded as a reversed form
of Maryculter, a name which, with Peterculter, has
never been satisfactorily explained.

Crois, a cross, appears in *Crois Catrion*, near Crois.
Tain; probably also in *Crosshills*, and *Corslet*.

A' Chananaich, the place of Canons, Chanonry, Cananaich.
is the Gael. name of Fortrose. A Roman Catholic
term.

Sgìr, a parish, is a loan from Ang. Sax. scír, a Sgir.
county, now shire.

Other ecclesiastical terms occasionally found in Manach.
place names are *manach*, a monk; *sagart*, a priest; Sagart.
cliar, clergy; *cléireach*, a cleric; *ministir*, a minister Cleireach.
—the last a presbyterian term. *Cf.* Ard-mhanaidh, Ministir.
Priesthill, Dochnaclear, Dalnaclerach, Clach Airigh
a' Mhinistir.

Traces of ecclesiastical establishments found by Norse
the Norsemen on their arrival are Inverkirkaig, Church
from *kirkju-vik*, Church Bay; Mungasdale, Monk- terms.
dale, both in Lochbroom; Pabay, Pope or Priest
Isle; Bayble, Priest-stead; Mungarsta, Monk-
stead, in Lewis.

The saints commemorated in Ross are Columba, Dedications.
Moluag, Donnan (contemporaries of Columba),
Colman, Iurnan, Malruba (already mentioned),
Fillan, Congan, Kentigerna, Fionn, Brìgh, Curitan,
Ferchar, Dubhthach or Duthac, and perhaps Cormac.

No dedication to St Columba appears on the Columba.
mainland of Ross. In Lewis the old church of
Lochs, on Eilean Chalum-Cille (St Columba's Isle),
was dedicated to him.

Moluag.   *Moluag* shows the honorific prefix *mo*, my, common with saints' names.   Lu-óc itself is a pet form
of *Lugaid*, root *loug*, win, whence the Celtic sun-
god Lugos.   The saint was Bishop and Abbot of
Lismore, and tradition says that he was buried at
Rosemarkie.[1]   His name survives in Davach-Moluag,
Fodderty.

Donnan.   *Donnan* of Eigg (from *donn*, brown), has his
name preserved in Kildonan on Little Lochbroom,
Seipeil Donnain or St Donan's Chapel in Kishorn,
and probably in Eilean Donnain, Donnan's Isle,
Kintail.

Colman.   *Colman*, "little dove," was a favourite name
among the Irish clerics, and in the multitude of
Colmans it is impossible to be sure of the particular
saint who is commemorated in the names Kilmachalmag, G. Cill-mo-Chalmaig, and Portmahomack,
G. Port-mo-Cholmaig, and to whom the parish
church of Tarbat was dedicated.   In Portmahomack
is *Tobair Mo-Cholmaig*, St Colman's Well.   At
Kilmachalmag, near the right bank of the burn not
far from its mouth, there are still traces of a very
small chapel adjoining a disused and sadly neglected
burying-ground.   East of it is Achnahannet, noted
above.

Iurnan.   For Iurnan *v.* under Killearnan.

Fillan   *Fillan*, G. *Faolan*, little wolf, was the son of
Kentigerna.   Hence *Kilillan*, G. Cill-Fhaolain, in
Kintail.

[1] Aberdeen Breviary.

Congan, brother of Kentigerna, is the patron Congan. saint of Lochalsh, and appears also in *Kilchoan*, now Mountrich, in Kiltearn.

Kentigerna, Ir. Caintigerna, kind lady, crossed Kentigerna. from Ireland to Lochalsh, according to the legend, c. 615, accompanied by her son, Fillan, and her brother, Congan. Her name is kept in Cill-Chaointeort (Glenshiel), in 1543 Kilkinterne, 1727 Kilchintorn, 1719 Killiwhinton. It will be seen that the place-names support the legend.

The existence of *St Fionn* is guaranteed by the Fionn. name Killin, G. Cill-Fhinn, at Garve, taken together with Loch Maol-Fhinn, Loch of the shaveling of Fionn, which is the G. for Loch Garve.

Brigh, a female saint; *Cladh mo-Bhrigh* is a Brigh. small burial place with remains of chapel between the public road and the sea, two miles east of Dingwall.

Curitan, G. Curadan, Latinised Queretinus, and Curitan. sometimes called Boniface, was a native of Scotland, for he is referred to as Albanus Queretinus (*i.e.*, Curadan Albanach), cf. St Duthac. Curitan was an important personage, who flourished c. 700, a contemporary of Nechtan, son of Derili, that King of the Northern Picts who promulgated the edict of conformity to Rome in the matters of Easter and the tonsure. It is probable that Curitan was of the Romanising party, and was Nechtan's adviser in things spiritual. In Ross we have *Cladh Churadain*, St Curitan's graveyard, a small rectangular burying-ground north of the farmhouse of Assynt,

Novar, used within living memory, and stated to
have contained stones with inscriptions and car-
vings.[1]   *Cnoc Churadair*, north of Ardoch, Alness,
is St Curitan's Hill (the *n* of Cladh Churadain is
sometimes heard as *r*); as the place is thickly
wooded, it would be difficult to search for remains
of a chapel, and I have heard no tradition.   Other
traces of Curitan are *Cladh Churadain* and *Suidh
Churadain* at Lochend, Inverness; *Cladh Churadain*
at Struy, Strathglass; *Cladh Churadain*, *Tobair
Churadain* and *Croit Churadain* in Glen-Urquhart.
The old church of Fearnua, in Kirkhill parish, was
dedicated to " Corridon."

Ferchar.   *Ferchar* (Ver-caros, very dear), is known only by
a small deserted burial-place opposite Shiel School,
called Cill-Fhearchair.

Dubhthach.   *Dubhthach* or *Dubtach* (Dubotācos), from *Dubh*,
black, was a name not uncommon.   Dubhthach,
contemporary with St Patrick (432), was one of the
nine compilers of the Seanchus Mór; another was
Abbot of Iona (850-870), and there were others
besides.   It is generally agreed, however, that St
Duthac of Tain is the one whose death is thus
recorded in the Annals of Ulster under date 1065:—

> Dubtach Albannach, prim Anmchara Erinn agus Albain in
> Ardmacha quievit.
> Dubtach of Alba, chief soul-friend of Erin and of Alba rested
> in Armagh.

St Duthac is the patron saint of Tain, where may
be seen the ancient chapel "quhair he was borne,"

---

[1] This venerable spot was inadvertently planted, but is now cleared and
tended by order of Novar.

and Tain in G. is *Baile-Dhubhthaich*, Duthac's Town.
Hugh Miller notes St Duthus' well near Cromarty.
In Kintail there are *Clachan Dubhthaich* on *Loch
Duich*, and *Cadha Dhubhthaich*, the name of the
Bealach leading into Glen Affric.

The name of *St Cormac* may be commemorated Cormac.
in *Tobair Cormaig*, Nigg. A Tain fair was also
named after him (*v.* Tain). Cormac was the name
of the brother for whom Columba sought the protection of King Brude, and who reached Orkney in
his voyaging.

All the saints above mentioned belong to the Roman
Celtic Church, though by Duthac's time relations Catholic
Dedications.
with Rome were closer. To the subsequent period,
when under the influence of Queen Margaret and
her sons the Scottish Church was made in all
respects to conform to the Church of Rome, belong
such dedications as *Kil-muir, Kirk-michael, Kilchrist*, and names like *Tobair Eadhain Bhaist, Port
Eadhain Bhaist*, Well and Port of St John the
Baptist. St Cowstan's Chapel, on the Eye Peninsula, shows a dedication to St Constantine.

VIII.

It may be useful to add a short analysis of the
principal terms connected with natural features,
artificial structures, old occupations, plants, animals,
etc., found in the names of Ross. As the Norse
names of Lewis are so arranged in the text, it will
be unnecessary to include them here.

Streams.   The general name for a river is *abhainn*, applied to all relatively large streams, and often to smaller ones, whose course is tolerably smooth. The obsolete word *abh*, stream, is seen in Av-och, stream place. *Allt*, in Irish means a wooded valley or glen, a cliff; in Welsh, a wooded cliff; connected with Lat. *altus*, high. Our meaning of "stream, burn," is peculiar to Scottish Gaelic, and is probably of Pictish origin. The original meaning appears in the common Leth-allt, half-burn, really half-height, applied to a burn with *one* steep side. *Caochan*, from *caoch*, blind, is applied to a small stream which is sometimes almost hidden by the heather. Another term for stream is *glais*, more common in Ireland than in Scotland. With us it occurs in Glen-glass, in Fowlis G. Fólais for fo-ghlais, and in Allt Fólais on Loch Maree. A slender rivulet is *feadan*. The very general term *uisge*, water, is met in Uisge Bhearnais, water of the cleft, Kintail. A still, narrow channel between two waters is *uidh*, a water isthmus, from Norse eið. The nearest Gaelic equivalent is *eileach*. *Fèith*, literally a vein, is applied to a bog channel. The O. Ir. word *bir*, denoting water, well, is seen in Poll a' Bhior, in the Applecross river. O.G. and Pictish *dobur*, water, gives Dòbhran, Dourag, Eddirdover. A fall is *eas*; a combination of two or more is *coneas*. *Cuingleum*, Coylum, narrow leap, gut.

Marshes.   The Pictish name for a marsh appears to be *Allan*, from the root seen in Lat. *pal-us*. Alness, G. Alanais, means 'the place of the marsh.' *Riasg* means a boggy place, where dirk grass grows. *Bogradh* is a soft place; *glaodhaich*, a miry, gluey place ; *càthar*, a place of broken, mossy ground. A damp meadow is *lòn* usually ; once we find *cala*.

The Pictish for confluence is Contin, in G. Cunndainn, *cf.* Gaulish Condāte, Contion-ācum. Another Pictish term is *obair*, for *od-ber*, out-put, out-flow, corresponding to the Gael. *inbhir* for *in-ber*, in-put, in-flow. The real term for a junction is *comar*, from *con-ber*, joint-flow ; also, though rarely, *comunn*. In Lewis the regular term for a river mouth is *bun*, bottom. The Norse for confluence is *ár-mót* or *á-mót*, river-meet, appearing as Amat. {Confluences.}

A ford is *àth* ; a ford-mouth, *beul-àtha*, pro- {Fords.} nounced quickly apt to be confounded with *baile*. A place where crossing was wont to be made on planks sometimes involves *clàr*, a board, *e.g.*, Poll nau Clàr. A place for crossing on stones is *clacharan*, in Lewis *starran*.

Camas means a bay, bend ; *òb* from Norse *hóp* is {Sea Terms.} the same ; also *bàgh*, a late word not much used in place-names. A sound, firth, or narrow is *caolas* or simply *caol*, *e.g.*, Caolas Chromba', the Cromarty Firth ; an Caol Arcach, the Orkney Narrow, *i.e.*, the Pentland Firth. A tide race is *sruth*, *e.g.*, Sruth na Lagaidh ; or *stròm*, from Norse *straumr*. Parts of the Minch are called *linne*, pool, *e.g.*, an linne Sgith-eanach, an linne Ràrsach. The Minch itself is a' Mhaoil, the Moyle ; also an Cuan Sgìth, the sea of Skye ; Cuan Uidhist, the Little Minch. A shore is *cladach* ; a stony beach, *faoilinn* ; a sea bank, scaup, *oitir* ; *port* means a harbour on the west coast ; on the east a ferry, usually ; *aiseig*, a ferry. *Feadhail*

is an extensive beach, or a place between islands
uncovered at low tide ; pl. *feadhlaichean.* *Bòdha,*
Norse *boδi,* is a sunken reef ; *iolla,* a fishing rock,
usually covered at high tide. *Saothair,* from saobh-
thìr, false-land or side-land, is a low promontory
covered at high water, or the similar bank between
an *Eilean Tioram* and the mainland. The shelving
slope between the old raised beach and the present
beach is on the west coast called *faithir,* probably
from *fo-thir ; Tairbeart* is a portage, isthmus.

Flats.   The level land by a river side is *srath,* a strath,
Norse *dalr,* dale. The term *srath* is much commoner
in Scotland than in Ireland, and may be rather
Pictish than Gaelic. A narrow strath is *gleann,*
a glen ; a rounded glen is *coire,* a cauldron, corry ;
often narrow at the mouth. *Innis,* primarily an
island, means commouly a haugh, river-side meadow ;
fàn is a level place or a gentle slope ; hence *fànaich,*
place of the flat. *Dail* is a dale, usually by a river
side ; it is to be compared with Pictish *dol,*
dal, dul, plateau. A plain is *magh* ; a sea-plain
is *mor'oich,* from *mur-magh* ; a mossy flat is *blàr.*
Machair is an extensive low-lying fertile plain ;
monadh, tolerably level hill ground. In Lewis the
land between machair and monadh, the strip where
the houses stand, is the *gèarraidh,* from Norse
gerδi, an enclosure. Another word for a plain is
clàr, primarily a board. A little plain is *rèidhlean ;*
a wet plain or lea, *lèana,* diminutive *lèanag,* or
with us *lianag,* e.g., Lianagan a' Chuil-bhàicidh.
Faithche means a lawn ; *àilean,* a green ; *cluan,*
meadow.

In dealing with names of lochs, straths, glens, and corries, it is well to remember that the Celtic custom is to name each after the stream that flows through it.

A gap or pass between hills is *bealach ;* a cleft is Hollows. *bearn* or *bearnas.* A chasm is *glòm, e.g.,* Eas na Glòmaich, Falls of Glomach. *Eag* is a sharp notch ; *lag,* a rounded hollow ; *slacan,* a circular depression like a kiln ; *poll,* a wet miry hollow, also, a pool ; *sloc,* a pit, slough ; *còs,* a nook ; *clais,* a narrow shallow ravine.

Beinn (an oblique case of *beann*) with us means Heights. a high hill ; in Ireland applied only to hills of medium size. Its primary meaning is pinnacle, horn, which is still kept in *Eilean na Binne* and in the adjective *beannach,* pointed. *Sliabh,* applied in Ireland to mountains, is very rare with us, and means rather a mountain moor. A hill of medium height is *cnoc ; sgùrr* is a high sharp pointed hill ; *sgor,* a peak. A low smooth hill or ridge is *tulach ;* the highest tulach is *Tulach Ard* or *Ard-tulach* in Kintail. *Tom* is a rounded knoll, with diminutive *toman ;* a one-sided *tom* or *toman* is a *tiompan.* A great shapeless hill is *meall,* a lump ; *sgonn* is similar, but rare ; *maol, maoil,* means a great bare rounded hill. *Aonach* is (1) market place, (2) high moor ; *aoineadh,* a very steep hill side. A broad slope is *leathad ; leacainn* and *leitir* have much the same meaning. A level shelf in a hill side where one would naturally rest is *spàrdan,* a roost, or *suidhe,* a seat. *Pait,* a hump, sometimes a ford.

Two words remain : *sìthean* and *cathair*. *Sìthean* means a fairy mound ; in some of the very few cases in which it occurs with us it applies to a big rounded hill. The fairy mound is always called *cathair* on the West Coast, and conversely almost every *cathair* is a fairy mound.

The following parts of the body are found used to denote shape, position, and appearance :—*Ceann*, head ; *claigionn*, skull ; *aodann*, face ; *sròn*, nose ; *beul*, mouth ; *teanga*, tongue ; *fiacail*, tooth ; *bile*, lip ; *sùil*, eye ; *feusag*, beard ; *bràghad*, neck, upper part of the chest ; *uchd*, breast, with its diminutive *uchdan* ; *cioch*, *màm*, a pap ; *druim*, a back ; *gualann*, shoulder ; *achlais*, arm-pit ; *ruigh*, forearm ; *meòir*, fingers ; *ionga*, nail ; *dòrn*, fist, cf. Dornie ; *màs*, buttock ; *amhach*, neck ; *tòn*, rump ; *slios*, side.

Woods. Trees. Plants. The generic term for wood is *coille* ; *doire* means a grove, primarily of oaks ; *bad*, diminutive *badan* and *badaidh*, is a clump ; *gar*, a thicket, is rare ; *preas*, in modern G. a bush, is in place-names better translated clump. The Pictish *cardden*, a brake, occurs in Kincardine, Urquhart, and Glen-Urquhart. A tree is *crann*, whence Crannich. Of individual trees we have *call*, hazel (the modern *calltuinn* never appears), *darach*, oak ; *ràla*, oak ; *beithe*, birch ; *caorunn*, rowan ; *giuthas*, fir ; *cuilionn*, holly ; *fiodhag*, bird cherry ; *fearna*, alder ; *sgiach*, hawthorn ; *draigheann*, blackthorn ; *seileach*, willow ; *uinnsin*, ash, is rare ; *leamh*, elm, also rare and somewhat doubtful. From *fiodh*, wood, comes

Achnegie, G. Achd-an-fhiodhaidh, with which may be compared the Pictish *Balkeith*.

Among the smaller plants are *aitionn*, juniper ; *bealaidh*, broom ; *eidheann*, ivy ; *roid*, bog myrtle ; *raineach*, also *rainteach*, bracken ; *fraoch*, heather ; *luachair*, rushes ; *creamh*, wild garlic ; *borrach*, rough hill grass ; *giùran*, cow parsnip ; *suibhean*, raspberry ; *dris*, bramble ; *samh*, sorrel ; *feartag*, sea-pink ; *carrachan*, wild liquorice.

The regular words for promontory are *rudha* and Promon- *àrd* or *àird*, corresponding to Norse *ness*. *Ros*, a tories. point, occurs in Rosemarkie and Rosskeen. Sometimes, chiefly in Lewis, *gob*, a beak, occurs. A little promontory at the end of a rounded bay is *corran*, very common on the west coast. *Ploc* is a lumpish promontory. *Maoil*, a loan from Norse múli, is rare, *cf.* the Mull of Cantyre.

The various names for horse are *each*, *marc*, Animals. *capull* ; a mare is *làr*, and is often difficult to distinguish from *làr*, floor, low ground ; and *làr*, middle. *Tarbh* is a bull ; *bó*, a cow ; *laogh*, a calf (of cow or hind) ; *gamhainn*, stirk ; *gabhar*, a goat ; *boc*, buck ; *meann*, kid. *Caor*, a sheep, does not occur, though *mult*, wedder, appears as applied figuratively to sea rocks ; also in the Pictish Multovy ; Norse, *sauða*, sheep, *hrútr*, ram, give Syal and Strath-rusdale ; *muc*, pig, is common ; *torc*, boar, is applied sometimes to hills from their appearance, *e.g.*, Meall an Tuirc ; sometimes from the wild boar ; *cat*, a cat, indicates haunts of wild cats ; *broc*, badger, is rare ; *cù*, dog ; *cù odhar*, otter, appears in Altchonier, G.

Allt a' choin uidhir ; *madadh* may mean either fox
or wolf.   Of the deer tribe, we have *damh*, stag ;
eilid, hind ; *agh*, hind ; *mang*, fawn ; *earb*, roe.
Moigheach, a hare, occurs once.

The following names of birds are found :—
Coileach, a grouse cock ; *clamhan* and *clamhag*, a
kite ; *speireag*, a sparrow-hawk ; *seabhag*, a hawk ;
fitheach, a raven, also the old word *bran*, raven ;
iolair, an eagle ; *feadag*, a plover ; *druid*, a thrush ;
còrr, a crane ; *lach, tunnag*, a duck ; *leirg*, black
throated diver ; *gèadh*, a goose ; *calman*, a pigeon ;
eala, a swan ; *sgarbh*, a cormorant.

Dwellings.   A house is *tigh*.   The regular word for a homestead is *baile*, so common in Ireland.   The distribution of this term in Ross is remarkable.   In
Easter and Mid Ross it is extremely common,
occurring over eighty times.   On the west there are
only four instances, Balmacarra in Lochalsh, Baile
Shios, Baile Shuas, and am Baile Mór (= Flowerdale) in Gairloch ; in Lewis there is only Balallan.
The absence of *baile* in Lewis is natural : the town-
ships are denoted by the Norse *ból-staðr* and *staðr*.
On the West Coast its place is taken by *achadh*, a
cultivated field, which is correspondingly rare in the
east.   The distribution of achadh is over forty in the
west, to about twelve in the east.   The Pictish *pett*
so common in Easter Ross has already been noted.
Both, a booth, hut, occurs only in *na Bothachan*,
Boath, and perhaps in *Claonabo* in Kintail.   This is
another term the distribution of which throughout
the Highlands deserves investigation.   It is very

common along the valley of the Caledonian Canal,
also in certain regions of Perth and Stirling,
extremely rare north of Inverness. The obsolete
fasadh, a dwelling, is frequent ; outside of Ross it
occurs in such names as Fassiefearn, Teanassie, Foss.
Another much less common term of the same
meaning is *astail*. A shieling hut was called *longphort*,[1] which appears in Loch-luichart, and in the
form of Longard, Lungard. *Treabhar*, as a collective
noun in common use in Easter Ross, meaning farm
buildings, is found once only in Tornapress, G.
Treabhar nan Preas. The ancient fortified places
are represented by *dùn*, *ràth*, *lios*. The site of a
ruined house is *làrach* ; a ruin with walls standing
and roof fallen in is *tobhta*.

A cultivated field is *achadh* (shortened into *ach*, Cultivation
and
Enclosures.
acha, *achd*), the distribution of which has been
noted above. Another word in common use for
field is *raon* ; a lea field is *glasaich* ; a park is
pàirc, an early loan from English ; *bàrd*, very common
in Mid Ross, means, usually, enclosed meadow.
Iomair is a ridge or rig ; *feannag*, a lazy-bed ; *gead*,
a narrow strip of land. *Gart* is enclosed corn-land ;
diminutive *goirtean* ; *ceapach*, a tillage plot. Terms
connected with enclosures are *eirbhe*, now obsolete,
a fence, or wall ; *dìg*, a moat ; *crò*, a sheep fold, with
its variant *crà*, a cruive ; *buaile*, a cattle fold ; *fang*,
a fank ; *geata*, a gate ; *cachaileith*, a field gate, or
hurdle. A tidal weir for catching fish is *cairidh* ;
an arrangement for catching fish in a stream by

---

[1] Taylor, the Water Poet, who travelled in Scotland in 1618 and saw a
hunting in Marr, mentions the "small cottages, built on purpose to lodge in,
which they call Lonquhards."

means of the *cabhuil* is *eileach*, applied also to a
narrow shallow stream joining two lochs, or to a
mill-lade. *Eileag*, now obsolete, appears to have
been a V-shaped structure, wide at one end, narrow
at the other, into which deer were driven and shot
with arrows as they came out.[1]

Crops. Together with the general term *arbh*, corn,
which occurs thrice, there are several names
involving *seagail*, rye ; *Lainn a' Choirc* is the Oat-
flat ; *lìon*, flax, occurs twice.

Occupations and Customs. In connection with the preparation of corn for
food are *àth*, a kiln ; *eararadh*, the process of
parching ; *muileann*, a mill. *Sabhal*, a barn, is
fairly common, as also *bàitheach*, a cow house.
Cnagan na Leathrach, and possibly the *Sutors*, are
connected with tanning. *Allt* and *Muileann
Luathaidh* commemorate the fulling of cloth.
Gobha, a smith, occurs in Balnagown and Ledgowan. *Ceardach*, a forge, smithy, has sometimes
reference to ancient smelting works. The seven-
teenth century works on Loch Maree side give
a' Cheardach Ruadh, the red smithy, Fùirneis,
Furnace, and Abhainn na Fùirneis, River of the
Furnace. The old practice of making peat charcoal gives rise to Meall a' Ghuail. The shieling
custom gives the numerous names involving
àirigh. Flax was steeped at the Lint-pools
and Tobair nam Puill Lìn, and linen was bleached
at Balintore. Balleigh means Leech's or Physician's stead. Baronies with power of pit

---

[1] Another name, not found in Ross, for a similar arrangement, but not
necessarily artificial, is *Elrig*, G. Iolairig.

and gallows have left traces in the not uncommon
Cnoc na Croiche, where men were hanged, and *Poll
a' Bhàthaidh*, where women were drowned.

The old standard measure of land in Pictland was
the *dabhach*, originally a measure of capacity, 'vat.'
The extent of the *dabhach* varied according to the
land and the locality. It is usually given as four
ploughgates, but must have been often less. Many
names involving *dabhach* are found all over the
mainland part of Ross. Lewis was divided into
fifteen davachs. The word usually appears in
English as Doch ; in E. Ross the Gaelic form is
do'ach. A half-davach is *leith-do'ch*, Englished
Lettoch, or sometimes Halfdavach, whence Haddach,
Haddo. Further divisions of the davach appear to
have been the *ceathramh*, fourth part, and the
ochdamh, eighth part, whence Balcherry, Ochto or
Ochtow.

Land
Measures.

The old Gaelic practice of division into fifths
survives in the name Coigach, Place of fifths.

The oxgate appears doubtfully in Midoxgate ;
the rental of 1727 gives Mickle Oxgate and Middle
Oxgate as divisions of Ruarach in Kintail. The
merkland survives in Drumnamarg in the Black
Isle, and in 1538 appear "the four merklands of
Eschadillis" (Eskadale, Ashdale), somewhere in
Strathconon. But apart from the davach and its
divisions, the representation in place-names of these
old land measures is trifling.

Aon, one, is found in Leathad an aon Bhothain,
Hillside of the one hut. Names involving the
numerical *dà*, two, are not uncommon on the West

Numerical
Combin-
ations.

Coast, *e.g.*, Achadh dà Tearnaidh, Field of two Descents ; Cnoc dà Choimhead, Hill of two prospects ; Ach' dà Dòmhnuill, Field of two Donalds ; Ach' dà Sgaillt, Field of two bare places ; Poll dà Ruigh, Wet hollow of two slopes. In the eastern part the only examples met are Cnoc Dubh eadar dà Allt a' Chlaiginn, Black hill between the two burns of the Skull, and Ach' dà Bhannag, Field of two Cakes. *Trì*, three, is found in Sgeir an Trithinn, Trinity Skerry, a sea rock with three humps. *Cóig*, five, is the base of Coigach, Place of Fifths. *Seachd*, seven, occurs in Fuaran seachd Goil, Well of seven Boilings. *Leth*, half, is frequently prefixed to denote one-sidedness. *Lethallt*, half-burn, really half-height, describes the valley of a stream with one steep side ; *leth-ghleann*, half-glen, is of similar meaning. *Leth-chreag* is a one-sided rock ; *leitheach*, a one-sided place, half-place, *e.g.*, the narrow strip of land between loch and hill ; Norse *skiki*. So *lethoir*, half-border, similar in meaning to Welsh *lledymyl* = G. *leth-iomall*, border near the edge, which exactly describes Learnie, on the south side of the Black Isle, sloping down to the sea-cliffs. The very common *leitir* is probably for *leth-tìr*, half-land, sloping hill-side.

Historical Events and Personages. Fights of olden times are commemorated in such names as Blàr nan Ceann, Knocknacean, Ath nan Ceann, Moor, Hill, and Ford of the Heads ; Allt nan Cnuimheag, Burn of Worms ; Bealach nam Bròg, Pass of the Brogues ; a more recent battle (1719) has left its mark in Sgùrr nan Spàinteach, Peak of the Spaniards. Cadha na Mine, Path of the Meal, and other names near it, are connected with the '45. Leac na Saighid and Sgùrr na Saighid recall old feats of archery. One of the most interesting names is Scotsburn, G. Allt nan Albanach, in connection with which are Càrn nam Marbh, Dead men's Cairn ; Lochan a' Chlaidheimh and Bearnas a' Chlaidheimh, Sword Lochlet and Sword Cleft. That a considerable battle was fought here is practically certain ; also that *Albanaich*, " Scottis men," were engaged in it. The curious thing is that the burn should have been named from the *Albanaich*, Scots, and not from their opponents, as might have been expected. It looks as if from the standpoint of the namers the *Albanaich* were regarded as strangers. They may have been Lowland Scots.

The great Pictish name *Nectan* appears in the obsolete Dalvanachtan, *i.e.*, Nectan's davach, also in Cadha Neachdain, Nectan's Path. The latter is one of the many steep paths in Nigg Rocks, and from the fact that near it is a cave called Uamh an Righ, the King's Cave, one is inclined to connect it with the Pictish King Nectan, son of Derili, who flourished circ. 715. This king had a remarkable and chequered career, one of the incidents in which was his joining the Church or becoming a recluse. The scene of his *clericatus* is unknown, but it may be plausibly conjectured that he spent some part of it in Uamh an Righ.

The great forest or hunting ground of Freevater, G. Frìth Bhàtair, Walter's Forest, in which Leabaidh

Bhàtair, Walter's Bed, occurs twice, most probably derives its name from Walter, that son of the fourth Earl of Ross who fell at Bannockburn, *v.* p. 12.

Glaic an Righ Chonanaich, Hollow of the Strath-conon King, is a somewhat surprising name, for which *v.* p. 249. The West Coast names are rich in references to local men and events of note. Of legendary heroes we have Fionn, Diarmad, and Oscar, all of the Fenian cycle. The widely spread story of Diarmad's tragic death is located with considerable circumstance in Kintail. A reference to Fionn seems to be contained in *Suidheachan Fhinn.* Fenian legends are attached to Fèith Chuilisg, Loch Lurgainn, Cnoc Farrel, Clach nan Con Fionn, Coulin, but several of these have obviously been invented to explain the names. The Fenians appear in *Coire na Féinne,* and legends of their huntings are connected with *Sgùrr nan Conbhairean.* The hero Oscar's name is found in *Buillean Osgair,* Oscar's Strokes—certain *claisean* or gaps on Little Lochbroom. From the great battles of modern time we get Camperdown, Waterloo (near Dingwall), and Balaclava (or Balnuig). Maryburgh, near Dingwall, was named from Queen Mary, wife of William of Orange. A good deal of fancy nomenclature has arisen in Easter Ross within the last century and a half, *e.g.,* Mountgerald, Mountrich, Petley, Arabella, Invergordon, and others, in English—not to the same extent in Gaelic—displacing the old names.

Under this head may be noted our one certain instance of *druidh,* a Druid, *viz., Port an Druidh,* the Druid's Port, with *Cadha Port an Druidh*, the Druid's path near it, both in Nigg, old names doubtless. The term *druineach*, which occurs with us in *Airigh nan Druineach*, *Cladh nan Druineach*, *Druineachan*, *Poll* and *Drochaid Druineachan* is frequent elsewhere, *e.g.*, *Càrn nan Seachd Druineachan* in Glen Fintag, *Inistrynich* is Lochawe, *Cladh nan Druineach* in Iona, *Tigh Talmhaidh nan Druineach* (Earth House of the D.), a round house or broch in Assynt. The word is sometimes equated with *druidh;* it is based on O. Ir., *druin*, glossed *glicc*, wise, clever ; and *druinech* in Ir. means an embroideress. The exact significance of it in our place names is far from clear. Logan[1] takes it to mean cultivators of the soil as opposed to hunters, which may represent a genuine tradition. Martin makes mention of little round stone houses in Skye capable only of containing one person, and called " Tey-nin-druinich, *i.e.*, Druids' House." Druineach, says Martin, signifies a retired person much devoted to contemplation.

Some miscellaneous terms omitted above follow. *Croit*, a croft, with its variants *creit, crait, cruit*, is common in Easter Ross. The Exchequer Rolls supply an interesting record of the crofts held by the minor officials of a great castle, *v.* p. 146. *Linne*, besides meaning a pool in a river, is used to denote a part of the sea near the shore, also a bay.[2] *Crasg*, a crossing, generally, if not always, applies to a

---

[1] *Scottish Gael*, II., 72 (ed., Dr Stewart).

[2] The Greek equivalent λίμνη has exactly the same meanings in Homer.

crossing over a ridge.   *Gasg*, diminutive *gasgan*, is
explained at p. 208.   *Cadha* is usually a steep,
narrow path, but is sometimes applied to steep parts
of a regular road, *e.g.*, an Cadha Beag and an Cadha
Mór, near Gruinard.   By *Bac* we mean in E. Ross a
peat moss ; in the west the primary sense of bank,
ridge, is preserved ; Norse bakki.   *Grianan* means
a sunny hillock, or a place, *e.g.*, good for drying
peats.   *Roinn*, a point, occurs in Roinn an Fhaing
Mhóir.   *Botag* is a wet or soft channel in a peat
moss.   *Rabhan*, after much search, I took to mean
water lily, and from one description of it that seemed
correct.   But another and better authority had no
hesitation in defining it as a long grass growing in
shallow, muddy parts of lochs or pools, and formerly
used for feeding cattle, an account of it which I
have had since confirmed beyond doubt.   The word
is almost certainly a Pictish loan, to be compared
with Welsh *rhafu*, to spread ; *rhafon*, berries
growing in clusters.   It occurs frequently in Sutherland place-names.   A similar kind of grass growing
in pools and lochs is *barranach*, from *barr*, top.

PLACE-NAMES

OF

ROSS AND CROMARTY

PLACE-NAMES OF ROSS AND CROMARTY.

KINCARDINE.

Kincardine—Kyncardyn 1275—G. Cinn-chàrdain ;
'cinn' is the locative case of 'ceann,' head ; càrdain
is of common occurrence in names on Pictish ground.
cf. Adamnan's Airchartdan, now Glen-Urquhart,
Plus-carden, Carden-den, and the various Kin-
cardines and Urquharts. Though not found in
Gaelic, it appears in Welsh as 'cardden,' a wood,
brake, whence Kin-cardine means Wood-head or
Wood-end. The name originally no doubt
applied only to the immediate neighbourhood of
the church ; whence it extended to the district
served by the church, *i.e.*, the parish. Such is
the origin of most parish names. The parish falls
into two divisions : the part drained by the
Carron and its feeders, and the part beyond the
watershed, toward Sutherland. We shall begin
with the former.

Carron—There are two rivers Carron in Ross, and
some half-dozen elsewhere in Scotland, all characterised by roughness of channel. The root is
kars, rough, and, on the analogy of Gaulish rivers

1

such as the Matrona, the primitive form of Carron would have been Carsona. It is doubtless pre-Gaelic, that is to say, Pictish ; cf. Carseoli in Italy.

Pools in Carron are : *Poll na muic,* sow's pool, opposite Gledfield ; *poll a' chapuill,* horse pool, near Braelangwell ; *linne sgàinne,* pool of the burst, a large dam-like pool opposite Dounie ; *poll an donnaidh,* pool of the mishap ; *poll an t-slugaid,* pool of the gulp or swallow. With the last named we may connect Braghlugudi, which appears in 1529 as belonging to the Abbey of Fearn, and no doubt refers to the bràighe or brae-face above the pool. In 1623 appears " part of Carron called Polmorral," still known as Poll-mòral. Mr Macdonald (Place-names of West Aberdeenshire) collects the following instances of this name : Balmoral, Polmorral on Dee near Banchory, Morall in Stratherne, Drummorrell in Wigtown, Morall and Lynn of Morall in the lord-ship of Urquhart, Morall mòr and Morall beag on Findhorn. Mr Macdonald suggests mòr choille, great wood, which is far from suiting the phonetics. The examples collected above may not all be of the same origin (Morel at Tomatin, for instance, is in Gaelic Móirl), but the second part of Poll-mòral above can hardly be other than mòral, majestic, noble. The pool in question is one of the largest on the river. Craigpolskavane appears on record in 1619, and appears to refer to a pool somewhere below Craigs, near Amat. There is a Loch Sgamhain in Strathbran.

Esbolg—Waterfall of bubbles, appears on record in 1657. On one of T. Pont's maps it is located on the river now known as the Blackwater, which joins the Carron at Amat, but on the old map called Ayneck (perhaps from confusion with the Eunag, a tributary of the Oykell). There is a large waterfall on this stream near Croick, now *Eas a' mhuilinn.* Perhaps, therefore, Esbolg is the "Big Fall" on Carron. Balgaidh, bubbly stream, is the name of a river in Applecross ; cf. also the better known Strathbhalgaidh. Strathbogy. Working from the eastern part of the parish along the south side of Carron, we have

Ardchronie, G. àrd-chrònaidh, an obscure name ; àrd, of course, means height or promontory ; crònaidh may be from either crón, dark brown, or crón, a hollow, both found in Irish names. Dr Joyce gives Ardcrone in Kerry as meaning brown height, and Ardcrony appears in the "Four Masters."

Gradal—G. Gràdal, Norse Grá-dalr, gray dale ; now usually called Badvoon.

Allt Eiteachan—(O.S.M. Allt na h-éiteig), probably from éiteach, root of burnt heather. Hence 'an fhéill éiteachan,' the Kincardine market.[1]

---

[1] The old-established Feill Eiteachan, the winter market still held at Ardgay, is said to owe its name to a certain quartz stone (clach éiteag), the old custom being that the market was held wherever this stone happened to be at the time. The stone was sometimes shifted west by the Assynt men, and east by the men of Ross, but finally it was built into the wall of the present Balnagown Arms Hotel at Ardgay, and so the market has ever since been held there. I give the story for what it is worth. Ma 's breug bhuam e, is breug thugam e. But éiteachan cannot be based on éiteag, which is a loan word from English *hectic* (Macbain).

Tigh'mhadaidh—Dog's (or wolf's) house.

An garbh choille—The rough wood.

Ardgay—G. ard gaoith, windy height. A deed,
granted in 1686 to erect it into a burgh of barony,
was never carried into effect.

Near it is *Carn Deasgan*, apparently the remains
of a broch. There are numerous mounds near it.
Less than half-a-mile away is *Cnoc ruigh griag*,
hill of the pebbly slope. It bears marks of forti-
fication on its western brow, and this side is
studded with tumuli.

Badavoon—G. bad a' mhun ('n' long). This is
the highest lying place with traces of cultivation
in the locality. 'Mun,' with long 'n,' seems to
be a dialectic form of 'muine,' just as 'dun,' with
long 'n,' is heard for 'duine;' muine means,
according to O'Reilly, thorn, brake, mountain, and
the last, if it can be relied on, would suit the
situation—mountain clump. Joyce, however,
gives muine only in the sense of 'brake,' and
Lhuyd has it 'thorn-tree;' cf. Bad a' mhuin bheag
and Bad a' mhuin mhòr in Coìgach.

Gledfield—A translation of G. leth'-chlamhaig, half
(*i.e.*, half-strath) of the buzzard. The word
is usually clamhan, a masculine diminutive,
while clamhag is of feminine form. The place is
known also as 'lòn na speireig,' sparrow-hawk
mead, but the other form is supported by the
records: Lachelawak, 1529; Lawchclawethe, 1561,
as belonging to the Abbey of Fearn; Lachclawy,
1606; Lachclaveig, 1643. A third form given me

is Leac 'chlamhaig, which also satisfies the written forms.

An t-sean bhaile—Old town, a very common name.

Clais a' bhaid choille—Wood-clump dell.

Lòn dialtaig—Bat-meadow (Upper Gledfield).

Dounie—Dùn, fort, with extension. There are traces of an ancient fort.

Ruigh na mèinn—Ore-slope. The epithet ' na mèinn,' literally ' of ore,' is usually applied to places where the water shows signs of oxide of iron.

An àirigh fhliuch—The wet shieling.

Alltan Domhnuill—Donald's burn.

Gruinard or Greenyards, Croinzneorth 1450, Gruinyord 1528 : Norse grunnfjörðr, shallow firth ; cf. Gruinard in Lochbroom and Gruineart in Islay.

Na h-òrdan—The heights, from àrd, high. The common tendency to change 'a' into 'o' is particularly strong in Strathcarron.

An fhànaich—The declivity ; fànach, of which fànaich is locative, is a derivative of fàn, a gentle slope, which is itself a common element in place-names, e.g., Balnain (but Balnain in Badenoch is beul an àthain, ford-mouth) ; cf. also na fàna, the Fendom, Tain.

Bun an fhuarain—Well-foot.

Croit na caillich—Old wife's croft.

Dal na crà—Dale of the (sheep) fold, or, possibly, cruive ; crà is a variant of crò, and is here feminine, if, indeed, it is not, as it may well be, for dal nan crà (gen. pl.)

Grianbhad—? Sun clump; but it may be Norse grunn-vatn, shallow loch.

Dalbhearnaidh—Dale of the cleft.

Bail' an achaidh—Town (*i.e.*, homestead) of the cultivated field.

Amat—Amayde 1429; Almet 1643, G. àmait, from Norse á-mót, river-meet, confluence, to wit, of the Carron and the Blackwater rivers. There are also Amat in Strath-Oykel and Amat in Strath-na-sealg, Brora, while the records show an Amot in North Kintyre 1643 (Reg. Mag. Sig.), in Islay 1614. Amat in Strathcarron is in two divisions, Amat na' tuath (of the husbandmen) to the south of the Carron, and Amat na h-eaglais (of the church) on the north side. There is still a tradition of a church having once stood on the 'claigionn,' above the present Lodge, and in 1609 there appears 'Amott Abbot under the barony of Ganyes, called of old the Abbacy of Fearn'; also in 1611 Ammoteglis, and Amad Heglis, T. Pont. 1608. The spelling Almet is of no significance beyond that the 'l' shows that the initial vowel is long.

Bail' an fhraoich—Heather-stead.

Baile Chaluim—Malcolm's-stead.

Bail' an dounie—G. bail' an donnaidh, town of the mishap. Near it is a pool in Carron, poll an donnaidh, so called, doubtless, from some drowning accident.

Bail' an lòin—Town of the damp meadow.

Baile mheadhonach—Mid-town.

Bail' uachdarach—Upper-town.

Dal-ghiuthais—Fir dale.

An garbh allt—The rough burn.

Gar nan aighean—Thicket of hinds; from gar comes the diminutive garan, thicket. On it is *Drochaid chaolaig*, bridge of the little narrow place, over the Carron. The green place (lùb) on the Glencalvie side was known as *bail' bean an dro'idich*, town of the bridge-wife, but a still older name for it is said to have been *Tuitim-tairbheach*. There may be here a confusion with the well-known place of that name at Oykell : my informant was born and bred at Gar nan aighean. Also *Coylum*. *i.e.*, cumhang-leum, narrow leap : cf. Cuilich in Rosskeen.

Glencalvie—G. Gleann Cailbhidh, cf. Loch Cailbhidh in Lochalsh. A Glencalvie man (there are still such, but not in the Glen), is known as a 'Cailbheach.' Glencalvie was, and is, noted for its herbage, and so are the shores of Loch Calvie : the root may therefore be calbh, colbh, plant-stalk ; Ir. colba, wand ; Latin culmus, stalk, calamus, reed.

Coire mhàileagan—V. Glenshiel. The waterfall at the mouth of the Corry was given by two informants, both natives of Glencalvie, as Eas càraidh and Eas càdaidh.

Dibidale—'The half-davach of Debadaill' 1623, G. Dìobadal, from Norse djúpr, deep ; dalr, dale, djúpidalr, 'deep-dale,' which accurately describes this beautiful, but now solitary, glen. There is a

Glen Dibidil in Rum, Mull, Skye, and Lewis; cf. also Dìabaig, Gairloch.

Sallachy—Salki 1529, on record as pasture land of the Abbey of Fearn : from saileach, the old form of 'seileach,' willow : Ir. sail, saileóg, with meaning 'place of willows.' For formation cf. Lat. salictum, from salicetum, a willow copse, cf. Sallachy on Loch Shin, Sallachy in Lochalsh, Sauchie-burn : also Salachar in Applecross, Salacharaidh, Loch Nevis. At the head of Strathcarron, forking off to the right, is

Alladale—G. Aladal, probably Ali's dale, from Ali, a Norse personal name.

Glenmore—Glenmoir, 1619 ; great glen.

Deanich—G. an dianaich, the steep place ; a locative of dianach from dian, steep, a name which well fits the place.

Meaghlaich—A place where the road crosses by a ford to Dianich ; locative of mang-lach, place of fawns ; cf. *coire na meagh*, between Dibidale and Lochan a' Chàirn. On one of Pont's maps it is marked Meuloch. Above it is *sròn 'n ìngaidh*. Near it is

An giuthais mosach—Pont's Gewish Moussach : Gyrissmissachie 1619, Reg. Mag. Sig. (where the transcriber is surely at fault), the nasty fir wood.

Toròigean : òigean, from òg, young, is used as a sort of nick-name ; the name therefore means Oigean's torr, or the youth's knoll. On the north side of the Carron we have

Invercarron—Estuary of the Carron.

Baile na coite—Boat-town ; cf. Sròn na coite on Loch Maree.

Langwell—Norse, lang-völlr, long-field.

Cornhill—G. Cnoc an airbh ; Knokinarrow. 1642 : O. Ir. arbe, corn ; later Ir. arbar, genitive arba, whence our modern Gaelic arbhar. The form ' arbh " occurs also in Cnoc an airbh, Urray, and in Ard-arbha, Lochalsh.

Syal—Seoll 1578, Soyall 1642 ; G. saoidheal : locally explained as ' suidhe fala,' seat of blood ; but it is Norse sauða-völlr, sheep-meadow.

Culvokie—G. culbhòcaidh ; hobgoblin's nook ; it has an uncanny reputation ; so has Poll-bhòcaidh at the foot of Glenmore ; cf. Culboky in Ferintosh.

Cadearg—G. an cadha dearg, the red steep path.

Culeave—G. Cul-liabh, apparently for cùl-shliabh, back (or nook) of the mountain moor : cf. for formation Cul-chàrn, Culcairn.

Balnacurach—Town of the curachs or hide boats ; cf. Balnacoit above.

Hilton—Bail' a chnuic.

Corvest—G. coire-bheist (accented on first syllable), locally explained as ' the monster's corry.' There is a very deep gully at the place, which gives colour to this, but the accent is against it.

An t-allt domhainn—Deep burn, flowing through the corry just mentioned.

Braelangwell—G. bràigh-langail, upper part of Langwell.

Bàrd an asairidh—Asair, or fasair, good pasture : bàrd is a somewhat uncommon word, but known

in Badenoch in the sense of 'meadow.' In Boath,
Alness is Bàrd nan laogh, and in Glen-Urquhart
is a meadow called 'the Bàrd.' The present name
therefore means 'the meadow of good pasture.'
Near Bàrd nan laogh in Boath there is curiously
enough 'an asaireadh,' the Assarow. Bàrd seems
borrowed from Norse barð, meaning first, beard,
then fringe, edge (cf. a hill, etc.,) hence applied to
the land on the edge of a river, which is the
situation of the Strathcarron, Boath, and Glen-
Urquhart 'bards.'

Scuitchal—Scuittechaell 1642, Skuittichaill 1657,
? Skatwell 1584, Skuddachall, Pont, G. Sguit-
chathail. Scuit is a locative of sgot, a piece of
land cut off from another, a small farm ; cf. the
Scottish 'shot,' a spot or plot of ground. The
second part of the compound is most probably the
personal name Cathal, Cathel, the meaning of this
being Cathel's section or croft.

Craigs—G. Tigh na creige, Rock-house, from the
rocky hill behind it. Pont's map shows Kreig-
skawen about this spot, and in 1619 we have
Craigpolskavane.

Glaschoille—Green wood ; Glaischaill 1619.

Lub-cònich—Mossy bend.

Lub-na-mèinn—Bend of the ore (irony water).

Letters—Na leitrichean, the hill slopes.

Croick—G. a chròic ; 'gillean na cròic' occurs in a
Strathcarron song ; the word is thus feminine.
It may be a locative of cròc, an antler, thus
meaning 'a branching glen, or side glen,' which

would suit the locality; a locative of cròg, paw, hand, is also possible, in which sense the common 'glaic' might be compared. The latter meaning suits the Croick in Glencasley, Sutherland. A diminutive of crò, sheep-fold, has been suggested, but the difficulty here is that crò, being masculine, would give crò-an, unless, indeed, we may sup- pose crò to have been dialectically feminine.

Strathcuillionach means as it stands, 'holly strath;' there is, however, a strong local tradition that the older Gaelic was 'srath cuireanach,' from 'car' a turn; hence, winding strath. The stream which flows through it is certainly very winding, and the change from 'r' to 'l' is quite possible. In its upper reaches this stream is called *Allt a ghlais àtha*, burn of the wan ford. In the high ground adjoining Strathcarron are

Garvary—G. garbhairigh, rough shieling. The termination -ary is usually best regarded as an extension of the adjective, but as there actually were shielings at Garvary, it may be taken as àirigh.

Meall na cuachaige—Cuckoo hill; possibly hill of the little 'cuach,' or cup-shaped hollow.

Meall Bhenneit—Apparently Bennet's Hill; cf. Bennetfield in the Black Isle, G. Baile Bhenneit.

Coire bog—The wet or soft corry.

Sròn na saobhaidhe—Point of the den; usually called sròn saobhaidhe.

Càrn Bhren—So often in Gaelic, but a Glen- calvie man, who ought to know, called it Càrn

Bhreathainn. There is a legend connecting it with Fingal's dog Bran. He entered a cairn there, and was never seen again. It means Raven's Cairn.

Càrn salach—'Dirty' cairn, from the broken and boggy nature of its surface.

Càrn an liath-bhaid—Hill of the grey clump.

Creag na ceapaich—Rock of the tillage plot. Ceapach (Keppoch) is one of the commonest names in the Highlands.

Cnoc na Tuppat—Locally derived from the English tippet, from the appearance of the vegetation on its rounded top; but it is more likely from 'tap,' a rounded mass or lump, which gives in Ireland Topped, Tapachan, Toppan, &c. (Joyce).

Creag Riaraidh—So the O.S.M., but G. creag(a)-raoiridh, the rocky termination of the ridge behind the old lodge of Glendibidale. There is in Tarbat a famous cave called toll-raoiridh, and below Achtercairn, Gairloch, is Leac raoiridh. This somewhat difficult name may be from roithreim (O'.R.) a rushing (ro, very, and rethim, run), and may have reference to the very stormy nature of the place.

Leaba Bhaltair—Always called Leabaidh Bhàtair. Walter's Bed, is on a hill on the south side of Glendibidale. There is another similar place bearing the same name on Alladale ground. Who the Walter in question was may be considered doubtful; but in any case the name must be connected with Frivater, 'fridh Bhàtair,' or Walter's forest. The probability is, and I

believe there is a tradition to the effect, that the
Walter whose name we find among these wild
hills was one of the early Rosses of the line of
Ferchar Mac an t-sagairt. The name is old, for it
is stated in the Chronicle of the Earls of Ross
that Paul Mactyre (fl. circ. 1360) acquired *inter
alia* Friewatter. Sir Walter Ross, son of William,
the fourth Earl, fell at Bannockburn, and, as he
was evidently a noted man, being recorded as the
dear friend of Edward Bruce, he may be the
eponymus of Walter's Bed and Walter's Forest.
The next choice would be Sir Walter de Lesley,
who married Euphemia, daughter of William, the
sixth Earl. and regarding whom William, in 1371,
addresses a 'querimonia' to King Robert II.,
complaining of the way in which his lands had
been given to Lesley. But the reference in the
Chronicle of the Earls of Ross, though perhaps
not decisive, points to the existence of the name
before Sir Walter de Lesley's time. With regard
to Paul Mactyre, I may say in passing that tradition makes him a freebooter. He may have been,
and probably was, a man of his hands, but he is
said to have been a great-grandson of the King of
Denmark, and he certainly married the niece of
Hugh of Ross, Lord of Fylorth, and obtained the
lands of Gairloch by grant of William, Earl of
Ross. in 1366 ; and in 1365, by grant of Hugh of
Ross, the lands of 'Tutumtarvok, Turnok, Amot
and Langvale in Strathokel.' His pedigree, as
given by Skene, connects him closely with the

Rosses or Clan Anrias, for it makes him fourth in descent from Gilleanris (modern Gillanders). He was therefore highly connected, and held a respectable position, and his descendants, the Polsons, have no reason to feel ashamed of him.

Creag Illie—G. Creag-illidh. ' Illie ' has exactly the same sound as in Bun-illigh, Helmsdale, where it represents Ila, the Ptolemaic name of the Helmsdale river. Creag Illie stands just about the west end of Glendibidale, not far from the source of the stream, now nameless, which runs through the glen, and though, of course, the case does not admit of certainty, 'Illie' may here also be the old river name ; cf. the rivers Isla, and for root German ' eilen,' to hurry. Cf. also G. ' èaladh ' (Macbain's Dict.).

Creag Ruadh—The red rock ; near Creag Illie.

Dùnach liath—The grey place of dùns ; Leac Gorm, the green hillside ; and the Dùnan liath, grey little dun, are beyond Coire Mhalagan.

Càrn Speireig—The sparrow-hawk's cairn.

Leab' a' Bhruic—The badger's lair.

Beinn Tarsuinn—' The cross hill,' which bars the head of Dibidale and of Coire Mhalagan.

Feur mòr—The big grass.

Cròm Loch—The bent loch—descriptive of its semi-circular shape.

Lochan Sgeireach—The little rocky loch.

Meall na Raineich—Hill of bracken.

An Socach—The snouted hill.

Sròn gun aran—Bread-less point—a quaint name.

Allt a mheirbh ghiuthais—(O.S.M., allt a mhòr ghiuthais). T. Pont, phonetically but accurately, has it 'alt very gewish,' 'burn of the slender pine-wood.' Mearbh is a variant of meanbh.

Loch Sruban—G. Loch Struaban. 'Lochen Stromannach so cald from great golden heared trowts' (Pont). What 'heared' means I cannot conjecture; the letter rendered *h* is doubtful, otherwise the MS. is perfectly clear. It is interesting, however, to know that 'struabanach math bric' is still locally used to denote a good-sized trout, such as are the trout of Loch Struaban. The root may be sruab, to make a paddling noise in water (H.S. Dict.); a 'sruabanach' would thus mean a fish that lashes the water.

Coire mòr—The great corry.

Meall am madadh: prop. Meall a' Mhadaidh—Dog's, or perhaps wolf's, hill.

Bodach mor and **Bodach beag**—The big and the little old man.

Meall nam fuaran—Hill of springs.

Allt a' chlaiginn—Skull burn. A 'claigionn' is usually a skull-shaped hill; but sometimes it means the best field of a farm.

An Sgaothach—'Sgaoth,' swarm; place of swarms; cf. 'sguabach,' place of 'sweeps' (of wind).

Allt a' ghuail—Coal burn; what the coal is, I have not learned; but cf. meall a' ghuail.

Creagloisgte—Burnt rock.

Càrn a' choin deirg—Cairn of the red dog.

Sithean rùarach--Sithean. a round hill, diminutive of sìth, a fairy seat ; rùarach. an extension of ruadh. red : cf. Ruarach in Kintail.

Coir' an t-seilich--Willow corry.

Cnoc an tubaist--Hill of the mischance.

Corriemulzie--G. coire mùillidh, mill-corry ; cf. Corriemulzie in Contin and in W. Aberdeenshire, Mulzie in Kiltarlity. Mr J. Macdonald suggests 'maoile.' corry of the hill brow, but the Gaelic pronunciation at once negatives this. In Corriemulzie. it appears from local information. there were at one time or other no fewer than seven mills. the sites of five of which can still be pointed out. The Garve Corriemulzie is also a place of old habitation. where there were, doubtless, mills. Muileann, a mill, has a genitive muilne, which readily becomes muille.

Abhainn dubhach--Sad river.

Mullach a' chadha bhuidhe--Stop of the steep yellow path.

Allt rappach--Noisy or dirty burn.

Creag Eabhain--Gladsome rock ; cf. Beinn Eibhinn in Badenoch, which is a hill with good outlook.

Allt Tarsuinn--Cross burn, from *loch na bìthe*, pitch loch (from pine wood) ; cf. Blarnabee in Strathconon.

Allt coir an rùchain--Probably from rùchan, throat, gullet ; corry of the throat, a narrow opening.

Strath Seasgaich--Probably a derivative of ' seisc,' reed, seasgach, loc. seasgaich, reedy place. There is also seasgach, a yeld cow, but this ought to give srath na(n) seasgach.

Allt Ealag—Ealag, properly eileag, is puzzling ; it looks like a diminutive of the feminine proper name Eilidh, only in point of fact this diminutive does not seem to be found. It may well be from ail, stone, meaning ' the little stony burn.' There is also Mointeach Eileag, a dreary stretch of moor on the Lairg and Lochinver road.

Sgonnan mòr—The great lumps : sgonn, block, lump.

Loch coir' na meidhe—There is meidh, a balance, and meidhe, a stem, stock. trunk, the latter of which is more likely to be in point here.

Coir' a' chonachair—Conachar means uproar ; also, a sick person who gets neither better or worse. It may be the proper name Conachar ; there is really no means of determining ; cf. Badach-onachair in Kilmuir Easter.

Lubcroy—G. an lùb-chruaidh, the hard bend ; cruaidh is applied to hard, stony ground, or to firm ground as opposed to bog.

Oykell has been happily identified with Ptolemy's Ripa Alta, High Bank, the exact location of which has long been matter of dispute. It must also be identified with the Norse Ekkjals-bakki, *i.e.*, Oykell Bank, which Skene strangely makes out to be the Grampians. Oykell represents the Gaulish uxellos, high, seen in Uxello-dunum, high fort. The word appears in Celtic in two forms—(1) Welsh uchel, high, which gives the Ochil Hills and Ochil-tree, high town ; (2) Gaelic uasal, high, and, without the -llo- suffix, uaise, height, majesty,

2

whence Beinn Uaise, Wyvis. Oykell follows the
Welsh form. It will thus be seen that Ptolemy's
Ripa Alta is a part translation of Oykel, which is
echoed by the Norse Ekkjalsbakki. The word for
bank is gone, but it evidently existed in Ptolemy's
time, and it looks as if it survived to the time of
the Norse occupation, and was translated by the
Norsemen into bakki. It is worth noting that the
high ground on the Sutherland side of the Oykell
estuary is Altas, G. Allt-ais, an extension of alt,
eminence; cf. Welsh allt, wooded cliff, hillside:
also O. Ir. alltar, heights.

Inveroykell is the confluence of the rivers Oykell
and Casley.

Einig—A tributary of the Oykell; G. Eunag. Pont
makes Avon Ayneck flow into the Carron at Amat.
Dr Joyce gives ean, water, as the basis of eanach,
a marsh. The streams falling into the Eunag
are—*Allt Rappach*, noisy or 'dirty' burn;
Abhainn Poiblidh, river of the booth, pubull;
Abhainn Coire Muillidh, the Corriemulzie river;
Abhainn Dubhach, the sad or gloomy river.

Amat—At the junction of Eunag and Oykell; cf.
Amat in Strathcarron above. The Oykell Amat
was distinguished as Amat na gullan, *i.e.*, na
ncuilean, of the whelps.

Lochan Phòil—Paul's lochlet, is probably a reminiscence of Paul Mactyre, who held these lands, as
above stated.

Langwell—Cf. Langwell, Strathcarron.

Beinn Ulamhie—Cf. ulbh (Sutherland), a term of
reproach, from Norse úlfr, wolf.

Meoir Langwell—The 'branches' of Langwell; *i.e.*, hill streams that converge there.

Loch Mhic Mharsaill probably contains the name of a son of 'William Mareschal, armiger to Hugh of Ross,' who was granted by the said Hugh, between 1350 and 1372, the lands of 'Dachynbeg in Westray' (Edderton) for good and faithful services. He received also lands in Tarbat and elsewhere; but he could hardly have held lands in the Oykell district, for it was held by Paul Mactyre. This, however, does not necessarily affect the argument.

Brae—G. a bhràigh.

Doune—Downe, 1657; a township on the Oykell; dùn, fort.

Oape—òb, creek; Norse hóp; it is near a bend in the river; cf. Oban.

Innis nan damh—Ox, or stag, meadow; cf. the other well-known Inshindamff.

Ochtow—G. an t-ochdamh, the eighth-part, to wit, of Davach-carbisdale (1623), which included most of this district.

Birchfield—Formerly Ach na h-uamhach, field of the cave, probably from the chambers of the broch, now much broken down, a little to the west of the farm-house.

Kilmachalmag—Sic 1548, Colman's cell; v. Church names. Within a short distance of it, on the edge of the wood, is the foundation of what seems to have been a broch of rather small diameter.

Achnahannet—G. achadh na h-annait, field of the 'mother church,' v. Church names.

An ruigh cruaidh—The hard slope.

Meall Deargaidh—G. Meall dheirgidh, from deargadh, redness ; Hill of redness.

Badandaraich—Oak copse.

Achnagart—Field of the corn enclosure ; cf. Garty, Goirtean.

Creag 'Chait—Cat's rock.

Lamentation Hill (O.S.M.)—G. creag a' chòinneachan, rock of the mossy place. Cf. the continuation of the " History of the Earldom of Sutherland " with reference to the defeat of Montrose, which took place here in 1650 :—' This miraculous victorie hapned the twentie seaventh of Aprill one thousand six hundreth fiftie years at Craigchoynechan, besides Carbesdell.' As this is a contemporary account, it effectually disposes of the popular notion, officially adopted on the O.S. Map as above, that the place meant Rock of Lamentation (Còineadh). The name was given long before the battle took place.

Poll cas gaibhre, Goat's foot pool, is a deep rounded hollow situated near the Kyle between Stamag and Riantyre (ruigh an t-saoir, the carpenter's slope). There is another of the same kind near the Church of Dunlichity, Inverness. These curious cup-like depressions are explained as the result of swallow-holes in glaciers.

Culrain—Of old Carbisdale ; Carbustell, 1548. The modern name is said to have been imposed from Coleraine in Ireland. Carbisdale is Norse kjarr-bólstaðr, copse-stead, with the suffix dalr, dale.

Rhilonie—G. ruigh an lòin, slope of the wet meadow.
Balnahinsh—Town of the meadow; near it is the site of Càrn nan Conach (O S.M. Carn nan Conacht).
Achagilliosa—Gillies' field; Sithean an Radhairc. Prospect Hill.

From a retour of 1623 it appears that at that date Strathkyle (Slios a' Chaolais) as far west as Ochtow was included under the term Davoch-carbiṣtell. We have 'the lands of Achnagart, belonging to Davoch-carbistell,' also 'the western bovate of Davoch-carbistell, called Ochtow, with the croft and arable land lying near the Meikill Cairne, called Cairne Croft, above the east side of the burn called Auldualeckach under the Barony of Kilmachalmag.' The names of burn and croft have now disappeared. The Meikill Cairne perhaps refers to the Birchfield broch. In 1657 we have 'the lands of Dalvanachtan [*i.e.*. Davach-nachtan] and Downe, extending to six davach lands, whereof four davach lands lye benorthe the water of Oichill and two davach lands on the south side.' Davach-nachtan is also gone. Nachtan is, of course, the personal name Nectan, so common among the Picts, still surviving in the surname Macnaughton. In 1619 (Reg. Mag. Sic.) we have the lands of Auchnagullane, Glaischaill, and Tormichaell; the forest of Frawatter, adjacent to them; the lands of Glenmoir, Glenbeg, Drumvaiche, Brynletter, Correvulzie, Knokdaill, Dovaik; the lands called

' the thrie Letteris,' viz., Letterinay, Letternaiche, Letterneteane, and Corremoir under the said forest of Frewatter; the scheillings of Mullach, Craigpolskavane, Gyrissmissachie, Tokach, Laikgarny, Alladul moir, Straithfairne, Alladill na nathrach, and Cairnehondrig. Pont marks Achanagullann on Avon Ayneck, near Esbulg, above noted. Tormichaell is somewhere in Strathcarron. The three Letters may, perhaps, be Letters noted above; they appear to stand for Leitir an fheidh, Leitir 'n eich, and Leitir na teine. Mullach is Meaghlaich noted above. Craigpolskavane seems to be the present Craigs. Gyrissmissachie is An giuthais mosach above noted. Alladul moir and Alladul na nathrach are clear. Cairnehondrig is Carn Sònraichte. Brynletter, Tokach, Laikgarny, Drumvaiche I do not know. The fishing of Acheferne and Stogok 1341; Achnafearne and Sloggake 1657. Downlairne 1604 appears on Pont's map as Downilaern, a little west of Layd Clamag (Gledfield).

EDDERTON.

Edderton — Ederthayn 1275 ; Eddirtane 1532 ;
Eddirthane 1561 ; G. Eadardan, with accent on
eadar. The traditional explanation is eadar-dùn,
between forts. In confirmation of this view may
be adduced the various brochs referred to below
and the hill fort of Strathrory. The name
applies especially to the part near the old church,
now the U.F. Church, which stands on the left
bank of Edderton Burn, and it would seem that
the old name for the district as a whole was
Westray ; cf. below ' Dachynbeg in Westray ' and
Blaeu's Dunivastra.

An luachar mhòr—' The big rashes ' (rushes), a
large swampy tract of moor.

Cnoc an t-sabhail—Barn-hill ; in the face of it,
above Raanich, is *clach meadhon latha*, mid-day
stone. There are two stones, some distance apart,
and which of the two is the real mid-day stone is
hard to say. The position is such that the sun
shines on them about noon.

Raanich—G. an ràthanaich ; the root is ràth, a
circular enclosure or fort, the rest being extensions (-n-ach), meaning ' place of raths.' South
of Raanich is *baile nam fuaran*, well-town.

Ramore—G. an ràth mòr, the great rath. These
raths were, probably, simply farm-houses fortified

for security in troublous times. Behind Ramore
is *an linne bhreac*, the dappled pool. Near it is
Galanaich, from gallan, a standing-stone. There is
a striking perched block not far off ; cf. Gallanaich,
Argyll ; Achagallon in Arran.

An t-uisge dubh—Black water.

Cadha nan damh (O.S.M. Casandamff)—Stags'
pass.

Gluich (Meikle and Little)—G. an glaodhaich ;
Glaodhaich àrd agus Glaodhaich iosal ; from
glaodh, glue, E. Ir. glaed, with -ach suffix ; hence
the soft, sticky, miry place, which applies well to
the lower Gluich. There is another Gluich in
Altas, Sutherland, also wet, and a third in Glenconvinth. Local tradition ascribes the name to
the ' glaodhaich' or lamentation of the Edderton
women on occasion of a battle with the Danes,
and a similar origin is assigned to Raanich (bha
iad a' rànail an sin).

Bailecharn—G. beul-atha chàrn, ford-mouth of the
cairns, a ford on the Edderton Burn, above *Eas
an tairbh*, the bull's waterfall, which latter is
reputed to be the haunt of a tarbh-uisge, water-
bull.

Inchintaury—The Gaelic hesitates between innis
an t-samhraidh and innis an t-sea'raigh, but the
latter seems to be the common local form, probably for seann ruigh, old shieling.   Innis an
t-samhraidh means summer-mead, *i.e.*, a grassy
meadow on which cows grazed in summer.

Rhibreac—G. an ruigh breac, the dappled slope.

Bogrow—G. am bogaradh, a derivative of bog, soft, wet—wet place ; it is a soft place by the water side. Also *leathad a' bhogaraidh*, broad slope of the soft place. In 1634 appears on record (Reg. Mag. Sig.) ' magnus limes lapideus vocatus Clachnabogarie,' the great march stone called, etc., to the east of Edderton Burn. The stone is still there, and known by the same name, but it is no longer a march stone, the burn being now the march.

Cambuscurrie — G. camus-curaidh, bay of the curach, coracle ; possibly currach, marsh. The Gaelic has certainly been affected by the modern English form. Locally said to have been the landing place of Curry or Carius (v. N. Stat. Acc.), the Danish prince whose prowess caused the ' glaodhaich ' and ' rànail ' above referred to. Cf. Cambuschurrich on Lochtayside.

Carrieblair—G. blàr a' charaidh ; the farm-stead is bail' a charaidh ; caraidh means ' grave-plot.' Cf. clach 'charaidh, the name of the fine sculptured stone at Shandwick, Nigg (see Nigg). There is a sculptured stone on Carrieblair also, still standing and depicted in Dr Stuart's ' Sculptured Stones of Scotland,' near which ancient graves have been excavated. According to local tradition, this stone marks the grave of Carius referred to above.

Edderton Farm—G. baile na foitheachan (final ' a ' open). The formation of ' foitheachan ' seems parallel with that of Guisachan, etc., and suggests as the base ' faidh,' a beech, which in Scottish

Gaelic is 'faidhbhile,' beech-tree. The name would thus mean Place of beeches.

Balleigh — Ballinleich 1550, Ballinleich, *alias* Litchstoune 1666 ; G. bail' an lighe (also lighich), Leech's or physician's town. Locally said to have been the place where the wounded were treated after the battle of Carrieblair.

Ardmore—G. an t-ard mòr, great promontory.

Rudha nan sgarbh—Cormorants' point ; here is a large round cairn. '*càrn màthaidh*,' where mathaidh is perhaps a proper name, near *loch nan tunnag*, duck loch.

Requill—G. ruigh Dhùghaill, Dugald's slope.

Pollagharry—G. poll a' ghearraidh, pool of the 'gearraidh.' There is no pool here now, but there was once, according to local evidence, a small loch. Gearraidh is Norse gerδi, a fenced field, borrowed, very common in Lewis, and meaning the strip of land between machair and monadh, plain and upland moor.

Garbad—G. an garbh-bad, the rough chump ; also, coille a' gharbh-bhaid, Garbad wood.

Meikle and Little Daan—G. Dathan mhòr and Dathan bhig ; 'Dachynbeg in Vestray' was granted circ. 1350 by Hugh of Ross to his armiger, William Marescal ; Daane 1429 ; Little Dovane 1578. These forms may possibly point to its being a diminutive of 'dabhach,' the old Celtic measure of land, and at the Reformation Dathan Meikle was three-fourths of a davach, and Dathan Lytle one-fourth—a davach in all. The place, however, stands at the confluence of two streams, and as there is an O. Ir. word ' an,' water, the name may really be dà-an, two waters. The joint stream is called the Daan burn, and the traditional explanation of Daan is da-àthan, two fords, which is quite possibly right. Near Daan is *Torr a' bhil*, edge-hill. Also, ' *an dòbhran*,' which seems to be a derivative of O.G. dobur, water, meaning ' the wet place.'

Balblair—G. bail' a' bhlair, plain-town ; near it is ' *an ruigh bhreac*,' spotted slope ; and east of it, ' *leac an duine*,' man's flat stone ; and ' *àrd mhanaidh*,' monk's point.

Little and Meikle Dallas—Doles 1560 ; G. Dalais mhòr and Dalais bhig. It is never used with the article. The old form, as compared with the modern Gaelic, shows the common transition from ' o ' to ' a '; cf. Culboky, G. cul-bhàicidh ; -ais is the Pictish ending seen in Allt-ais, etc. (v. Introd.), and the first syllable is to be equated with ' dol ' in dolmen, used in place-names in the sense of ' plateau.' Dallas is thus a Pictish word, meaning ' place of the plateau,' which describes its situation ; cf. Dallas, Elgin ; perhaps also Dalkeith.

Dounie—from dùn, fort.

Hilton—G. Bail' a' chnuic.

Craigroy—a chreag ruadh, red rock.

Cartomie—G. càthar-tomaidh ; càthar, a moss or bog, and tom, hillock ; compounded on the same principle as Balaldie, etc. (v. Introd.)

Polinturk—G. poll an tuirc, boar's pool.

Cnocan na goibhnidh — (O.S.M. Cnoc àl na gamhainn), smithy-hillock, near Polinturk.

Muieblairie — Moyzeblary 1429. G. muigh-bhlàraidh, spotted plain ; locative of magh, compounded with blàr, spotted, with the -idh ending so common in Easter Ross. Blàr is not nearly so frequent in place-names as its synonyms riabhach. breac, ballach.

Alltnamain—G. allt na mèinn, burn of ore, with reference to its irony water. There are strong traces of iron in most of the Edderton burns and wells, and there are even said to have been iron-workings in Edderton burn.

Struie—G. an t-srùidh ; rathad na Strùidh, the road from Alness to Bonar, which attains its highest point at Cnoc na Strùidh. Before railways this was the usual route from the south, so John Munro of Creich in his ' Oran Ducha,' on leaving Glasgow to visit his native place, says—

> O théid sinn, théid sinn le suigeart agus aoidh,
> O théid sinn, théid sinn gu deònach,
> O théid sinn, théid sinn thairis air an t-Srùidh
> Gu muinntir ar daimh, is ar n-eòlais.

Strùidh appears to be best regarded as a contracted form of sruth-aidh, an extension of the root of sruth, stream ('t' euphonic). From the base of Cnoc na Strùidh streams flow in all directions ; cf. Struy in Strathglass, which is also a place of streams. At *Lòn na Strùidh*, moist flat of Struie, is *fuaran an òir*, a well strongly impreg-

nated with iron, and reckoned to possess healing
properties, but it has been insulted (chaidh tàmailt
a chur air), and is not what it once was ; so called
from a gold ring having been lost in it in course
of cleaning.

Lechanich—G. an leachanaich (Leachanaich àrd and
L. iosal) ; locally interpreted as leth Choinnich,
Kenneth's half, but the presence of the article
does not countenance this. The place is a sloping
hill-side, and the name is, most likely, Leacanaich
(with 'c' aspirated), from leac, a sloping hill-face ;
v. Macbain's Dict., s.v. lethcheann.

Cnoclady—G. cnoc leathadaidh, hill of the 'leathad'
or slope ; formed like Bal-aldie. Near it is *badan
binn* (*'n*) *coin*, where 'eoin,' as in other cases
where it occurs, seems to be the genitive singular
of èun, bird.

Craggan—G. an creagan, the little rock ; behind it
is *allt na corrach*, burn of the places of corries ;
there are three small corries drained by it.
Beyond this again, leading towards Fearn, is ' *an
cadha iosal*,' the low pass, over Struie.

Cnoc an liath bhaid—Hill of the grey clump.

Beinn clach an fheadain—Hill of the whistle
stone or of the spout (of water).

Carr Dubh—G. an càthar dubh, a hill ; càthar,
usually a moss or bog, is here used to mean ' a
rough, broken surface.'

Cnoc Bad a' bhacaidh—Hill of the moss-clump.

Cnoc an Ruigh ruaidh—Hill of the red slope.

Chulash—A' chùlais, the recess.

Cnoc Thorcaill—Torquil's hill.

Cnoc 'Chlachain—Hill of the clachan, with reference
to the Monastery of Fearn, the original site of
which was not far off.

Meall na siorramachd—(O.S.M. Cnoc Leathado
na siorramachd)? Shire-hill, on the Kincardine
boundary.

Beinn nan oighreagan—Hill of the cloud-berries ;
the usual plural is oighrean, implying a singular
oighre, ot which oighreag is diminutive.

Easter, Western, and Mid Fearn—Feàrn' àrd,
Feàrn' ìochdarach, literally High Fearn and Lower
Fearn, and Feàrna meadhonach. Blaeu's Atlas
has Faern Iera, Faern Meanach, Faern Ocra ;
from Feàrna, alder. The Monastery of Fearn
was originally founded 'near Kintarue, in Strath-
charron' (Chron. of Earls of Ross), probably,
therefore, at Wester Fearn, about 1225, and
about twenty years later, in the founder's life-
time, 'for the more tranquillitie, peace and
quietnes thereof translated' to the spot it still
occupies, where it was called at first Nova Farina,
New Fearn, then simply Fearn.

Allt Grùgaig—The little surly one, the burn of
Wester Fearn.

According to the New Stat. Acc. (1840),
" there is a complete chain of those round towers
called Dunes surrounding this parish ; none
of them, however, in a state of even tolerable
preservation. One of these, situated at Easter
Fearn, and known by the name of Dune-Alliscaig

(from Dùn-fair-loisgeadh, or the beacon watch
tower), was about fourteen feet in height within
the last thirty years, and had vaults and a spiral
staircase within the wall." It was destroyed for
dykes, etc., about 1818. The site is still to be
seen, and the name is still current in Gaelic as
Dùn Alaisgaig. Falaisg, moor-burning, which
seems hinted at in the derivation offered above,
suits the phonetics exactly, but the word is
probably Norse. Blaeu has it Dun Alliscaig.
East of it he marks Dunivastra, i.e., Dounie of
Westray, now Dounie, where there are also the
ruins of a broch still known as the ' càrn liath.'
There is a third, nameless, at Lechanich, said to
have been six or seven feet high, with chambers,
within living memory. Càrn màthaidh, on Rudha
nan sgarbh, may have been another.

There are no Norse names in Edderton, except
the obsolete Westray, and possibly Dùn Alaisgaig.

TAIN.

Tain—Tene 1227 ; Thane 1483. The Gaelic form
is not available, as Baile Dhubhaich, St Duthac's
town, has in Gaelic displaced Tain. The existence
of another Tain, near the head of Dunnet Bay in
Caithness, suggests the name to be Norse, but it
is difficult to offer a satisfactory etymology. The
guesses of Rev. W. Taylor and others need not be
repeated, nor have I arrived at anything certain.
In Reg. Mag. Sig., under date 1612, the annual
markets of Tain are given as follows :—Midsomer
or St John's, 26 June ; S. Barquhani, 4 August ;
[St Berchan] S. Duthosi, 30 December, 6 March ;
S. Makharboch, 20 November. The Calendar of
Fearn gives only three fairs, on 18 March, 9
August, and 20 December, the last being 'Mak-
carmochis day.' (St Cormac ; cf. Tobar Cormaic
in Nigg).

The girth of Tain, marked out by four crosses
(Charter of James II., 1457), appears to have
been roughly co-extensive with the bounds of
the parish. In 1616 (Reg. Mag. Sig.) appears
' the girth croce dividing the common lands of
the Burgh of Tayne from Ulladil,' and Rev.
W. Taylor notes *clais na comraich*,[1] hollow of the
girth or sanctuary, on the southern boundary of

[1] It is at " The Canary."

the parish, towards Scotsburn (of old Ulladale).
Crois Caitrion, Catherine's Cross, to the north of
Loch Eye, may have been another girth cross.
The revenues of the Collegiate Church of Tain,
which dates from 1487, were derived from the
lands of Tain, Innerathy, Newmore, Dunskaith,
Morynchy, Tallirky, and Cambuscurry. Of these
places, the last five were chaplainries, and the
last three were within the girth of Tain.

Meikle Ferry—G. am port mòr, of old Portin-
coulter. The Little Ferry is at the mouth of
Loch Fleet, between the parishes of Dornoch and
Golspie.

Ardjachie—G. àird-achaidh, promontory of the
cultivated field.

Tarlogie—Tallirky 1487 ; Tarlogy 1529 ; Tallarky
1559 ; Talreky 1580 ; G. Tàrlogaidh. Talorg,
diminutive Talorgan, was a Pictish proper name,
from tal, brow, and the root arg, white, seen in
argentum, airgiod, Argos. The Gaulish proper
name Argiotalus shews the same elements. The
name of a Pictish saint Talorgan survives in Kiltarlity, G. Cill-Taraghlain. As a place-name,
white brow is, of course, quite appropriate.

Pitnellies—Petnely 1512 ; G. Bail' an ianlaith,
Birds' town. The plural form has arisen from the
division of Pitnely into two—north and south.
The English form is an instructive corruption.

Balcherry—G. Bail' a' cheathraimh, town of the
quarter (davach), cf. Balcherry, near Invergordon,
also Ochto.

Pithogarty—Petogarthe 1548 ; Pettogarty 1560 ;
Betagartie 1574 ; G. Bail' shogartaidh, Priest's
town. The true Gaelic form would be Bail' an
t-sagairt or Baile nan sagart ; cf. Pitentagart and
Balhaggarty in Aberdeenshire.

The Fendom—G. na fàna (fánoo), from fàn, a gentle
slope, or, usually in Scottish topography, a flat,
low-lying place, the Scots ' Laigh.' Fàn is seen
as an adjective in Rob Donn, ' an rùm a's fhàine
fo 'n ùir,' the lowest room beneath the earth, *i.e.*,
the grave. The English form is a curious corruption.

Balkeith or **Balkil**—Ballecuth 1548 ; G. Baile na
coille, town of the wood ; keith looks like Welsh
gwydd, wood, which would make the modern
Gaelic Baile na coille a direct translation of an
original Pictish Pit-keith. Similarly Dal-keith,
which is on a flat-backed ridge, may mean
' plateau of the wood.'

Plaids—Plaiddes 1560 ; G. a Phlaid, from Norse
flatr, the flat or low land. The plural form is
English ; cf. Pladday, Flat Isle. Fladay, off
Barra, retains the Norse form. Near Plaids is
said to have been a court-hill of Paul Mactyre.

Morangie—Morinchy 1487, Morinch 1507, Morin-
schie 1618 ; G. Mòr(a)istidh. The ' t ' of the
modern Gaelic form is, doubtless, developed after
' s ' (cf. *an dràsd* for *an tràth sa* ; *cùlaist* for
culais), and from the old forms it may be inferred
to be of fairly recent origin. This leaves us with
Mòr(a)isidh, where ' is ' is the reduced form of

'innis,' haugh, and the rest is termination, the whole meaning Big-haugh.

Kirksheaf—Kerskeith 1560, Kirkskeith 1607; Croskyth. Pont ; now in G. a chroit mhòr, the big croft. The old forms suggest cathair, seat or fort, and either sgàth, dread (cf. Dunskaith in Nigg), or sgèith, hawthorn. The place is close to the ancient Chapel of St Duthus.

Cnoc nan aingeal, or Angels' Hill—The small hill, now cut through by the railway, north-east of the old chapel. The road to Inver crosses the cutting by a bridge. Cf. Cnoc nan aingeal at Kirkton of Lochalsh. The name may equally well mean knoll of fires, from G. aingeal, light, fire.

Knockbreck—G. an cnoc breac, the spotted hill.

Cnocanmealbhain—Knoll of the white lump.

Aldie—G. Alltaidh. burn place, from allt, with extension.

Garrick Burn—Muirs and Moss of Garrack, 1690 ; also Ben Garrick, Beindyarrok 1632, and drochaid Gharaig, Garrick Bridge.

Knocknacean—G. cnoc nan ceann, hill of heads, with probable reference to a battle.

Glastullich—Green hillock ; locative of tulach.

Blarleath—G. am blàr liath, the gray plain.

Ardival—Height of the home-stead.

Loch Lapagial—A tiny lochlet in the heights, the Gaelic form of which I have failed to verify.

Loch Uanaidh—(O.S.M. Lochan Uaine); Loch Owany, Pont ; perhaps from uan, lamb, but there is also O. Ir. uan, foam.

An t-allt clachach—The stony burn.

Beinn na gearran—of O.S.M. should be Binn Garaig, the hill of Tain.

Lairg—'The Lairgs of Tain'; G. lairig, a sloping hill, moor.

Kingscauseway—G. cabhsair an righ; but, according to Rev. W. Taylor, rathad an righ; probably the road by which James IV. so often rode to St Duthac's shrine.

Balnagall—Balnagaw 1560, town of the strangers; scarcely likely to be a reminiscence of the Norseman.

Bogbain—G. am bac bàn, white moss.

Hunting Hill—G. druim na sealg.

Morrich more—G. a mhoraich mhòr, a large, low-lying sandy flat by the sea shore. Moraich, better mor(mh)oich or mor'oich, is from Ir. murmagh, sea plain; cf. a mhor'oich, the Gaelic of Lovat; Morvich, Kintail, &c. It is usually applied to a plain by the sea shore, yet we have a moor so called in Badenoch. A sand bank off the coast, accessible only at low tides, is called '*an aideal*,' from Norse vaðill, ford.

Loch Preas an uisge, Loch na Muic, Loch nan Tunnag, Loch of the Water-bush, Sow Loch, and Duck Loch are small lochs in the Morrich More.

An innis mhòr, big isle, and an innis bheag, small isle, off the coast.

Whiteness—Apparently Norse, white point.

The Gizzen Briggs[1]—A dangerous sandy bar guard-
ing the entrance to the Dornoch Firth. G.
drochaid an obh (ow). Taylor, however, gives
drochaid an aobh, and says he had also heard
drochaid an naomh, with a nasal sound. The
local explanation connects with baobh, or baogh,
hag, in Easter Ross called ' a vow,' and specialised
into the meaning of water-sprite, or possibly
mermaid ; in any case, a malicious spirit. Gizzen
Briggs is connected by Taylor with Norse Geyser,
a boiling spring, which suits neither the sense nor
the phonetics. Brig, for bridge, is so utterly
foreign to the English of Ross that it is most
reasonable to regard it as a Norse survival, as also
the ' meikle,' so common in Easter Ross farm
names. The name is, doubtless, the Norse
' gisnar bryggja,' leaky bridge. In Easter Ross
the term ' gizzened,' leaky, is still commonly
applied to tubs or barrels that have shrunk in the
sun.

Inveraithie—Now practically obsolete ; in a Retour
of 1652 appears as ' within the liberty of Tain,
and having salmon fishings and stells.' ' The
tradition is that the town of Tain was once built
much nearer than it is at present to the mouth of
the river, on land that has been in great part
swept away by the sea, but that was called in old
charters and is sometimes remembered still as

---

[1] " Most of the Norwegian fiords are partially obstructed at their entrance
by the remains of old moraines, which in the north are called *havbroen*, sea
bridges " (*Reclus, Univ. Geog.*).

Inver-Eathie, or in Gaelic Inbhir-àthai' (Taylor).
The Gaelic form here given, though it cannot now
be verified, is doubtless right, for Eathie Burn
in the Black Isle is Allt àthaidh.   Evidently
àthaidh was also the old name of the Tain river.
The word is probably based on àth, a ford.

Inver—G. an in'ir (inbhir), the confluence, or mouth
of a stream.   Rev. W. Taylor says that it appears
in old documents as Inverlochslin, which would
imply that Lochslin, now drained, sent its waters
in this direction.

Na h-oitrichean—The mussel scalps, from G. oitir,
sea bank.

Culpleasant—A hybrid of comparatively recent
origin ; cùil, nook.   Near it is *Fuaran Dhà'idh*,
St David's well, the principal source of the Tain
water supply.

The Canary—So called, it is said, from a drinking
place which once existed here.

Queebec—Bridge and Brae, on the Scotsburn road
about two miles from Tain ; the name arose from
the fact that a gentleman who had made money
in Quebec settled near.   The Gaelic name is
Muileann Luaidh, Fulling Mill, and the burn
is *Allt Luaidh*.

Commonty—Once the common lands of the burgh
of Tain.

The following names appear to be obsolete :—
The two Thesklaris (on west side of Tain),
Enycht, Croftmatak, Poltak, Neclacanalych, Bal-
natouch, Petgerello, Skardy with its mill, Auley

(? Aldie), the Buttis, Gorlinges, Clerk Island, and
Priest Island, the last three 'belonging to the
Burgh from time immemorial (confirmation of
1612 by King James VI.)

FEARN.

Fearn was until 1628 included in the parish of
Tarbat. The name was transferred with the monastery from Fearn, Edderton. The monastery, on
its new site, was styled Nova Farina, New Fearn,
but in Gaelic the parish is Sgìr na Manachainn,
Parish of the Monastery, also simply A' Mhan-
achainn. As distinguished from Beauly (Manachainn 'Ic Shimidh), it is called Manachainn Rois, the
Monastery of Ross.

Cadboll—Cathabul 1529; Norse kattar-ból, cat-
stead; from this and similar names in Tarbat
it appears that the rocks facing the Moray Firth
were of old a haunt of wild cats. Cf. Cattadale,
Islay. Below Cadboll are *Tobar a' bhaile duibh*,
Well of the black town, and *Tobar Suardalain*,
Well of Suardalan; also *Creag na baintighearna*,
the Lady's rock.

Cadboll Mount—The curious story of Cadboll
Mount is told by Bishop Forbes. The Laird of
Cadboll was on bad terms with his cousin,
Macleod of Geanies, and built the 'mount' to
look down on his lands. Geanies replied by
planting a belt of trees which in time shut out
the view. The mound, which still exists, was
made quadrangular, built in steps like a pyramid,
and about 60 feet high.

Hilton—Balnaknok 1610 ; G. bail' a' chnuic.

Balintore—G. bail' an todhair, bleaching-town ; cf.
Balintore in Abriachan and in Kirkhill. The
name goes back to the time when flax was cultivated in the north. The old name of Balintore
is given locally as Port an Ab, Abbot's Port, and
Blaeu shows Abbotshaven here.

Tullich—Tulloch 1606 ; G. an tulaich (locative),
at the hillock.

Clasnamuiack—Glasnamoyache 1647 ; G. Clais na
maigheach, Hares' hollow.

Balmuchy—Balmochi 1529 ; Balmoch 1561 ; G.
Baile mhuchaidh. The meaning is uncertain ;
muc, pig, is out of the question ; perhaps Ir.
much, mist, or mucha, owl. Pendicles of
Balmuchy were Bellewallie (Broomtown), Ballin-
reich (*Bail' an fhraoich*, Heather-stead, between
Fearn U.F. Church and Manse, north of the road),
and Glasnamoyache above.

Pitkerrie—Pitkeri 1529 ; G. Baile-chéiridh ; not
the same as Balcherry, Tain, which has short e.
The local derivation is céir, wax : the place was
covered with whins, from which the bees made
only wax. This is quite possible, though it looks
somewhat fanciful. But at least equally possible
is a derivation from ciar, dark, whence céiread,
duskiness, hoariness. Behind it is *Waterton*, G.
Baile nam fuaran, Well-town.

Rhynie—Rathne 1529 ; G. ràthan (mhòr and bheag,
meikle and little) ; a derivative from ràth, circular
enclosure or fort. Rhynie in Aberdeenshire is

of different origin—Ryny 1224, Rynyn 1226;
from roinnean, diminutive of roinn, headland, as
Mr James Macdonald thinks (Place-names of
West Aberdeenshire).

Poulfock—G. poll a' phoca, pool of the bag.

Locheye—G. loch na h-uidhe; uidh, from Norse
eith, isthmus, is common in place-names, where it
may mean (i.) isthmus, cf. the Eye peninsula at
Stornoway, or (ii.) according to some, slow running
water between two lochs. Here, from the fact
that we have 'an uidh' (see below) near the
outlet of the loch, uidh seems to be used with the
second meaning.

Mounteagle—G. cnoc na h-iolaire, also, an uidh, as
above, but the 'uidh' is strictly the western part
of Mounteagle, near the outlet of Loch Eye.

Lochslin—G. Loch-slinn, from slinn, a weaver's
sleye. Lochslin, as a loch, has disappeared, and
survives only in the names Lochslin Farm and
the ancient ruin of Lochslin Castle. It must
have been a small loch, at the eastern end of Loch
Eye, v. Inver.

Knocknahar—G. cnoc na h-aire, watch-hill.

Loandhu—G. an lòn dubh, black 'loan' or wet
meadow.

Balnagore, probably baile nan gobhar, Goats' town,
which is confirmed by a well, Tobar nan gobhar,
Goats' well, noted by Rev. Mr Taylor, and
appearing on record as Tobarnayngor. Formerly
a number of small crofts.

The Talich—Dallachie, in the barony of Geanies,
1676 ; G. loch an dàilich, ? loch of the meeting.

Allan—Allan Meikle 1479 ; G. Alan mhòr (broad
'l'). In the parish of Knockbain there are three
Allans, Allan-grange, Allan nan clach, and Allan
fhraoich ; there is also Alan-ais, the Gaelic of
Alness, all pronounced alike in Gaelic, v. Alness.

Ballinroich—Munro's town. William Munro, son
of Andrew Munro of Milntown, obtained the lands
of Meikle Allan about 1570.

Balblair—G. bail' a' bhlair, town of the plain.

Balindrum—G. bail an druim, town of the ridge.

Muldearg—G. a' mhuil dearg (locative). the red
rounded eminence.

Midoxgate—G. an (t-)uchd meadhonach, the mid
hillock or terrace. In view of the Gaelic it would
be unsafe to regard this interesting name as a
genuine survival of the bovate or oxgate, the old
land measure. The place is on the 100 foot ridge
between Hill of Fearn and Loch Eye, and 'uchd
meadhonach' is therefore quite applicable. In
the absence of old forms, it seems more reasonable
to suppose Midoxgate to be an ingenious mis-
translation of the Gaelic by some one of anti-
quarian tastes, than to regard ' uchd ' as a Gaelic
attempt at ' ox.'

At **Hilton of Cadboll** stood a chapel, dedicated to
the Virgin ' Our Ladyis Chapell ' 1610, in connection with which appears in 1610 (Reg. Mag.
Sig.) Litill Kilmure, Toir of Kilmuir, a well called
Oure-Lady-well, situated near the angle of the
kailyard dyke occupied by And. Denune of Balnaknok ; also the heavin called Our-Lady-heavin

of Kilmure. Some of these names survive : Creag na baintighearna, Lady's Rock, is under Cadboll ; Tobar na baintighearna, Lady's Well, is (or was) near a small graveyard east of Hilton used for unbaptized children ; Port na baintighearna, Lady's haven. The name Kilmuir, curiously enough. seems to have gone, but there is Bàrd Mhoire, Mary's meadow or enclosure. I have met with no other clear instance of bantighearna in the above sense of ' Our Lady.'

TARBAT.

Tarbat—Arterbert 1227 ; Terbert 1529 ; Tarbat 1561-66 ; G Tairbeart, a crossing, portage, isthmus. The land of Estirterbate stands first in the list of lands given in the Exchequer Rolls as belonging to John, last Earl of Ross, which passed to the Crown on his resignation in 1479.

Tarbat Ness—G. rudha Thairbeirt, cf. Arterbert above, where Ar(t) is for àirde, promontory. Cairns near the lighthouse are named *Bodach an rudha,* the old man of the point ; *an Cailleach,* the old wife ; *a' Bhean-mhuinntir,* the servant lass. A rock in the sea is called *Steolluidh,* Norse stagl-ey, rock-island.

Port a' chait—Cat's port ; cf. Cadboll. There is also *Gót nan cat,* hole or cavern of the cats, from Norse gat, hole ; English gate. Near it is *Gót nan calman,* hole of the pigeons.

Port Buckie—G. Port nam faochag.

Wilkhaven—A translation of Port nam faochag. Near it is *na h-àthan salach,* the nasty fords, a small burn, which appears on record as Allan-sallach, with a chapel dedicated to St Bride.

Blàr a' chath--The battlefield.

Brucefield—G. cnoc an tighearna, the laird's hill, probably from Robert Bruce Macleod, a former proprietor. North Brucefield is in Gaelic *Loch*

Sirr'. Near it was *Loch nan cuigeal* ; cuigeal, a distaff, is also the name of a water plant.

Port Uilleam—William's port.

Hilton—G. Bail' a' chnuic ; near it is *Cnoc beall-aidh.* broom-hill.

Bindal—G. Bindeil ; Norse bind-dalr, sheaf-dale, The name occurs in Norway. Near it is *Stiana Bleadar* or *stoney-blather,* Norse stein-blettr, stone-spot.

Portmahomack—Portmaholmag N.S.A. ; G. Port ma Cholmag, Colman's port. *Tobar ma Chalmag,* Colman's well, is near the Library. Behind it is *Pitfaed,* G. Baile Phàididh, of doubtful meaning.

Gaza—So called (i.) because it is desert, being mostly sand-hills (cf. Acts viii. 26), or (ii.) because a minister of Tarbat once referred to its people as " muinntir Ghaza," men of Gaza, *i.e.,* Philistines, because of their irregular attendance at church. Such are the local explanations.

Balnabruach—Town of the banks.

Rockfield—G. a' Chreag, or Creag Tarail beag.

Castle Corbet—G. an Caisteal dearg, Red-castle. In 1534 James Dunbar of Tarbat sold one-third of the lands of Arboll to John Corbet of Estir Ard, and the Corbets appear on record thereafter as proprietors in Tarbet.

Balachladich—Shore town ; further inland is *Seafield.*

Drumancroy—G. an druim(a) cruaidh (locative), the hard ridge.

Petley—So called in the first decade of last century by Sheriff Macleod of Geanies, who married Miss Jane Petley. The old name was Mulbuie, yellow height ; Mulboyeid 1535.

Tarrel—John of Tarale 1373, Tarall 1561 ; G. Tarail. Probably 'tar,' across, over, and 'ail,' rock—Over-cliff. There are high cliffs at Tarrel and at Rocktown (Little Tarrel), as there are at Geanies. Gaelic has 'Tarail mhòr, is Tarail bheag, is Tarail fo na chreag.'

Meikle Tarrel included in 1529 Royeindavoir, Renmasrycshe, Creitnacloyithegeill, Creitmantae. Kilpottis, Rownakarne, Rownaknoksenidis, and near it were Callechumetulle, Kandig, Kilstane.

Geanies—Gathenn 1529 ; Eistir Gany, Wastir Gany, Midilgany 1561-1566 ; G. Gàan. The modern form is thus an English plural. Gàan is most probably a Gaelic plural of Norse 'gja,' a chasm, from the precipitous rocks on the coast. From the same root we have also 'gaw,' a furrow or small trench ; cf. 'yawn,' Ger. 'gahnen,' Scottish 'gant.'

Balaldie—'Baile,' town ; 'alt,' burn, with -ie ending—Burn-town.

Balnuig—G. bail' an aoig, town of death ; *Baile na h-àtha*, Kiln-town, is part of it.

Toulvaddie—G. toll a' mhadaidh, dog-hole.

Loch Clais na crè—Loch of the clay hollow.

Arboll—Arkboll 1463 and 1535 ; Norse ork-ból, ark-stead, but possibly from orkn, seal, which in Skye gives Or-bost. Near Arboll were Knokangirrach, on the coast, 1633 ; also Lochanteny and Loanteanaquhatt, *i.e.*, Lòn tigh nan cat, Cats'-house mead.

Gallow Hill—G. cnoc na croiche, about a mile from Balloan Castle.

Skinnertown—G. baile nan Scinnearach. Skinner is a surname very common in the coast villages of Easter Ross.

Innis Bheag—Small Isle—off the north coast.

A' Chreag Mhaol—Bare or blunt rock, below Tarrel.

Teampall Earach—Easter Temple, a cave on the south coast, east of Bindal, opposite a moor now cultivated between Bindal and Wilkhaven, called *Blàr-Earach* ; there is also *Cruit Earach*, easter croft ; cf. cùil earach, easter recess, in Islay. There is a tradition that the cave, which is but small, was once used for purposes of worship. Rev. Mr Taylor quotes a description, which applies not to it but to a much more imposing cave near it.

Balloan Castle—Two causeways lead to it, *Cabhsair an righ*, King's causeway, and *an cabhsar mòr*, the big causeway. Near it is *Cnoc Dubh*, Black Hill, where stone coffins have been found, also *Cnoc druim(a) langaidh*.

Port a' Chaisteil—Castle-haven, whence the title in the Cromarty family of Viscount Castlehaven. In a rock to the west of it is *Gót a choire*, hole of the cauldron.

Toll Raoiridh is a cave on the north-east side of Tarbat Ness. Its mouth is now blocked, but some cattle which entered it long ago came out in Caithness! Cf. Creag Raoiridh in Kincardine and Leac Raoiridh below Achtercairn, Gairloch.

Kilpots, which appears as Kilpotis, is a sea-mark; there is also *oir na poit,* edge of the pot.

Cillean Helpak is a fishing bank in the Moray Firth, called in Cromarty Geelyum Melpak. There is another 'Geelyum' nearer Cromarty. Helpak is said to have been a witch.

The following names, probably belonging to Fearn or Tarbat appear to be obsolete :—Hardnanen and Ardnadoler, Port na cloiche, Port nagrigack, Portnawest[1] alias St John's port—all described as small ports, and the last three near Arboll ; Innerladour, Rochani, Knokydaff, Arthreis, Coillen, Kandig, Rownaknoksenidis, Elviemore, Ballinsirach, and, near Arboll, a port called Camray.

---

[1] This is probably *Port a' bhaist,* still known.

NIGG.

Nig—Nig 1227 ; G. 'n eig, the notch (locative of
eag). The notch in question may be that cut by
the bay of Nigg ; but it is noteworthy that the
parish church, which has always apparently occupied the same site, stands on the edge of a
V-shaped gully, and on the analogy of other
parish names it is perhaps safer to regard this
gully as the notch which gave its name first to
the church and then to the parish ; cf. Eigg, and
Nigg near Aberdeen.

Broomtown—Ballewallie ; G. bail' a' bhealaidh.
Between it and Balintore is *Dorus na(m) bà*,
door, or pass, of the kine.

Shandwick—G. seannduaig, from Norse sand-vík,
sand-bay. In Islay the same combination gives
Sanaig. A plan of the land about Shandwick,
dated 1786, shews the following :—*Tobar na
slainte*, well of health ; *Stronmore*, the big point ;
Walter's Seat ; *Craggan*, the little rock ; *Cull
lish*, back or nook of the enclosure ; *Crot kerk*,
Hens' Croft ; *Crot Ganich*, Sandy Croft ; *Crot
Oich*; *Fisher Crofts*; *Ballnamorich*, Fisher-town ;
Cromlet, the bent slope ; *Leatcaum*, the bent hill-
side ; *Clasinore*, ? *Claisean mòra*, the big furrows :
Rhindow, black slopes ; *Cocli kinich* (*i.e.*, Cachaileith Coinnich), Kenneth's gate.

Rarichie (Easter and Wester)—Rarechys 1333,
Raricheis 1368 ; G. Rath-riachaidh shios agus R.
shuas. Fort of scratching (as by brambles), satisfies the phonetics. The foundations of a circular
fort still exist on a hillock, with well-marked fosse
at foot, near the farmhouse of Easter Rarichie.
The former existence of wood is proved by its
name, *Cnoc coille na tobarach*, Well-wood Hill.
Cf. Dunriachie, a hill fort in the parish of Dores,
Inverness. The latter part of the compound may,
however, be riabhach, dappled, with -idh extension. The local derivation is as follows :—The
Picts lived at Cadha 'n ruigh, and in spring-time
they would say, ' tiugamaid 'bhàn 'dheanamh
rotha riachagan,' ' let us go down to make rows
of scratches' (to sow seed in).

Easter Rarichie includes *Cnoc Coinnich*, Kenneth's Hill; an Torran shuas and an Torran shios,
the wester and the easter hillock.

Lower Rarichie—G. Bail' a' phuill, Pool-town.

Drumdil—G. Druim(a) daol, Beetle-ridge, west of
Wester Rarichie. Below it is *Croit Bhreunan*,
the little rotten croft.

Pitcalnie—Pitcahan 1662 ; G. Baile-chailnidh ; ' l '
silent in English ; an obscure name.

Pitculzean—Revived as the name of Westfield,
which was of old Meikle Pitcalzean ; Pitcalzeane
1581, Pitcalzean 1598 ; G. Bail' a' choillean, town
of the little wood, as is proved by *Tobar na coille*,
well of the wood, on the place.

Culnaha—Culnahaw 1611 ; G. Cul-na-h-àtha, Kiln-
nook or Kiln-back, for it is practically impossible

in such cases to distinguish cùil, recess, from cùl,
back. With it goes *Cadh' a' bhreacaich*, path of
the spotted place.

Culinald—Culnald cum ustrina lie kill die Nig,
1634 (Culnald with the kiln, called the kiln of
Nigg); Burn-nook, now part of Nigg Farm. The
streamlet in question flows through the gully at
Nigg Church.

Strath of Pitcalnie—Culderare 1611; G. Srath
chuilt-eararaidh; eararadh is the process of
parching corn; cuilt occurs *passim* in Perthshire
and elsewhere, *e.g.*, a chuilt rainich, the ferny
'cuilt'; doubtless the Aberdeenshire Cult-s. The
meaning of this obsolete word seems to be something like 'nook'; it may be cùil, O. Ir. cuil, with
excrescent 't.' Cuilt-eararaidh would thus mean
the nook of parching. In this Strath is *Cnoc
Ghaisgeach*. From a loch in the hill above it
flows *Allt an damhain* (O.S.M. Aultandown),
burn of the little ox.

Balnabruach—Kindeis Wester, within the barony
of Ballinbreich, 1650 Ret.; Bank-town. Near it
is *Cnoc na h-iolaire*, Eagle-hill.

Balnapaling—A hybrid, Paling-town; there were
a number of small plots of land separated by
'palings.'

Castlecraig—G. Caisteal Chrag (*sic*); now the
name of a farm, on which may yet be traced the
lines of the castle built by William the Lion in
1179. Its name was *Dùn Sgàth*, fort of dread,
now English Dunskaith. The farm of Castlecraig
includes several holdings formerly distinct: *an*

Annaid, the Annat (Annot 1611 ; *Rhidorach*, the
dark slope ; *Culbinn*, back (or nook) of the hill,
and *Dùnsgàth*, Dunskaith.

Bayfield—Formerly Meikle Kindeace ; G. Cinndéis
mhòr, or Cinndéis Rob'son shuas, Wester Kindeace of Robertson, from William Robertson, a
burgess of Inverness, who bought it and the following in 1629. The name was changed to
Bayfield by John Mackenzie, commander of the
' Prince Kaunitz,' who bought the estate about
1788 (v. Nevile Reid's ' Earls of Ross."').

Ankerville—G. Cinn-déis bhig, Little Kindeace ;
also Easter Kindeace ; bought in 1721 by Alexander Ross (locally known as Polander Ross), late
merchant at Cracow, who changed the name (v.
' Earls of Ross ' and N.S.A.)—v. Kindeace in
Kilmuir Easter.

Carse of Bayfield—G. Mor'oich Cinndéis, Carse of
Kindeace, or simply, a Mhor'oich.

Culliss—Culisse 1296 ; Culuys 1351 ; Culliss alias
Cullenderie, 1642 ; G. Cùl an lios, back of the
' lios ;' lios, now garden, formerly meant an
enclosure or fort with an earthen wall ; cf. Lismore. Rare in northern place-names. Near
Culliss was Muileann Ach-ràilean, Achrailean
Mill, cf. Badrallich in Lochbroom.

Blackhill—G. an cnoc dubh.

Hill of Nigg—G. Binn Nig ; of old ' the Bishop's
Forest.'

Big Audle—A channel in the bay, from Norse
vaðill, a ford. There is also *an oitir*, the sea-
bank.

The Three Kings—G. Creag Harail, Harold's Rock.
This skerry off the Nigg coast is called in the
N.S.A. The King's Sons. The story goes that
three sons of a Danish prince, sailing to avenge
their sister's wrongs, were wrecked here. Their
graves were marked by the sculptured stones of
Hilton, Shandwick, and Nigg. Another legend
of their burial is given below.

Of all Ross-shire parishes, Nigg is, in proportion
to its size, the richest in wells. Most have
names, but some that appear in the following list
no longer rise to the surface at their proper
place :—

Tobar Cormaig—Cormac's well, at Shandwick farm-
house.

Tobar Cnoc Coinnich—Well of Kenneth's hill, *i.e.*,
the hill above Easter Rarichie.

Glagaig—Now closed, to the south of the road at
Torran shuas, 'the little noisy one;' cf. glagan,
the clapper of a mill; glagar, a prating fellow.

Sul bà—Cows' eye, *i.e.*, well-eye at which cattle
came to drink ; in front of the old curate's house
at Easter Rarichie.

Tobar na h-iù—At the wester side of Cnoc
coille na tobarach, Well-wood hill, which is the
Gaelic name of the so-called Fairyhill or Danish
fort, really a Celtic hill fort, at Easter Rarichie.
Hard by this well once stood a tree whose
branches bent over the water, and while the tree
stood, the well cured 'white swelling.' The tree
was cut, and the well struck. The following

rhyme in connection with this tale shows the sort of feeling with which such wells were regarded :—

> Tobar na h-iù, Tobar na h-iù,
> 's ann duit bu chumha bhi uasal ;
> tha leabaidh deis ann an iuthairnn
> do 'n fhear a ghearr a' chraobh mu d' chluasan.[1]

> Well of the yew, Well of the yew ![2]
> to thee it is that honour is due ;
> a bed in hell is prepared for him
> who cut the tree about thine ears.

Tobar nam puill linn—Well of the lint pools, above Wester Rarichie.

Tobar nan geala (or deala) mòra—Well of the big leeches, between Wester Rarichie and Culliss. This well was insulted and is not what it was.

Tobar Sèin Sutharlain—Jane Sutherland's well, at Drumdil.

Tobar a' bhaistidh—Baptismal well, at Ankerville, just above the old U.P. Church. Otherwise, tobair Eapaig Ghearr, Eppy Gair's well.

Tobar Eadhain Bhaist—John Baptist's well, beside Chapelhill Church.

Tobar a' Chòirneil—The Colonel's well (Colonel Ross), at Nigg Farm.

Tobar na coille—At Pitcalzean ; G. Bail' a choillean.

Tobar Alaidh Bhodhsa—Sandy Vass's well, supplies Westfield house.

---

[1] The two last lines would be rendered less rugged by reading
  tha leabaidh deis an iuthairnn do'n fhear
  a ghear a' chraobh mu d' chluasan.

[2] This translation supposes "iù" to represent Ir. eó, a yew tree.

Tobar Dun-Sgàth—Dunskaith well.

Tobar na h-éiteachan—On the top of Nigg hill, famous water, used by the Nigg smugglers.

Tobar cadha 'n ruigh—Ca'an ruigh well.

Tobar na slàinte—Well of health, near Shand-wick Village, and noted for its healing powers.

Tobar na' muc—Pigs' well, by the shore, west of Shandwick.

Leisgeig—The little lazy one, near Shandwick; its water comes in very small quantity.

Tobar a' chlaidheimh duibh an Eirinn, 's i air aghaidh na greine an port an Druidh (al. a dh-éirich an Port an Druidh)—Well of the black sword in Erin, facing the sun in the Druid's port (or, that rose in the Druid's port). It does not rise, but gushes out of the rock, and is excellent water. *Port an Druidh* is west of Shandwick.

Besides the old churchyard at the Church of Nigg, there are, or were, four other places of burial in the parish.

At **Nigg Rocks**, below Cadha Neachdain, there is a graveyard, now covered with shingle. Here the Danish princes were buried. Their grave-stones came from Denmark, and had iron rings fastened in them to facilitate their landing. So local tradition. This most unlikely spot for a graveyard was not selected without some good reason, the most probable being that hermits once lived in the caves, whence the place was reckoned holy ground.

At **Clach' charaidh**, the sculptured stone near Shandwick, all unbaptized infants of the parish were buried up till fairly recent times. It is now cultivated.

At **Easter Rarichie**—Here the curate of Nigg lived, and the field behind his house is called ' raon a chlaidh,' the graveyard field. The plough goes over it now, and formerly used to strike the gravestones, but these are now removed.

Near **Shandwick Farm-house**, to the south-west, between the sea and the rock was a graveyard, the name of which I failed to find. Some of the stones are still visible.

The following are the paths (cadha) leading to the shore beneath the rocks :—*Cadha nan caorach,* sheeps' path ; *Cadha sgriodaidh,* shingly path ; *Cadha nan suibhean,* path of rasp-berries ; *Cadh a' bhodaich,* the old man's path ; *Cadha a' bhreacaich,* pass of the speckled place ; *Cadha Neachdain,* Nectan's path ; *Cadha 'n ruigh,* path of the slope ; *Cadha cul lósaidh* ; *Cadha togail toinn,* a path with one difficult part where a push from behind is requisite ; *Cadha port an druidh,* west of Shandwick, path of the Druid's port ; *Spardan nan gobhar,* goats' roost.

LOGIE EASTER.

Logie—Logy 1270; G. Lagaidh; 'lag,' a hollow,
with -aidh ending. The O.S.A. correctly says that
the name is derived from the little hollow in
which the old church at Marybank stands.
That church is probably pre-Reformation, but
there must have been a still older church or
churches on the same site. The old grave-yard
around it was used within living memory, and has
some fine stones, but is unenclosed and disgrace-
fully neglected. On the Kilmuir side of the river
is *Cadha an t-sagairt*, the priest's path.

Calrossie (accented on first syllable)—Glossery 1476,
Calrosse 1479, Calrossie 1586. The 1476 record
(Reg. Mag. Sig.) runs :—' The lands of Mekle
Meithaute, Drumgill, Glossery, Mekle Alane,' &c.
The 1479 record (Ex. Rolls) is—' Alane Mekle,
Calrosse, Drummethat,' &c., so that there need be
no doubt that Glossery and Calrossie are one and
the same. Glossery has the advantage of being
intelligible—' glasaraidh,' green place, or, possibly,
green shieling ; but, if we assume this to be the
true original form, the change to Calrossie involves
a double metathesis, explicable perhaps in itself
(cf. Kiltarlity from Cilltalorgain), but startling as
involving a change from a well-known and significant combination to an obscure one. Of course,

Glossery may be an error of the scribe. Calrossie, as it stands, is extremely difficult, especially in view of its accent on the first syllable, which debars any explanation such as ' Coille Rois,' Wood of Ross, or ' Coille Rhois,' Wood of the Moor.

Arabella—Formerly 'the Bog.' It was reclaimed in the earlier half of the nineteenth century by Hugh Rose of Calrossie, &c., who named it after his wife, Arabella Phips. Hence also *Phipsfield*, near it.

Glastullich—Glastollich 1479 ; 'glas,' green, ' tulaich,' hillock. It is west of Calrossie, and the ' glas' may be an argument in favour of Glossery.

Pitmaduthy—Pitmadwy 1370, Pettecowy 1578 ; G. Pit 'ic Dhuibh, also Baile 'ic Dhuibh, Macduff's stead. Here, and also in the case of the Black Isle Belmaduthy, the modern Gaelic form is decisive against the common, and, at first sight, plausible, connection with St Duthac ; cf. Pett mal-duib (Book of Deer). Near it is *Baile na tòin*, Auchownatone 1623, " the part of Pitmaduthy commonly called Auchnaton," 1691. Next Auchnaton was Drumgill, now obsolete.

Lochan nan tunnag—Duck-loch.

Brenachie—G. Breanagaich (long ' n '); cf. Brinknach 1610. The 1610 reference (Reg. Mag. Sig.) runs :—" The house and lands of Logie, with the fields called Riharrald, Auldmuiramoir, Achimmoir, and the Bus of Preischachleif, and the mosses of Brinknach and Derrileane with the

shielings and grassums bounded by the cairn of
stones called cairnne na marrow alias Deidmannis-
cairne, and the burn (torrente) called Aldainal-
banache alias Scottismenisburne, in the barony of
Nig." Riharrald is ' ruighe-Harrald,' Harold's
slope, evidently from Norse times. It is a strip
of land near the river, towards the western
extremity of Marybank Farm, under the Heather
Park, still known as *Ri-horral*. There is also
Ri-horral Well, and, in the river, Ri-horral Pool.
The two following places may also have been part
of Marybank. The ' Bus' in its G. form means
' the bush of the gate'—' preas 'chachaileith,' a
word intelligible to few Easter Ross people now.
Derrileane is modern *Torelean*, G. Torr leathan,
broad eminence. The cairn must be that in the
wood north of Torelean. The burn, ' Scotsburn,'
is to the west of Marybank Farm, and is now
practically dried up. There are local traditions of
a battle fought here by the ' Scots,' supported by
cairns in Scotsburn Wood and by the names
Lochan a' Chlaidheimh, Sword Loch, and *Bearns
a' Chlaidheimh*, Sword Cleft (bearnas).

Marybank—G. Lagaidh (no article), from the ' lag,'
or hollow, which gives its name to the parish.
The modern name is from Lady Mary Ross of
Balnagown.

Ballachraggan—Rock-town ; otherwise Lòn nam
ban, the women's mead. In the wood near it is
the *Clootie Well*, or Fuaran bean Mhuiristean,
much frequented on the first Sabbath of May.

Creag a' Chait—Cat-rock.

Leinster Wood—So called, it is said, in honour of a Duchess of Leinster.

Loch Buidhe—Yellow loch.

Badnaguin—·G. Bad na' gaoithean, windy copse. It is near the top of Scotsburn Hill.

An Dùn—The Dùn, at east end of Strathrory. Old people know it as Dùn-gobhal, Fork-fort. They will have it, however, to mean Fort of Goll, the Fenian hero; but 'gobhal' is distinctly two syllables, and, besides, there is a typical fork at the spot, formed by two deep ravines. The name appears as Dungowill 1616 (v. Scotsburn), Dungald 1674. The dùn, or fort, is the second largest in Scotland (Christison's 'Hill-forts'), and was in its time an awkward place to tackle. Its fortifications are well worth examination (v. Trans. of Inverness Field Club, Vol. V.).

Coag—G. An Cumhag; 'cumhang,' narrow—the narrow place where the river enters Scotsburn ravine.

Garbh Leitir—The rough slope, just beyond the 'Cumhag.'

Dalrannich—Dale of bracken.

Scotsburn—The name has now shifted from the burn to the farm of Scotsburn, apparently of old called in part Cabrach, Cabreithe 1571, and in part Ulladale. In 1616 appear on record (Reg. Mag. Sig.) 'the church lands of Ulladill with their crofts called Rifleuche and Riddorache alias the Glen of Ulladill, the wood called Dungowill

between the Girthcroce dividing the common
lands of the Burgh of Tayne from Ulladill," &c.
The Glen is now called the Glen of Scotsburn.
"The Commonty" is still well known.

Parkhill—Site of the post-office near Balnagowan
Bridge. The name was transferred along with
the P.O. from the real Parkhill, two miles further
west.

Poll a' Bhàthaidh—Drowning pool, near the Free
Church Manse. This was the drowning pool of
the barony of Nigg. The hanging hill is near it,
G. Cnoc na croiche. Further south, near the
railway, is Cnoc a' mhòid, the Moot-hill.

Meddat—Drummethat and Mekle Methat 1479 ;
(Kilmure) Madath 1541, (Kilmure) Meddett 1575.
Local pronunciation has a tendency to Merret ;
G. Meitheid. For the terminal suffix cf. Ràt from
ràth-d, Bialaid from beul, Caolaid from caol,
Croaghat from cruach. This leaves a root 'meith,'
which is probably connected with maoth, soft ;
mèith, sappy ; meath, fail,[1] giving the meaning,
which is appropriate, of soft or spongy place ;
cf. Muthil.

Shandwick—Transferred from Shandwick, Nigg.

[1] 'Na h-alltaichean a' fàs, agus na h-aibhnichean a' meath,' 'the burns
growing and the rivers failing,' is a proverb applied to the growth of new
families and the decay of old ones.

KILMUIR EASTER.

Kilmor 1296, Kilmure Madath 1541, Kilmure Meddett 1575—G. Cill-Mhoir, Mary's Church.

Milntown—' Myltoun of Methat with its two mills' 1479 ; G. Baile-mhuilin or Baile-mhuilin Anndra, from Andrew Munro, who built Milntown Castle, c. 1500, or his son, Black Andrew Munro. Now officially known as Milntown of New Tarbat.

New Tarbat—So called by the Cromartie family, from Tarbat, where their former seat was (v. Castlehaven).

Kildary—G. Caoldaraidh, based on caol, narrow, and analysed caol-d-ar-aidh, "d" being euphonic. The 'narrow place' in question is doubtless the river gorge between Kildary Farm and the parish of Logie.

Apitauld (pron. Abijald)—G. Ath-pit-allt ; 'àth,' ford, 'pet,' baile, 'allt,' burn. The place is close to Balnagown Bridge. 'Pit' has survived here owing to the prefixing of ' àth,' ford, which caused the sense of ' pit' to be obscured. Were it not for this, the name would no doubt have become Balnault.

Balnagown—Balnegovne 1375, Smith's town ; the modern Gaelic is as the English form. Near the castle is a steep old bridge over the river, still in good order, known as ' the King's Bridge,' and traditionally associated with James IV. It leads to the King's Causeway—the old road to Tain.

Polnicol—Poll Neacail, Nicol's pool. Between the farms of Polnicol and Garty, on the north side of the road is a narrow strip called *the Lint-pools.*

Garty — Gorty 1368 ; ' gart,' standing corn ; ' goirtean,' small field of corn, W. ' garth.' Also Knockgarty.

Rhives—G. Na Ruigheannan; le Royis 1479, le Ruvis 1487, later Ruffis ; ' ruigh,' land sloping up to a hill in ridges. The G. form is peculiar, and looks like the pl. of a diminutive ' ruighean,' but the pronunciation does not countenance this. It is probably to be compared with such plurals as ainmeannan, léumannan, etc. Cf. Kin-rive. The present farm of Rhives contains, in addition to the ancient le Royis, three other tracts whose names appear in record and are not yet wholly lost :— *Auchoyle,* the northern part of the farm, partly a slope once heavily wooded, now rough pasture. Achawyle 1351, Achenwyl 1368, Achagyle 1619 ; ' achadh,' field, and ' gall,' stranger. Near it was Badferne, now obsolete. *Knoknapark* 1527 and passim in E.R. This was the hillocky part to the N.E. of Delny Station, where the P.O., ' Parkhill,' formerly stood. The P.O. and the name have now been shifted two miles east, just beyond Balnagown Bridge. *Badebaa* 1587, etc.; also Badebay. This is the part of Rhives lying south of the railway, still known locally as ' the Batty-bay.' Before being reclaimed, it was dotted with birch clumps ; hence ' bad a' bheith,' birch copse.

Delny—Dalgeny 1356 ; G. Deilgnidh, based on dealg, prickle, whence deilgne, thorns ; deilgneach, prickly ; ' place of prickles.' Here stood a castle of the Earls of Ross.

Tornabrock—G. Torr na' broc, Mound of the badgers.

Balvack—Bail a' bhac, Moss-town ; between Delny Station and the U.F.C. Manse.

Barbaraville—G. an cladach, the shore ; its east end is *Portlich*, G. port fhlich (loc.), the wet port —there being no proper place for landing.

Pollo—G. Am Pollan ; Estir Polga and Westir Polga 1479 ; diminutive of ' poll,' pool, or hole.

Balintraid—Balandrade 1479, Balnatraid 1507 ; ' baile ' and ' tràigh,' sea-shore, genitive, tràghad.

Priesthill—Cnoc an t-sagairt ; the pre-Reformation manse and glebe were here. Somewhere to the west of it is said to have been a drowning pool. Poll a' bhàthaidh, but its site can hardly be identified. *John the Baptist's Well* is, or was, west of Priesthill, near the burn.

Broomhill—Bromehill 1634 appears to represent Ardunagage 1479, Ardnagag 1487, Ardnagaag 1586 ; ' gàg,' cleft, chink ; hence, Height of the cleft. Cf. Gaick.

Inchfuir—Inchfure 1463, Petfure 1479, Inchfure alias Pitfure 1539, G. I's-fiùr (i's = innis) ; interesting as showing the unique, or at least very rare, change of ' pit ' to ' inch ' (innis) ; cf. Pitfure in Black Isle and in Rogart, Porin in Strathconan. Dochfour, Balfour, etc. In the " Book of Deer "

here occurs " nice furene," unto Furene, which
appears to be an aspirated Porin ; '-fure' is from
the root seen in Welsh ' pori,' to pasture, and
' poriant,' pasture.   Thus ' Inchfuir' means
pasture meadow.

Kindeace, G. Cinn-déis, has been transferred from
Nigg. William Robertson, of Inverness, acquired
the estate of Kindeace, in Nigg, in 1629.   The
Nigg estate was subsequently disposed of, and the
family acquired the estate now known as Kindeace,
in Kilmuir, of old Inchfure, retaining the style
" of Kindeace."   ' Cinn,' locative of ' ceann ;'
' déis,' perhaps loc. of ' dias,' an ear of corn ;
' corn-head ;' suitable, but doubtful.

Lonevine—G. Lòn a' bhinn ; ' lon,' marsh, or low
damp ground ; ' binn,' gen. of ' beann,' hill.

Tullich—G. An Tulaich, locative of ' tulach,' hillock.

Burracks—G. Na bùraich ; ' bùrach,' digging ;
' the diggings '—for peat and turf.   The place is
a rough peat-moss.

Dorachan—Extension of ' doire,' copse.   Cf. for
formation Giuthsachan, place of fir.

Driminault—Druim (n) an allt, ' ridge of the burns,'
one of which flows into the Balnagown Water.

Claisdhu—' Clais,' furrow, narrow and shallow
valley ; ' dubh,' black.

Torran—G. An Torran, diminutive of ' torr,' heap ;
of old Torran liath, grey hillock.

Badachonachar—Baddiequhoncar,Baddiequhonchar
1571 ; ' bad,' copse ; ' conachair, (1) uproar, (2) a
sick person who neither gets worse nor better

(Macbain's G. Dict.); a large peat-moss in the upper part of the parish. In this case it may be from the proper name Conachar. Cf. Coir' a' Chonachair (Kincardine).

Dalnaclerach — 'Dail,' dale, meadow; 'clerach,' cleric; clerics' dale. It appears to have formed part of the church lands of Kilmuir, and is probably included in the grant made in 1541 by "Master David Dunbar, chaplain of the chaplainry of the Virgin Mary in the parish of Kilmure Madath to Thomas Ross of Balintrait, etc., of the church-lands called Priestishill and Ulladule, reserving to himself and his successors one acre of the lands of Priestishill, lying near the manse on the south side for a manse and garden to be there constructed." Ulladule (v. Logie Easter) was the old name of Scotsburn, which is adjacent to Dalnaclerach.

Kinrive — G. Ceann-ruigh, Kennachrowe 1362, Candenrew 1547, Canderwiff 1549, Kenroy 1556; 'ceann,' head, 'ruigh,' ridgy slope. Kenrive is the hill to which the land slopes up from the sea in a succession of terraces. The various spellings are suggestive of the way in which the G. 'ruigh' became Anglicised—'rive' (pron. riv). Rhives, in the low part of the parish, shows the plural form in Gaelic and in English.

Cnoc-still (west of Inchfure)—Hill of the strip, *i.e.* strip of grass. 'Still' is genitive of 'steall,' which in O. Ir. is 'stiall,' and means a belt, girdle, strip, piece of anything. Cf. Loch Still : Caisteal Still (now Castlehill), Inverness.

Carn Totaig (north of Cnoc-still)—Diminutive of
'tobhta,' knoll.   The cairn has disappeared, but
the place is still counted uncanny.

Heathfield—G. Cal-fhraochaidh ; Kalruquhy 1479,
Calrechy 1586, Calrichie 1616, from cala, a wet
:adow (which exactly describes it), and fraoch,
neather.   Cf. Calatruim, hollow of the elder
(Joyce) ; Freuchie, now Castle-Grant.

Strathrory—G. Srath-uaraidh ; Strathury 1362,
Straithworie 1563, Strathworie 1628, but Strath-
rowrie 1571.   The modern English form is due to
the false analogy of the personal name 'Ruaraidh,'
Rory, which sometimes affects even the Gaelic.
The Old Stat. Acc. of Logie states (referring to
the Rory or Balnagown Water) ; " The only river
in the parish goes generally by the name of Abhor
or river," and in accordance with a custom so
general as to be almost a rule, the Strath should
take its name from the river.   'Srath-abharaidh'
might yield Srath-uaraidh ; cf. the dialectic change
of famhair, giant, into fua'r, e.g. Tigh 'n fhua'r,
Novar.   The New Stat. Acc. suggests uar, water-
spout, which is worth considering.   The river is
liable to sudden spates.

Druim na gaoith—Windy ridge ; a hill in the
extreme north-west of the parish.

Craskag—The name, now obsolete, of the burn
issuing from Achnacloich loch, and running at the
foot of Kinrive hill—the little cross (burn) ; cf.
Allt Tarsuinn (Kincardine).

Allt Rapaidh—Noisy burn ; north side of Strathrory; boundary between Balnagown and Kindeace.

ROSSKEEN.

Rosskeen—Rosken 1270, Roscuyn 1640; G. Ros-
cuithnidh ; ' ros,' headland, referring most probably to the promontory on which Invergordon
stands, now called ' An Rudha.' The latter part
is rather difficult. Dr Joyce notes in Ireland
such names as Quinhie and Feaghquinny, from
Ir. cuinche, pronounced nearly *queenha*, the
arbutus tree. This suits the phonetics of Ros-
cuithnidh, which would thus mean arbutus head.
In a field by the roadside, near the Parish Church,
is *Clach a' Mhèirlich*, the thief's stone.

Saltburn—G. Alltan an t-saluinn. Explained from
the tradition that cargoes of salt were hid here in
the times when there was a duty payable on that
article.

Ord—' Ord,' hammer, in root connected with ' ard,'
high ; secondary meaning, ' rounded hill ' ; but
the eminence in this case is very slight.

Inverbrekie—Inchbreky 1475, Innachbreky 1511,
Uvachbrekie 1608, Innerbreky, 1512, Innerbreke,
1533. The name is now applied to the farm lying
north of Invergordon, but formerly included the
site of the town. The ' inver' implies a stream,
which must have been called the ' Breakie,' from
' breac,' dappled, and is probably that which enters
the firth near Rosskeen church. The surface has

been much changed by cultivation and draining. Inchbreky is 'the meadow of the Breaky.'

Invergordon appears in Pocock's Tour in 1760. So called by a former proprietor, Sir Alexander Gordon.

The Cromlet — The slope behind Invergordon: 'crom-leathad,' sloping hill-side.

Kincraig—Kynnacrege 1479 ; G. Ceann na creige. Rock-end.

Achintoul—G. Ach an t-sabhail, Barn-field.

Achnagarron—Probably 'ach,' field, and 'carran,' spurrey ; Ir. 'carran,' scurvy grass. Locally from 'gearran,' a gelding, but the phonetics do not suit.

Rosebank—A modern name ; ancient Culquhnze 1477, Culkenzie 1586 ; 'cùil,' nook, 'Coinneach,' Kenneth ?

Newmore—G. An ne' mhòr, the great glebe (v. Church names).

Stoneyfield probably represents Feauchlath 1479. Feachclathy 1487, Feauchclachy 1507 — Faich nan clach, or, Féith nan clach.

Coillymore—Kellymmoir 1571 ; G. A' Choille mhòr, Big wood.

Rhicullen—'Ruigh,' land sloping up to a hill, and 'cuileann,' holly. There is a remarkably fine holly bush, which must be of great age.

Riaskmore—'Riasg,' morass with sedge or dirk-grass ; 'mòr,' big.

Tomich—'Tòm,' conical hillock, with collective suffix 'ach,' in locative—Place of hillocks.

Inchindown—Inchedown 1571 ; G. I's an dùin, Meadow of the Dun, innis, as often, being reduced to i's. There is no trace of a fort, but Kinrive hill in the part immediately behind the farm is precipitous, and covered with stones. Many large cairns were removed when the farm was extended about forty years ago.

Achnacloich and **Dalnacloich**—Fie'd and dale of stones ; from the large cairn on the hillside, northeast of the loch.

Dalnavie, Cnocnavie, Nonakiln, Inchnavie—(See Church-names).

Millcraig—Craigemylne 1479, Cragmyln 1507 ; also molendinum de Crag ; G. Muileann na creige —Rock-mill.

Badcall—Badkall 1571 and passim ; G. Bad-call, hazel-clump ; to the east of Millcraig, and fast becoming obsolete.

Mulnafua—' Fuath,' spectre—Goblin-mill.

Caplich—' Capull,' horse, mare—Place of horses. The name is fairly common.

Obsdale—Obstuill 1548 ; Norse hóps-dalr, bay dale.; from the small bay near it.

Culcairn—G. Cul-chàirn ; Culcarne 1571 ; ' back of the cairn,' i.e., Carn na Croiche, the hanging cairn, on the hill behind it.

Crosshills—Perhaps, in view of the nearness of Nonakiln, the name may be ecclesiastical.

Balnaguisich—Fir-wood stead.

Ardross—' Ard-rois,' height of Ross. Blaeu's Ardross is the water-shed between Easter and Wester Ross, which may have been correct in his day. In any case, Fear Ard-rois was in use to denote

Laird of Ardross (in Rosskeen) before Sir A. Matheson's time.

Cuillich—Culyeoth Mekle and Culyeoch Manach (Mid) 1479, Chwleauchmeanach and Chwyulaich-mor 1571, Cunlich (Retours and Reg. Mag. Sig. passim), 'Cumhang-lach,' the place of the 'cumh-ang' or narrow passage, with reference to the gorge of the river on which it is situated. Cf. Coy-lum, Badenoch; Cuag, in Kilmuir; 'cunglach' still means a narrow defile in modern Gaelic.

Dalneich—Horse-dale. Cf. Caplich.

Glaick—Locative of 'glac,' grip; it is, as it were, in the grip of the hills. Very common.

Loanreoch — 'Lòn,' low meadow; 'riabhach,' brindled—from copse alternating with grass and heather.

Balanrishallaich—Fraser's town.

Stittenham seems modern, as it does not occur on record. Gaelic accents the last syllable.

Strathy—G. an t-srathaidh—with -aidh ending.

Crannich—Locative of Crannach, place of trees, or abounding in trees; G. a' Chrannaich.

Srath-na-Frangach—? Tansy Strath, from Franga-lus or lus na frang. It was the abode of the noted cattle-thief, "Seileachan," the site of whose house is said to be still distinguishable. Near it is *Allt na fuaralaich*, burn of the cold place; Aldnaquhorolache 1571.

Coire-ghoibhnidh—Corryzewynie 1571, ? corry of the smithy; at the west end of Kinrive Hill; cf. Ard na goibhne in Tanera. But possibly, Corry of the wintry stream, O. Ir. gam, winter; cf. the Goineag, Badenoch.

Tolly—G. Tollaidh, probably here from ' toll,' hole ;
'place of holes.' Tollie-mylne, *alias* mylne-
chaggane appears on record. The lands of Tolly
were part of the patrimony of the Chapel of
Kildermorie. Above Tolly are *Coirc Thollaidh*
and *Braigh Thollaidh*.

Baldoon—G. Bail' an dùin, town of the dùn. There
is a hill fort in the wood near.

Inchlumpie—G. I's-lombaidh ; ' innis,' meadow,
' lom,' bare, with -aidh ending. The ' b' is
euphonic. The place is a narrow level strip by
the river-side. Above it is *am Breac'radh*, the
spotted place ; cf. am bog'radh. The ground rises
up to *Cnoc an t-seilich*, Willow-hill.

Strathrusdale—Strathrustell 1691 ; G. Srath-
rùsdail ; Norse ' hrúts-dalr,' ram's dale, with G.
srath prefixed. This name is interesting, and
suggestive as to the extent and the character of
the Norse occupation of Easter Ross.

Aultanfearn—Alder-brooklet. This and the four
following are in Strathrusdale.

Balnacraig—Rock-town.

Dalreoich—Spotted dale ; cf. Dalbreak.

Balanlochan—Loch-town.

Braeantra—Bràighe an t-sraith, Head of the strath.

Cnoc an t-sìthean beag and **Cnoc an t-sìthean
mòr** are hills north of Strathrusdale. ' Sìth,'
' sìthean,' hill, usually grassy ; especially a green
fairy hill ; but often (as here) applied to high
hills with rounded tops. Cf. Schiehallion.

Sìthean a' choin bhain—Hill of the white dog.

Doire leathan—Broad copse.

Beinn Tarsuinn—Cross hill. Very common.

Garraran—G. an gar(bh)aran, the rough place ;
from garbh, with double suffix ; cf. Cloch-ar-an,
Giuths-ar-an, &c

Càrn Cuinneag—'Cuinneag,' a milking pail. The
Cairn (3000 ft.) is double peaked, and I am
informed that the 'Cuinneag' proper is the
western and higher peak, the other being called
Carn Màiri, from the name of a girl who perished
there while crossing from Strathcarron to Kildermorie. In a rock on the Cuinneag there are
several clean-cut hollows, one or more of which
is tub or pail-shaped. They are really pot-holes
caused by wind action. From these the hill is
said to have got its name ; but it may be from
the fact that, when viewed from a distance, the
peaks may be considered. with the help of a little
goodwill, to represent a gigantic cuinneag with its
' lug.' This is the explanation of the Sutherland
Cuinneag.

The following names, belonging either to Kilmuir or to the border of Rosskeen, are obsolete :—
Rawsnye or Risaurie, Knokderruthoill, Ardachath
(a cultivated field on Newmore), Glascarne (a
cairn), Knocknasteraa, Abianemoir (a wood),
Kirkchaistull or Pollograyscheak (a hill), Alda-
naherar (burn), Tobirinteir (well in Kinrive),
Brakach, Rawcharrache, Rewchlaschenabaa, Chan-
deraig, Binebreychst, Correbruoch, Almaddow.
All these are taken from the marches of Newmore
as given in the " Origines Parochiales' for 1571.

ALNESS.

Alness—Alenes 1227 ; G. Alanais. Local tradition
has it that the name Alness applies primarily to
the spot where the Parish Church stands, which is
at once probable from analogy, and confirmed by
old maps and by the fact that south of the church
is Pàirc Alanais, Alness Park.[1] The name, therefore, has nothing to do with Norse ness, a point.
Its ending -ais is that seen in Dallas, etc., and the
first part is identical with Allan in E. Ross and
the Black Isle Allans. There are at least three
Scottish rivers called Allan, and this is supposed
to be the modern form of the Alaunos of Ptolemy,
who also mentions Alauna as a town of the
Damnonii. Two roots seem possible ; ail, a rock,
and that seen in Latin pal-us, a marsh, which in
Celtic would drop initial *p*. Culcraggie and
Balachraggan (below), which adjoin the Church
of Alness, favour ail ; one of the other Allans is
Allan nan clach. But another is Bog Allan.
Further, Allan in. E. Ross, while far from stony,
lies low, and was once, doubtless, marshy, while
close by Alness Church is a burn and a low damp
meadow. Local evidence therefore suggests the
meaning of Allan to be ' the bog,' and of Alness,

---

[1] Seawards of this park is a marshy place called An Inbhir, the estuary,
where the burn which flows by Alness Church enters the Cromarty Firth. It
is quite possible that this burn was once an " Allan Water."

'place of the Allan, or wet place.' Cf. the Welsh
and Cornish rivers Alun.

Ardroy—'Aird,' promontory; 'ruadh,' red; a point
west of Alness point. The 'stell,' or fishing
station of Ardroy is mentioned in 1479; also
"the Flukaris croft."

Teaninich—G. Tigh 'n aonaich, Moor-house, or
Market-house. The name appears in the Retours,
but not in the Ex. R., where the modern
Teaninich appears as "the two Culmelathquhyis"
(th = ch), 1479 and passim; Culmelloquhy 1526,
Culmalochie 1586, Ovir-culmalochie 1526. The
two Culmalochies were thus Over- and Nether-
Culmalochy.

Coulhill—G. Cnoc na cùil; the higher part of the
village, in rear of the main street. Balnacoule
1583.

Culcraggie—Culcragy 1479; G. Cuil-chreagaidh,
Rocky-nook, creagaidh being the old locative of
creagach. The banks of the burn which adjoins
the farm are steep, but not rocky. The reference
is rather to large boulders with which part of the
farm near the present house was once strewn.

Ballachraggan—Town of the little rock.

Balnacraig—G. Bail' na creige. Rocktown, so called
from the precipitous banks of the Alness River
close by.

Contullich — G. Cunntulaich; 'con,' together;
'tulach,' hillock; 'congeries of hillocks,' accurately
descriptive. Cf. Conachreig, Coneas, Contin, etc.
A park at the east side of the Boath road, near

the Contullich farm-servants' cottages, is called
An Triubhais, the Trews, probably because of a
resemblance to that article of dress at a time
when the field was only partly reclaimed.

Clashnabuiac—Cleft of the yellow flowers.

Tallysow (always with the article both in English
and Gaelic, which latter is sounded as the Eng.),
referred to in the New Stat. Acc. as Novar Inn.
The name appears in Jamieson's Scottish Dict. as
Tilliesoul, " a place at some distance from a gentleman's mansion-house, where the servants and
horses of his guests are sent when he does not
choose to entertain the former at his own
expense." He gives also the form ' tilliesow.'
Derived by Jamieson from French ' tous les souls,'
the place where all the drunkards congregate, or
' tillet les soulds,' soldiers' billet, a place where
soldiers are quartered out with money to pay for
lodging; or, G. ' tulach an t-sabhail,' barn-
hillock. The last is out of the question. The
Tallysow is by the roadside, near Novar House,
and there is another Tallysow near Maryburgh.

Novar—Tenuer, Blaeu. G. Tigh 'n fhuamhair,
Giant's house.

Fyrish (farm and hill)—G. Foireis; Fyrehisch 1479,
Feris 1539; the spelling varies almost with
each appearance, and sometimes becomes even
Fischerie ; probably from Norse ' fura ' or ' fyri,'
pine-tree. Fyrish is and was noted for its wood.
To the back of Fyrish hill, towards Ardoch, is
Poll a' Mhucainn, Poll of the place of swine.

Here, according to local tradition, was concluded
the Communion service held at Obsdale in 1675,
which was broken up on the approach of a party
of soldiers sent to apprehend the minister.

Ballavoulin—Bail' a' mhuilinn, Mill-town.

Assynt—G. Asaint; Norse 'áss,' rocky ridge;
' endi,' end.   Cf. Assynt in Sutherland.

Aultgrande—G. an t-allt-grannda, the 'ugly burn'
which flows through the famous Black Rock.

Cladh Churadain (see Church names).

Druim nan Damh—Stag ridge.

Redburn—G. an t-allt dearg.

Uig—G. an ùig, 'vik,' bay, but it is well inland, and
so is an extension of the primary meaning.

Sockach—G. an t-socaich, a locative from 'soc,'
snout, fore part of anything, with the suffix -ach.
Common as a name for places that project.

An Lainn—Loc. of lann, enclosure; very rare in
Scottish names, but cf. Lhanbryde; an Garbhlainn
(Anglicised Caroline) on the farm of Tullich,
Strathnairn.   Part of Lainn is *am blàr borraich;*
borrach is a species of rough grass.   Near Glen-
glass School.

Lorgbuie—G. an lorg bhuidhe, the yellow track.

Achnagou —' Gobhal,' fork; 'field of the fork.'

Balnard—Town of the height.

Eilean na Cabhaig—(In Val. Roll Ellancavie),
Island of the hurry.   With it goes *Bruach dian,*
steep bank.

Loch a' Chapuill—'Capull,' horse; Horse Loch.

Meall an Tuirc—'Torc,' boar; Boar's Hill.

Bendeallt (Bénnjullt), on O.S.M. Beinne na diollaide ; an un-Gaelic-looking name ; possibly corrupt.

Cnoc Léith Bhaid or, Cnoc an liath bhaid, hill of the grey clump. (O.S.M. Cnoc Liath Fad).

Cnoc Coille Bhrianain—(O.S.M. Cnoc a' Ghille Bhrònaich), now often simply ' Brianan ;' Hill of Brendan's wood ; but ' coille ' is almost certainly a recent corruption of ' gille,' servant, follower.

Loch a' Mhàgraidh—From màg, pawing, paw ; also toad, Loch of the place of toads (possibly of pawing) ; cf. Mucarach, from muc, pig.

Sgor a' Chaoruinn—Rowan-tree rock.

Meall nam bò—Cow-hill.

Kildermorie (see Church names). Above the old chapel is *Creag na Cille*, Church-rock, below which is *Glaic nan Clerach*, where the parson of Kilmuir was killed by the parson of Kildermorie (or *vice versa*) ; near the chapel is *Tobar Mhoire*, Mary's Well. A market, Feill Mhoire, was once held here. The waters of Loch Moir, G. Loch Mhoire, are locally reputed to have an underground outlet to Loch Glass, a tradition noted by Macfarlane (c. 1750), who says that its waters sanctify those of L. Glass. Between Kildermorie and Teaninich, on the north side of Loch Moir, is *Allt na Fuirrid*, Ir. furbaide, a cutting out ?

Leathad Riabhach—The ' brindled hill-side,' north of Loch Moir—a precipitous rocky face.

Am Màm—' Màm,' large round hill ; M.Ir. ' mamm,' breast. Cf. ' Cioch ' as a hill name

Kinloch—Loch-end ; at the end of Loch Moir.

Boath—Bothmore 1583 ; G. na Bothachan, the places of booths or huts. The name applies to the spacious strath, or rather half-strath, from *Cnoc a' Bhoth*, Hill of the booth, which runs north and south at its western end, to *Cnoc 'Chroisg*, Hill of the crossing. In Cnoc a' Bhoth is *Creag a' Bhoth*, Rock of the Booth, and under it, *Both-bhig*, with a field, *am Blàran Odhar*, the dun field, at the top of which is a sloping piece of grass called *am Bard*, the meadow, a name common in the district ; not yet obsolete in Badenoch speech. *Both-mhòr* is next to Glaick. The great cairns of Boath are noted below. There are hut circles and numerous tumuli on *Cnoc Alasdair*, and on the highest of the hillocks to the east of Strone are the ruins of a hill-fort or broch with many tumuli on its south-east side, and a hut circle to the west.

Poll na Cuilc—Reedy pool, in the river east of Kinloch.

Strone—Nose ; Cnoc na Sròin, the hill running to a point which separates Boath from Strathrusdale. West of the Strone peat road is *Druim na Ceardaich*, Smithy Ridge, with a curious circular ruin, said to have been a smithy. East of it *An Ruigh Dreighean*, Thorn-slope, with a small cairn.

Glaick—G. a' ghlaic, the hollow ; part of the farm so called is the highest cultivated land in Boath. Near it is *an t-Uchdan*, the terrace, breast-let.

Duchan—Probably based on dubh, black ; the little black place.

Ballone—Bail' an lòin, town of the loan, or wet meadow. Above the farm-house is *Am Bàrd*, the meadow.

Allt na' Cnuimheag—Burn of worms ; explained locally by reference to a skirmish with cattle-lifters which took place near it, after which the dead were left unburied.

Milltown—G. Baile-mhuilinn.

Cnoclea—G. An Cnoc-liath, grey hill, from the grey appearance given by the two great cairns on the moor. One of these has an oval megalithic chamber, once vaulted, and still over eight feet deep. The other is much destroyed.

Acharn—' Ach,' field ; ' càrn,' cairn. It is adjacent to the cairns ; ' field of the cairns.'

Clais na' mial—A small winding glen opposite the road leading to Acharn ; ' saltus pediculorum,' locally explained (1) from its convenient privacy, (2) from the poverty of its grass and consequent effect on cattle. But ' mial ' is used here in its old general sense of ' animal ' ; ' beasts' hollow.'

Balnagrotchen—Bail' nan croitean, croft-township ; the hill to the south west is *Cnoc na Leacachan*, Flag-stone hill ; corruptly, Cnoc ar Leacachan. (O.S.M. Cnoc liath na h-Acain).

Balmainach—G. Bail' meadhonach, Middle-town ; between Acharn and Loanroidge.

Loanroidge—G. An Lòn-roid, wet meadow of bog-myrtle, which is very plentiful here. East of the farm-house is a pretty meadow by the river-side, called *Bàrd nan Laogh*, calves' meadow. Further

6

along is *The Assarow*, G. an asaradh, a stretch of
pasture sloping up from the river, based on fasair
or asair, pasturage.   It has no connection with Ir.
Assaroe.   Below the Assarow is *Am Poll Ruadh*,
the red pool, the deepest in the Boath part of the
river.

Pollag Aitionn—Juniper pool ; in the river below
Loanroidge Farm.   Known also as *Poll nam
morbh*, Pool of the fish spears.   It is a good pool
for salmon and sea-trout.   East of it is

Poll na' Clàr—As this is a good place for crossing
by leaping from stone to stone, the meaning may
well be that seen in many similar Irish names,
Pool of the Boards, *i.e.*, planks to facilitate
crossing.

Cnoc 'Chroisg—'Crasg,' a crossing ; the hill over
which the road crosses into Boath.   The old road
crossed rather to the west of the present road.

Lealty—Lealdy 1622 ; G. Lethalltaidh ; 'leth-allt,'
half-burn, *i.e.*, the sloping land on one side of the
burn, common as Leault, but here it shews the
-ie termination.   A 'Leault' is usually a 'one-
sided' burn, and is so here.   East of Lealty
and north of Ardoch is a wooded hill, *Cnoc
Churadair*, a name which looks like "hill of
the sower," but it really stands for Cnoc
Churadain, St Curitan's hill.

An Corran—Dimin. of ' coire,' corry.

Ardoch—G. An àrdach, the high place.   Below it,
north of the present road, is *An Cabhsair fliuch*,
the wet causeway, part of the old road.

Baddans—G. Na Badanan, the little copses. A little south of the farm-house and east of the road is *Am Bàrd*, a nice flat field.

Clais druim bhàthaich—Cleft of the byre-ridge. Auchvaich and Ardache appear in 1608 as pendicles of Contullich.

Multovy — Multowy 1490 ; G. Multabhaidh, an extension of ' mult,' wedder ; place of wedders. Cf. Muckovie, place of swine. The termination represents an early -ab-, -ob-, -ub-. Cf. Cen-abum, Or-obis, Es-ubii.

Cnoc Duchary—Probably ' dubh-chàthraidh,' the black-moss-place. A great cairn containing cists stood on its easter slope.

Cnoc Céislein—Hill at back of Fyrish ; a derivative of Ir. ' céis,' sow. It is a broad-backed hill, and faces Meall an Tuirc (Boar's Hill) on the west. Cf. the Boar of Badenoch and the Sow of Atholl. East of it is Poll a' Mhucainn, noted above.

Averon—The local name of the Alness River. The local derivation is worth recording. Once on a time there lived at Kinloch a widow with two sons. One died suddenly, and not long thereafter the second was drowned in crossing the ford above Poll na Cuilc. When the sad news was brought to the mother, she exclaimed, " M' ath bhròn ! " (My second sorrow !), whence the river is called Averon to this day. A similar derivation is locally given for Carn-averon in Aberdeenshire. The name is best regarded as an extension of O. Ir. ab, river, with diminutive termination—

Abh-ar-an.   Strictly it is said to apply only to
the part from L. Moir to the junction at Strathrusdale.   An equation with the Gaulish Avara,
though tempting, would be rash.   Cf. Strathrory,
Avoch.

Ceann-uachdarach :   " lands of Candwachterach
with its brewhouse (cum brasina)," 1642—upper-
head ; beyond Kildermorie, but of old evidently a
less lonely place than it is now.   It was near the
drove road from the north to Dingwall.

Càrn Sonraichte—Cairnehondrig 1619 ; ' notable
cairn,' north of Kildermorie.

Loch Bad-a-bhàthaich—Loch of the byre-clump.
About a mile to the east of it is Clach àirigh a'
Mhinistir, Stone of the Minister's shieling.

Creachainn nan Sgadan—Bare hill-top of the
herring.   There is a local tradition of a shower of
herring, which may be founded on fact : for inland
places in Ireland similarly named, see Joyce
II., 312.

Bad-sgàlaidh—(Also Bothan Bad-sgàlaidh), about
five miles beyond Kildermorie, and noted for
ghosts ; Ir. scàl, spectre ; " Spectre-clump."   In
this direction, near the river, is *Braonan*, the
little wet place ; v. Fairburn.

KILTEARN.

Kiltearn—Kiltierny 1227, Keltyern 1296 ; G. Cill-tighearn. Usually explained as 'Lord's Kirk,' either in the sense of 'Church dedicated to the Lord,' or from some early chief of the Munros having been buried there. As for the first of these explanations, there seems to be no parallel for such a dedication, though we find indeed Cill Chriosd. As to the second, the burying-place of the family of Fowlis, from the earliest times of which we have any record, was in the Chanonry of Ross, and it is in any case extremely improbable that the church should receive its designation from the burial of a chief. A third theory is a dedication to St Ternan, who is supposed to have been a contemporary and pupil of Palladius. This also is unsatisfactory, for though Ternan's name is preserved in Banchory-Ternan, dedications to him are extremely rare, and, moreover, it is difficult to see how Ternan would suit the phonetics, for the last syllable, '-an,' could hardly have been dropped. The most feasible explanation is a dedication to Tighernach. Cf. Kiltierny in Ireland with Kiltierny 1227.

The parish includes in its western part the old parish of Lumlair ; Lemnelar 1227, Lymnolar and

Lumlar 1548 ; G. Luim na làr ; luim, locative of
lòm, a bare surface ; làr is most probably genitive
plural of làir, mare ; làr, the ground, not being
suitable in respect of meaning and gender.
Names from the various words for ' horse '—each,
capull, marc—are very common, arising from the
old practice of keeping the horses on a pasture by
themselves ; cf. Glenmark, Glenmarkie, Ardin-
caple, Kincaple, Caplich, Dalneich. The church
of Lumlair, according to the Old Statistical
Account dedicated to the Virgin Mary, and in
modern times known as St Mary's Chapel, stood
at Lumlair near the sea-shore. The site referred
to is close by the roadside, about two and a-half
miles east of Dingwall. The foundations of the
chapel are still visible, with an ancient and now
disused burying-ground, called Cladh ma-Bhrì
(Kilmabryd, Blaeu). This burying-ground is
doubtless called after the saint to whom the
chapel was dedicated, and who, moreover, from
the above well-known modern Gaelic form of the
name, could not have been Mary. Blaeu's Kilmabryd suggests Bridget, but her name in
Gaelic is always Brìd, never Brì. The only
name that satisfies the phonetics is Bríg, later
Brìgh. There were at least two Irish female
saints so called.

Fowlis—G. Fólais (narrow o) ; cf. Allt Fólais in
Gairloch (Loch Maree), Foulis in Aberdeen (G.
Fólais), Fowlis in Perth, Fowlis in Forfar. The
oldest forms of all are similar to the modern.

The phonetics indicate a lost 'g' or 'd' before
'l,' which suggests fo-glais, foghlais, from fo,
under, and O.G. glas, water, 'Sub-water,' or
'Streamlet'; cf. for meaning Welsh 'goffrwd,'
streamlet, the philological G. equivalent of which
is 'fo-sruth.' (For the phonetic process involved,
cf. 'foghnadh,' sufficiency, from O. Ir. fognam).
A small burn, Allt Fólais, runs through the Glen
of Fowlis, and there are burns near all the other
places of the same name.

Drummond—G. Druimein, locative of drum, ridge ;
cf. Drymen, in Stirling.

Balconie—Balkenny 1333 and 1341 ;[1] G. Bailcnidh,
based on bailc, strong ; Welsh balch, proud ; for
the extensions of the root cf. Delny. The Gaelic
form is decisive against baile, a town or stead, and
compels me regretfully to give up a former
identification (by myself) of Balkenny of 1333
with Petkenny of 1281.[2] The traditional explanation is Baile Còmhnuidh, dwelling place, to wit,
of the Earls of Ross ; but the meaning cannot be
other than ' the strong place.'

Teanord—G. Tigh 'n ùird, Ord-house.

Katewell—Catoll 1479 ; Keatoll 1608 ; G. Cladail ;
Norse kvi, fold ; dalr, dale ; cf. kvia-bolr, milking
place ; kvia-bekkr, fold-beck.

Swordale—Sweredull 1479 ; G. Suardal ; Norse
svörðr, sward ; dalr, dale.

[1] Charters granted at Balkenny by Hugh, Earl of Ross, and by William,
Earl of Ross.

[2] In 1281 William, Earl of Ross, granted a quarter of land, which was
called Petkenny, to the Bishop of Moray. Petkenny cannot be located.

Balachladich—Shore-town.

Ardullie—G. Aird-ilidh ; the latter part may represent ' ileach,' variegated, in which sense may be
compared the uses of breac, riabhach, ballach.,
blàr ; ' speckled height.' Dìlinn, as in leac
dhìlinn, natural rock, will not suit, as the *i* of
Aird-ilidh is short.

Pelaig—Pellock 1583 ; G. Peallaig. Rob Donn
uses ' peallag ' in the sense of ' rough garment '—
dimin. of ' peall,' hairy skin, borrowed from Latin
pellis, hide. But the meaning is not satisfactory
as a place-name, and the word may be non-
Gaelic—as is indeed suggested by the initial ' p.'
' Peallaidh ' is a Pictish river-name, seen in Obair-
pheallaidh, Aberfeldy. Peallaidh is used in Lewis
as the name of a water-sprite. (Cf. German quell,
a spring).

Clachan Biorach—' Pointed ' or ' standing stones
they consist of two equal ovals joined to each
other, and are described minutely by the late Mr
Roderick Maclean in his " Notes on the Parish of
Kiltearn" (Gaelic Society Transactions XV.)
North of the Clachan Biorach is Cnoc an
Teampuill, Temple Hill. There are also *Clachan
Biorach* at the head of Clare.

Fluchlady—Fliuch leathad, wet hillside, with -aidh
ending.

Bogandurie—Bogginduiry 1696 ; G. Bog an dùbh-
raidh, gloomy bog.

Culbin—Back of the hill.

Octobeg—G. An t-ochdamh beag, the small octave, *i.e.*, eighth part of a davach; cf. Ochto, Kincardine.

Cnoc Vabin—G. Cnoc Mhàbairn, a name showing the good Celtic termination -ernos, but otherwise obscure; perhaps a personal name.

Fuaranbuy—Yellow-well.

Strongarve—Rough nose or point.

Skiach (water) — Scraiskeith 1479; G. Allt na sgitheach; O. Ir. sce, G. sgeach, hawthorn; a common element in names; cf. Altnaskiach, near Inverness.

Culnaskiach — Culnaskeath 1546; nook of the Skiach, or, of the hawthorn.

Teachatt (so, 1608)—G. Tigh-chait, Cat-house; cf. Cadboll.

Knockancuirn—Cnocan, dimin. of cnoc; caorunn, rowan.

Rhidorach — Ruigh, slope; dorach, dark; dark slope.

Clare—Clearmoir 1608; G. An Clàr; but also, anns na Clàr; clàr, board, hence a flat place. But cf. Poll na' Clar in Alness.

Gortan—G. Goirtean, small field of corn.

Knockantoul—Barn-hill.

Druim—Ridge.

Achleach—Achlich 1608; Achleich 1633; G. Achleitheich, locative of "ach-leitheach," half-field, *i.e.*, field on a hill side. A cold sunless place.

Sgorr a' Chléi'—Creel peak; an exceedingly steep piece of land, where, according to tradition, manure, etc., had to be carried in creels.

Gleann and **Meall na Speireig**—Glen and Hill of
the Sparrow-hawk—'speireag.'

An Socach—The Snouted Hill ; a spur of Wyvis.

Cabar Fuais—The Antler of Wyvis.

Allt nan Caorach—Altnagerrack 1608 ; sheep-
burn ; its precipitous sides are dangerous for
sheep.

Loch Glass and **Glen Glass**—O.G. glas, water ; cf.
R. Glass in Strathglass ; Douglas Water, where
Eng. 'water' is a translation of 'glas ;' Glenfin-
glas (fionn-glas, white-water).   Findglais and
Dubglas appear in a list of 'healing waters' in
Ireland (O'Curry, M. and C. III. 97).   Dubglas
(Blackwater) is somewhat disguised in Inver-
uglas (L. Lomond).   The river flowing through
Glenglass is called in its lower reaches, where it
passes through the famous chasm of the Black
Rock, the Allt-grannda, Ugly Burn.   The old
name, at least of the upper part, must have been
Glass.   The river flowing into Loch Glass is now
known as Abhainn nan èun, Bird-river (O.S.M.)

Corrievachie—G. Coire-bhacaidh, an old locative
of Coire-bhacach, bent corry.

Cuilishie—G. Caolaisidh, the narrows.   "The
narrow passage at the lower end of Loch Glass.
Here is the ford of the old drove road that passed
that way."—Mr R. Maclean.   Cf. Lienassie.

Kinloch—At the eastern end of Loch Glass.

Eileanach—Place of islands ; it lies low by the
river side, and is liable to be flooded.

Allt na Cailce—Chalk Burn ; on its right bank is considerable deposit of lime, which is constantly added to by a tiny rivulet.

Cnoc a' Mhargadaidh—Market Hill. There is a tradition of a market, which is probably correct, in view of the nearness of the old drove road from Sutherland. Certain enclosures near the foot of the hill may be explained as connected with this market, or they may be very much older. There are numerous small cairns and some fine hut circles. There are traces of a road leading to the top, and on the top is black earth with charcoal fragments. At least one flint has been found on the top.

Coneas—The remarkable double waterfall below Eileanach. Con, together ; eas, waterfall : 'combination of falls' ; cf. Conachreig, Contullich, Contin, Conval, Conchra, Conglas, Conaglen.

Clyne—Clon 1231, Clonys, 1264, Clyne 1350-1372 ; G. an Claon, the slope ; now Mountgerald. 'Amadan a' Chlaoin' (the Fool of Clyne) was a well-known character in the earlier half of the 19th century.

Kilchoan—Church of St. Congan, now *Mountrich*.

Loch nan Amhaichean—Loch of the Necks ; Loch Gobhlach (O.S.M. Loch nan Gobhlag), Forked Loch ; Loch Coire Feuchain (?) ; Feur Lochan, Grassy Lochlet ; Loch Bealach nan Cuilean ; Loch na' Druidean (O.S.M. Lochan Driogan), Loch of the Starlings : Loch Mhiosaraidh (O.S.M. Loch Measach), Loch of dairy produce, are all in the uplands of the parish.

Allt Dubhag—The small black burn.

Ath a' bhealaich eidheannaich—Ford of the ivy-pass.

Balnacrae—G. baile na crè, clay-town.

Culcairn—G. Cul-chàirn, behind the cairn ; the cairn exists no longer.

Dun-ruadh—Red fort.

Teandallan—Explained by Mr Maclean as " house of swingle-trees or plough-yokes." " A carpenter lived here, who made a trade of them." Dallan also means a winnowing-fan.

Altnalait—G. allt na làthaid, burn of the miry place ; near Tulloch, and at the western boundary of Kiltearn. Based on root of làthach, mire, with ending seen in Bialid, &c.

Modern names are :—

Evanton—G. Bail' Eoghainn, or am bail' ùr, New-town, as opposed to the old village of Drummond on the west side of the river. Evanton dates from about 1800.

Fannyfield—Part of Swordale ; formerly am Bog-riabhach, brindled bog.

Mountgerald, formerly Clyne, so called, says Mr Maclean, by a Mackenzie who owned the place about the middle of the 18th century, in honour of the supposed Fitzgerald descent of the Mac-kenzies.

Obsolete are :—Arbisak, 1608, and Badnagarne, a pertinent of Keatoll.

DINGWALL.

Dingwall—Dingwell in Ross 1227, Dignewall 1263,
Dingwal 1308, Dingwall 1382. Norse, Thing-
völlr, Field of the Thing, the Norse general court
of justice. Dingwall was therefore the centre of the
Norse administration in Ross. The most southerly
Norse place-name in this direction is Eskadale
(Beauly), but Norse influence doubtless extended
further. A mound, supposed to have been the
actual meeting place of the Thing, is referred to
about 1503, when James, Duke of Ross, resigned
the earldom, and reserved to himself for life the
moot-hill (montem) of Dingwall beside the town,
in order to preserve his title as Duke. Dingwall
is in Gaelic In'ir-pheofharan, Inver-peffray, and
Inverferan appears in a Bull of Pope Alexander
IV., 1256 (Theiner Vet. Mon.).

Another term applied in a more or less familiar
way to the ancient town is Bail' a' chàil, Kail-
town, but of the antiquity or origin of this term
we cannot speak with confidence. Under date
1526 appear the following names connected with
the burgh of Dingwall :—Blakcaris-land, Gray
Stane, Mill of Brigend, Acris Scotte, Schortaker,
march of Fesallich (dirty bog channel), Thombane
(white-hillock). In 1655 we have the Boig of

Dingwall within the Burgh thereof, called Boig-moir, including Boigmoir or Westerboig, the Mid-boig and the Eister Boig, within the parish of Dingwall.

Tulloch 1507, Tulch 1563 ; G. tulach, hillock ; common also in locative case as Tullich.

Kildun—Thomas Dingwell of Kildon 1506, Kildun 1527 ; G. Cill-duinn, locative of Ceall-donn, brown church. Cf. Killin, from Cill-fhinn, white church ; Seipeil Odhar, dun chapel ; An Eaglais Bhreac, the spotted church (Falkirk).

Humberston — Formerly Upper Kildun. Major William Mackenzie, of the family of Seaforth, married Mary Humberston.[1]

Pitglassie—Petglasse 1526 ; G. Bad a' ghlasaich, Lea-town ; the change from ' pit' into 'bad' is very rare ; but cf. Pitenglassie, G. Bad an glais tir.

Kinnairdie—Kynnardy 1479 ; G. Cinn-àrdaidh, head of the high ground ; " the four Glakkis quhilkis are the ferd quarter of Kynnarde," 1539 ; " the demesne lands commonly called Kynnairdie, and the lands of Glakkis, a fourth part of the said demesne lands," 1584.

Drynie—Wester Drynee 1479 ; G. Droighnidh (no article) ; droigheann, thorns, with -aidh ending.

Other names in the lower part of the parish explain themselves : — Bakerhill, Blackwells, Knockbain, Allanfield, Croftandrum, Baddamh-roy (copse of the red stag or ox).

[1] *V.* A. Mackenzie's " History of the Mackenzies," p. 331.

In the uplands are Cnoc a' Bhreacaich (O.S.M. Cnoc a Bhreacachaidh), hill of the spotted place; Leathad a' chruthaich (O.S.M. Leidchruich), hillside of the quaking bog; cf. suil-chruthaich; Meall a' ghuail, Coal Hill, noted for excellent peats used for smithy charcoal, as was the regular custom before coals became available. Meall na speireig (hill of the sparrow-hawk, at the junction of Dingwall, Fodderty, and Kiltearn).

FODDERTY.

Fodderty—Ecclesia de Fotherdino 1238, Fotherdyn
1275, Fothirdy 1350, Fothartye 1548, Fedderdy
1561 ; G. Fodhraitidh (close 'o'). The spellings
of 1350 and 1548 still represent the common
English pronunciation. Fodder or fother, as a
prefix, is well known on Pictish ground. Fodderty itself is the most northerly instance ; in
Inverness-shire is Fodderletter (Tomintoul); in
Aberdeenshire, Fetterangus, Fetternear, and
Fedderat (Fedreth 1205, Feddereth 1265) ; in
Kincardine, Fetteresso (Fodresach, Pict. Chron.),
and Fordun, which in St Berchan's Prophecy is
Fothardun ; also Fettercairn (Fotherkern, Pict.
Chron.) ; and in Perthshire, Forteviot, the Foth-
uirtabaicht of the Pictish Chronicle. As a suffix
it appears in the Annals of Ulster, under date
680 A.D., "obsessio Duin Foithir," and again, 694,
"obsessio Duin Foter"—siege of Dunottar. The
change to 'Fetter,' seen in the Aberdeen and
Kincardine names, is curious, but mostly late,
and perhaps a matter of umlaut in Scots dialect.

Fodder, early Foter and Fother (in modern
Gaelic 'for' with close 'o'), is best regarded
as a comparative of 'fo,' under, and may be compared with 'uachdar,' upper, from the root seen

in 'uasal,' high. The strong accent on Fodder,
G. For, may have helped to obscure the second
part of the compound. The ending -ty(n) is not
uncommon on Pictish ground, and is always
troublesome ; cf. Cromarty, Navity, Auchter-
muchty, Buchanty. It is, however, probably safe
to say that the meaning of Fodderty must be
something like ' Lower place,' in contrast to
Achterneed.

The modern parish of Fodderty includes the
ancient parish of Kinnettes—Kenneythes 1256,
Kennetis 1561, Kynattas 1574 ; Gael. Cinn-it'ais,
' t' soft. The name is now applied to the farm
on the high ground to the west of the Spa.
' Cinn ' is the locative case of ' ceann,' head. The
ending, ' ais,' is seen in Allt-ais (Altas), Fearn-ais
(Farness), Forres, Durrais (Dores), Dallas, Geddes,
being practically a local suffix. The middle part
-it- is obscure, but may possibly be referred to
Welsh ' yd,' corn ; O. I. ith ; giving a meaning
' place of corn ;' Kinnettes, head of the corn-land.

Achterneed—Wethirnyde 1476, Ouctirnede 1479 ;
G. Uachdar-nìad, the high ground rising up from
the plain of Fodderty, Uachdar means ' upland' ;
nìad can hardly be explained from any Gaelic or
Irish source, but it would very well represent
Welsh ' nant,' valley ; cf. Welsh cant, Gael. ceud,
W. dant, G. deud. Achterneed would thus
mean, ' The land above the valley.' Above
Achterneed is a cup-marked stone called *a' chlach
phollach*, the stone full of holes.

7

Strathpeffer—G. Srath-pheofhair, 'Strath of the Peffer.' Peffer occurs as a burn name in Inverpeffray (Crieff), and there are two Peffer burns in Athelstaneford (Haddington), also a Peffer Mill at Duddingston. The initial 'p' indicates a non-Gaelic origin. Dr Skene, misled by the resemblance of Inchaffray (Insula Missarum, Mass Isle), has referred Inverpeffray and Strath-peffer to Ir. 'aifrend,' a mass, which is quite out of the question. The various Peffer streams are more likely to be connected with the root seen in Welsh 'pefr,' beautiful, fair ; 'pefrin,' radiant ; 'pefru,' to radiate.

Knockfarrel—G. Cnoc-farralaidh ; 'far' in composition denotes 'projecting' or 'high'; *e.g.*, 'far-bhonn,' fore-sole ; Ir. 'for-dorus,' porch ; G. 'far-dorus,' lintel ; 'for-all,' high cliff. In farralaidh, *a* of 'farr' is indefinite in quality, indicating that it has been affected by a succeeding slender vowel, which has become broadened in its turn. This gives an original far-eileach, in locative far-eiligh, 'high' or 'projecting stone-house,' or 'stone-place,' with reference to the important vitrified fort which crowns the hill. For 'eileach' in this sense, cf. na h-Eileachan Naomha or Garvelloch Isles, Jura ; also the great Irish Ailech. Cf. also Farrlaraidh, Rogart, from far-laraigh, old locative of làrach ; 'projecting site.'

Castle Leod—Contaneloid 1507, Kandinloid 1534, Cultenloid 1547, Cwltelloid and Cultaloid 1556,

Cultalode 1575, Cultelloud, 1609, Culterloud 1618. From these old forms it appears that Castle Leod is a corruption, facilitated doubtless by the presence of the 'castle,' which bears date 1616. Contaneloid and Kandinloid represent 'Ceann an leothaid,' Head of the sloping hill-side ; the other forms point to 'Cùl da leothad,' At the back of two slopes, to wit, the slope of Achterneed and that immediately to the west of the castle.

Ardival—Ardovale 1479, Le Tympane de Ardovale 1487, Ardwaill with its mill called Tympáne Myln[1] 1586, half davach of Ardauell 1655 ; G. Aird a' bhail', Height of the town or farm-stead.

Kinnellan—Kynellane 1479; G. Cinn-eilein, Island-head, from the small artificial island in Loch Kinnellan, "resting upon logs of oak, on which the family of Seaforth had at one period a house of strength"—New Stat. Acc.

[1] The site of the old mill is still well known, a little to the west of the present railway station, and just behind the stables. In 1681 it is mentioned as "Tympane mill, near Clach an Tiompan," the stone in the grounds of Nutwood near the public road, inscribed with an eagle and "horse-shoe" ornament. There seems now to be a tendency to the absurd corruption 'Muileann tiunndain' and 'Clach an tiunndain'—'turning mill' and 'stone of the turning,' a corruption arising from 'tiompan' not being understood in this connection. 'Tiompan' has two quite distinct meanings—(1) a musical instrument ; (2) a rounded, one-sided knoll. In this sense it is common in place-names, and may be compared in point of derivation with English 'tump,' Greek 'tumbos,' Lat. 'tumeo,' Gael. 'tulach,' Welsh 'twmp,' a mound. In this particular case the 'tiompan' is the knoll on which the house of Nutwood stands, and which is exactly all that an orthodox 'tiompan' should be. I have been told that 'tiompan' is used in a third sense—viz., a narrow gully, or even the nozzle of a bellows ; and in support of this was quoted the proverb : "Tha a' ghaoth cho fuar 's ged a bhiodh i tighinn a tiompan"—The wind is as cold as if it were blowing out of a bellows' mouth.

Ulladale—Elodil 1476, Ulladall 1479 ; G. Ulladal
is Norse, and probably means Ulli's dale.   Cnoc
Ulladail is the hill above Castle Leod.   Cf. Ulladale in Logie Easter, Ullapool, etc.

Park—Park 1476, le Park 1479 ; G. a' Phàirc.
The battle of Park, Blàr na Pàirce, between the
Mackenzies and the Macdonalds, took place about
1490.

Dochcarty—Dalcarty and Davachcarty 1541 ; G.
Do'ach-gartaidh : dabhach of the corn-enclosure.

Davochcarn—Dalfcarne 1479 ; G. Do'ach a' chàirn,
davach of the cairn.

Davochpollo—Dalfpoldach 1479, Dauchauchpollo
1526 ; G. Do'ach a' phollain, Davach of the pool.

Davochmaluag—Dalfmalawage 1497, Dalmalook
1584 ; G. Do'ach Mo-luaig, St Moluag's davoch.

These three were included in the farm of Brae,
1777.   On the moor to the west of the Heights
of Dochcarty, G. Brèigh Doch-gartaidh, are five
stone slabs, heavy, broad, and pointed, marking
an oval of about ten to twelve feet axis.   They
are called *Na Clachan Gòruch*, the silly stones,
and are evidently part of what was once the
central chamber of a large round cairn, now
almost quite removed.   They may be compared
with the chambered cairn near Acharn, Alness.

Inchvannie—Inchevaynel, Enchewany 1554, Inch-
vandie 1584 ; G. I's-mheannaidh, probably from
meann, a kid.   These *inshes* were places frequented
by cattle.

Blarninich—G. Blàr an aonaich, Plain of the meeting, or, of the moor. It is near the church of Fodderty.

Inchrory—Chapel of the Virgin Mary of Inchrory 1349, Inchrory 1583, Inchrorie 1609. G. I's Ruaraidh. On the right bank of the Peffery, immediately opposite the old burying-ground of Fodderty. Here stood the chapel of Inchrory. To the north of the burying-ground was ' Croit an Teampuil,' Temple Croft, where stone coffins have been found (O.S.A.). " Rory's Mead."

Dochnaclear—Dauachnacleir with the mill 1533, Davachnacleir 1533 ; G. Do'ach nan cliar, davach of the "cliar" ; cliar here has probably its old meaning of clergy ; in modern Gaelic it means poet or hero. The place is above the farm of Fodderty.

Keppoch—G. a' cheapaich, the tillage plot. Common.

Bottacks—G. na botagan (close ' o ') ; botag in place-names means a sun-dried crack, or narrow channel.

Creag an Fhithich—Raven's Rock.

Rogie—le Rew 1476, Rewgy cum le Ess (with the waterfall) 1472, Rewy 1527, Rowe, Rowy 1575, Rowy 1614 ; G. Roagaidh, name of burn and district ; ? Norse rok-á, splashing, foaming river ; cf. Loch Roag, Lewis. Doubtful ; cf. Errogie, Inverness.

Strathrannoch—Foreste de Rannach 1479, Strathrannoch 1542 ; strath of bracken. Cf. Rannoch and Loch Rannoch in Perthshire.

Allt a' choire ranaich—Burn of the bracken corry, in Strathrannoch.

Lùb a' chlaiginn—Skull bend; 'claigeann' is common in place-names, and is usually applied to a bare rounded knoll. When applied to a farm or field, it is said to mean the best arable land (New Guide to Islay, p. 42).

Allt coir a' chùndrain—I have failed to verify this name.

Meall a' ghrianain—Hill of the sunny knoll.

Beinn a' Chaisteil—Castle Hill; cf. Beinn a' Chaisteil, at the head of Glen Rosa, Arran.

Càrn nan aighean—Hinds' cairn.

An leathad cartach—'Cartach' may come from 'cairt,' bark of a tree, but in this particular connection it is, I think, more likely to come from 'cairt,' cleanse or scour; whence 'cairteadh,' muck. Thus the 'leathad cartach' would mean the 'scoury' hillside, i.e., liable to be scoured by water. 'Cairt' scour, is seen also in Glen Docharty, and Glendochart; cf. the rivers Cart.

Allt an eilein ghuirm—Burn of the green island; Meall nan sac, hill of burdens or loads.

Inchbae—G. I's-beith, Birch-haugh

Allt na Bana-Mhorair—Lady's burn.

Gleann sgathaich—Doubtful; 'sgathach' means lopped branches, brushwood, from 'sgath,' lop. The 'a' is short, otherwise we may think of a derivative from 'sgàth,' fear—'uncanny place.'

Ben Wyvis—G. Beinn Uais (but prosthetic 'f' seen in Cabar Fuais); High Hill; 'uais,' from the root seen in 'uas-al,' high, noble; Gaulish ux-ellos; Gaulish 'x' becomes 's' in Gaelic, but in Welsh it becomes 'ch.' Thus 'ux-ellos' gives in Welsh 'uch-el,' high, whence Ochil, Oykel, Achilty. The height of Wyvis is perhaps best appreciated from the higher parts of Inverness and neighbourhood.

Bealach Collaidh—An ancient drove road to the west of Wyvis; hazel-gap or pass; an extension of 'coll,' the old form of 'call,' hazel, representing a primitive *Coslacum*. The forest of Colly, in Kincardine, appears in 1375, modern Cowie; cf. Kilcoy, and Duncow in Dumfriesshire.

URRAY.

Urray—Owra 1476, Urra 1479, Kingis Urray c.
1560 ; G. Urrath.   The New Stat. Acc. suggests
ùr-àth, new ford, from the tendency of the rapid
Orrin, near which the church and churchyard are
situated, to shift its fords.   This, however, does
not satisfy the phonetics either in respect of the
quantity of the 'u' or the quality of the 'r.'
The first syllable is rather the preposition 'air,'
O. Ir. ar, air, Gaulish are-, meaning 'before,' and
cognate with the English 'fore.'   In Gael. compounds it appears as 'ur-' in 'ur-chair,' a shot
(i.e., something cast forward), 'ur-sainn,' a door-
post (i.e., something standing forward), 'ear-ball'
or 'ur-ball,' a tail.   It is seen in such Gaulish
names as Are-brignus ('brig,' hill) and Are-morica
('mor,' sea).   The second part may possibly be
'àth,' a ford, which would give the not very satisfactory sense of 'projecting ford'; more probably
it is 'ràth,' a circular enclosure or fort, 'fore-fort,'
or, 'fort on a projecting place.'   For phonetics cf.
urradh, person, security, = air + ráth (Macbain).

Brahan—Browen 1479, Bron 1487, Branmore 1526,
Brain 1561 ; G. Brathainn, as if loc. of bràth, a
quern.   W. brenan, handmill) ; "place of the
quern" is the local tradition, which may be
correct.

Tollie—G. Tollaidh, from 'toll,' hole. There was a chapel and also a burying-ground at Tollie. Cf. Tollie, Ardross, and Tollie, Gairloch.

Jamestown—G. Baile Shiamais.

Bealach nan Còrr—Cranes' pass.

Moy—Half davach of Moy 1370, le Moye 1479, Moymore 1542; G. a' mhuaigh, locative case of magh, a plain. Moy Bridge is *Drochaid Mhuaigh*, and the ferry which existed before the bridge was *Port Mhuaigh*. (Moy, Inverness, is a' Mhoigh).

Ussie (loch and district)—Usuy 1463, Ouse 1476, Housy 1527, Lytill Usui and Mekill Usui 1583; G. ùsaidh; an obscure name, Pictish or pre-Pictish.

Balnain—G. Baile 'n fhàin, from 'fàn,' a low-lying place or gentle slope, not uncommon in place-names; cf. na fàna, the Fendom (Tain); am fàin Braonach (Aultbea), Forsinain (Sutherland).

Fairburn[1]—The two Ferburnys 1476, Fairburneglis 1527, Eistir Farbrawne 1538, Kirkferbrune 1542, Farabren 1555, Avon Forbarin (Orrin River), Blaeu; G. Farabraoin, or simply Braoin; from 'far,' over, as in Cnoc Farrail, and braon, water, which in place-names is used to denote a wet spot, *e.g.* Brin, Daviot, G. Braoin; cf. Lochbroom.

---

[1] Local tradition connects the burning of the women of the Finn by Garry with the fort on Cnoc Farrail, and it is curious to find several old Gaelic poems on that subject, entitled "Losgadh Brugh Farbruin," the Burning of Fairburn Fort. A fragment of one is printed in "Reliquiæ Celticæ," I. 226. Another version with same title is printed in Campbell's "Leabhar na Feinne," p. 176.

Arcan—Arcoyn 1479, Arckyne 1561, Arcan 1584 ; from Old Gael. ' arc,' black ; Welsh ' erch,' dusky. In a West Highland Fingalian tale, one of the characters is Arc dubh, where ' dubh ' is a translation of ' arc.' Cf. Loch Arklet, in Stirling ; Loch Arkaig, in Inverness-shire ; and Arkendeith, in Black Isle.

Clachandhu—Black stones.

Achtabannock—G. Ach-da-bhannag, field of two cakes.

Aultgowrie—G. Allt-gobhraidh, Goat-burn. The regular Gaelic form would of course be Allt nan gobhar ; but the formation seen here is not uncommon in Easter Ross ; cf. Invergowrie, identified by Dr Reeves with " flumen Gobriat in Pictavia," Acta SS. Mart. II., p. 449.

Balloan—G. Bail' an lòin, town of the low damp place.

Teanafruich—Tigh 'n fhraoich, Heather-house.

Achnasoull—Auchansowle 1479, Auchnasoill 1538, Auchnasowle 1542—Barnfield.

Blackdyke—G. An Gàradh dubh, of which the English is a translation.

Clachuil—G. Clach-thuill, Hollowed stone. The name comes from a stone hollowed out as if for ' crocking' barley—' clach an eorna,' the barley stone—which may still be seen at the Inn of Clachuil. Cf. Clach-toll in Assynt.

Cornhill—G. Cnoc an airbh ; cf. Cornhill in Strathcarron (Ardgay), formerly Knockinarrow.

Auchederson—G. Achd-eadarsan ; it lies between the Gowrie burn and the Orrin, not far from their

junction. The meaning is obviously ' the field
between' (eadar), but the last syllable is puzzling.
Perhaps with the extension of 'eadar' shown
in Auchederson, we may compare ' tarsuinn,'
from 'tar,' across, and ' ur-sainn,' from ' air,'
before, in both of which the ending represents
a primitive ' -stan,' from root ' sta,' to stand.

Stronachro—Point of the fold or enclosure ; on the
opposite side of the Orrin is

Cnoc an òir—Gold hill.

Auchonachie—Ach Dhonnachaidh, Duncan's field.
In the birch wood south east of it is *Cnocan nam
Brat*, hillock of the mort-cloths, near a very small
burying-ground, now disused and nameless.

Cabaan—Cadha bàn, white steep path.

Rheindown—Ruigh an dùin : Slope or stretch of
Dun ; adjacent to Dunmore.

Teandalloch—G. Tigh an dalach, House of the
dale ; cf. Ballindalloch.

Aultvaich—Byre-burn.

Aradie (in Glenorrin)—G. Aradaidh. It is at the
junction with the Orrin of a stream flowing from
a loch marked on the O.S.M. Loch Annraidh, but
which is locally called Loch Aradaidh. The
stream is also Allt Aradaidh. Aradie is thus a
stream name, and we are safe in comparing it
with Inverarity (Inuerarethin 1250), in Forfar,
now the name of a parish, but primarily the
junction of the Arity streamlet with a small burn.
There is also Arity Den, in Fife. The various
streams Arity are probably to be connected with
the Gaulish river Arar, of which Cæsar says that

its current is so extremely slow that the eye can
hardly distinguish in which direction it flows.
This again points to the root seen in the Welsh
'araf,' slow, still. Another Gaulish stream,
apparently from same root, is the Arabo, and
there is a personal name Arabus. The ending -ty
is not uncommon on Pictish ground.

Dunmore—Great fort; there is a hill fort, of the
usual type.

Tarradale—Taruedal 1240, 1278 ; Constable of
Taruedale 1278 ; Ouchterwaddale and Onachter-
vadale 1275-94 ; Taruedelle 1309, Tarridil 1372,
Tarredill 1479 ; Norse ' tarfr-dalr,' bull-dale.

Balvatie—Bail' a' mhadaidh, Dog's or Wolf's town.

Hughstown—from Hugh Baillie, son of a former
proprietor; formerly ' Cnocan cruaidh.'

Hilton—Hiltoun 1456, Balnoknok and Hiltoun of
Tarradaill 1586 ; G. Baile-'chnuic.

Gilchrist—Kylchristan 1569 : ' Christ's Kirk.'

Balnagown--Ballingovnie 1476, Balngoun 1479 ;
Smith's town.

Blair—Balliblare 1475, Belblare 1479 ; G. Bail' a'
bhlàir, town on the plain.

Carnaclasser—Cf. Kinkell Clairsair 1527 ; G. Càrn
a' Chlàrsair, the Harper's cairn.[1]

---

[1] The cairn is now gone, and its site matter of some uncertainty, but the
oldest tradition available to me places it in the garden of the present schoolhouse of Tarradale. The clarsair, according to the story, was slain by Iain
Dubh Ghiuthais to prevent disclosure of a theft of mill-stones, of which he
was unfortunate enough to be the spectator. But as this gentleman's father
died about 1619 (Hist. of the Mackenzies), and we have seen the term
' clarsair' attached to Kinkell in 1527, it follows that, whoever killed the
clarsair, if indeed he was killed, Black Fir John must be held innocent.
Perhaps the origin of the name is, like the cairn, gone beyond recovery.

Fiddlefield—Recent and English.

Ardnagrask—Height of the crossings. 'Crasg' is usually applied to a crossing place in the hills; cf. Cnoc chroisg, Boath, Alness. Here, however, it is locally explained as from the old system, practised in Ardnagrask up to comparatively recent times, of cross rigs. On this system the arable land of the township was held in common, and allotments of rigs made at fixed periods in such a way that no two adjacent rigs fell to the same man, the idea being that so every man got his fair share of good and bad land. This is likely to be correct, and is favoured by the fact that in Ardnagrask 'crasg' is genitive plural, not singular as is usual elsewhere.

Broomhill—G. Cnoc a' bhealaidh, or An cnoc bealaidh.

Caplich—G. Caiplich; from 'capull,' horse, or mare—'place of the horses'; a name of frequent occurrence.

Croftnallan—G. Croit an àilein, croft of the green flat.

Balavullich—Bail' a' mhullaich, town of the summit.

Torris Trean—A pathetic attempt at G. torr a' phris draigheann, hillock of the thorn-bush.

Culach—The back place.

Highfield—G. Ciarnaig; a word of doubtful meaning, which may perhaps be compared with Achiarnaig (Aviemore),

Glaickerduack—G. Glaic an dubhaig, hollow of the small black burn ; ' dubhag' is a fairly common burn name.

Chapeltown—G. Bail' an t-seipeil.

Dreim—The farm of Dreim (ridge) has swallowed up some small holdings such as Culblair, where some friends of Ewen Maclachlan's once lived, while modestly curtailing its own ancient name to a monosyllable. A reference to Blaeu's and Pont's maps shows it to be identical with Hilculdrum 1476, Kynculadrum 1479, Kilquhilladrum 1707. With the old forms may be compared Kincaldrum, in Inverarity, Forfar ; Kingoldrum, Forfar.

Balvraid—Ballibrahede 1476, Belbrade 1479, Esche (waterfall) of Balbrait 1527, Ballivraid 1648 ; G. Bail' a' bhraghaid, town of the upper part.

Tormuick—Swine's hill.

Febait—G. an théith bhàite, drowned, or wet bog.

Balno—Am baile nodha, new-town.

Ord—Le Ord 1479 ; G. An t-Ord ; Muir of Ord is *Am Blàr Dubh.* Near it are standing stones called ' na clachan seasaidh.'

Milton—G. Bail' a' mhuilinn.

Teanacriech—G. Tigh na criche, march-house.

Corriehallie—G. Coire shaillidh, fat corry ; noted for its grass ; cf. Coire feòil, Contin. In Corriehallie Forest is Creag a' Bhainne, Milking-rock.

Droitham—Anglicised form of Drochaid riabhan, or Drochaid cheann a' riabhain, connected with

Canreayan—G. Ceann a' riabhain; 'riabhain' is a derivative from root of 'riabhach,' meaning 'dappled, speckled place.'

Lettoch—G. an Leithdach, *i.e.*, leith dabhach, half davach. There are several Lettochs. Cf. Haddo, in Aberdeen, from Half-davach; Lettoch, Knockbain.

Teanalick—G. Tigh an t-sluic, bog-house; also given as Tigh-an-luig, house of the 'lag' or hollow.

Claisdarran—G. Clais an torrain, hollow of the hillock.

Tenafield—G. Tigh na fidhle, Fiddle-house.

Derrivorchie—G. Doire Mhurchaidh, Murdoch's copse.

Sron na saobhaidh—Point of the den.

Cnoc-ùdais—A hill at the entrance to Glen Orrin, with a large cairn on top, locally asserted to mark the grave of Judas! The ending -ais (open 'a') is that noted above in Kinnettes, and means 'place of.' The meaning of the root ùd- must be conjectural; but cf. Welsh 'ud,' howl, blast, which suggests 'place of blasts'—appropriate in point of sense.

Cuthaill Bheag and **Cuthaill Mhòr**. ? N. kúa-fjall, cow-fell. Hills near Cnoc-ùdais.

Orrin River—G. Abhainn Orthainn, which would point to a primitive Orotonna or perhaps Orsonna. We may perhaps compare the Orrin with such names as the Fifeshire Ore, with which has been connected Ptolemy's Orrea, a town of the Vernicones; and with Or-obis, a river of Gallia

Narbonensis ; there was also a Gaulish highland
tribe called the Orobii.   The root syllable in all
seems to be 'or,' which may or may not be the
same as Latin ' or-ior,' start.   The Orrin is
notorious for shifting its channel during the
sudden spates to which it is liable.   The junction
of the Orrin and the Conon is *Poll a' choire,*
kettle-pool.   Cf. Joyce II., 432.

URQUHART.

Urquhart — Utherchain 1275, Urquhard 1498, Wrchart (Blaeu) ; G. Urchadain, from the preposition ' air,' on, in front of, which in composition frequently becomes ' ur-'; and ' cardden,' a wood, brake ; a word not found in Gaelic or Irish, but preserved in Welsh as above—Urquhart thus meaning ' wood-side.' The Pictish name Urquhart is closely paralleled by the Gaelic Kinkell (woodhead), which appears below as occurring in this parish. ' Cardden' is a frequent element in names of places on Pictish ground, especially in the compounds Kincardine passim (wood-head), and in Urquhart ; cf. Glen-Urquhart, Inverness, Adamnan's Airchartdan ; Glen-Urquhart in the parish of Cromarty (though this has been connected with the Urquharts of Cromarty), and the parish of Urquhart in Elgin. We have also Pluscarden in Elgin, and Carden-den in Fife.

The modern parish of Urquhart includes the old parish of Logie Wester (united about 1669) ; Logy 1498, Logy Westir 1569, Logwreid 1600. In 1238 it seems to appear as Longibride (Theiner's Vet. Mon.) and again in Baiamund's Roll we have Dunthard and Logynbrid, 1275. Logy, G. lagaidh, is from ' lag,' a hollow, with

8

the '-aidh' ending. It forms the south-west portion of the united parish, and the name still appears in Logieside, half-a-mile or so north-east of Highfield Home Farm.

In 1430 the King confirmed to Donald, Thane of Caldore (Cawdor in Nairnshire), the lands of Estirkynkelle and the mill of Alcok in the county of Ross. In 1476 the King united and incorporated into the one complete thanage of Caldor (unum et integrum thanagium de Caldor), having the liberties and privileges of a barony, certain lands in Nairn and Forres, as also the two Kinkells, Kindeis, Invermarky, Mulquhaich, and Drumvoourny in the county of Ross, all which he granted to his faithful William, Thane of Caldor. This explains the origin of Ferintosh, G. An Tòisigheachd, or an Tòis'eachd, 'The Thaneship,' from 'tòiseach,' the ancient Celtic dignitary ranking next to the 'mormaer,' who, in the language of feudalism, was translated into thane, while the mormaer became 'Comes,' or Earl. Ferintosh, 'land of the Toiseach,' is still the popular designation of the parish in English, as 'An Tòisigheachd' is in Gaelic. Of the places mentioned in the grant of 1476, the two Kinkells, Mulcaich, and Dunvorny are in Urquhart ; Invermarky, now obsolete, was near Rosemarky. If there was a Kindeis in the Black Isle, I have failed to identify it, the only Kindeis known to me having been in Nigg, where it has now become obsolete, and whence it has been transferred to Kindeace in Kilmuir Easter.

Kinkell — Kynkell 1479, Kinkell Clarsair 1527, Kinkell Clarshac 1542, Kinkell Clairsheoch 1556 ; G. ceann na coille, wood-head. The similarity in meaning to the name Urquhart is worth noting. There are two Kinkells — Easter Kinkell and Wester or Bishop's Kinkell ; and Kinkell Clarsair of the records is doubtless the wester one, which is nearer Muir of Ord, or Càrn a' Chlàrsair.

Mulchaich—Mulcach 1456, Mulquhaich 1476, Mulquhaisch 1507 ; G. Mul-caich ; from 'mul,' rounded eminence ; the ' -caich,' or ' cathaich,' is doubtful.

Alcaig—Mill of Alcok 1430 ; "the Alcaikis with their pendicles, viz., Crostnahauin, and Bogboy, with the mill of Alcaik and the yare of Alcaik called Corrinagale," 1611 ; G. Alcaig; from Norse Alka-vík, auk's bay.

Bogboy is modern Bogbuie, yellow bog, two miles from Alcaig, beyond Easter Kinkell.

Crostnahauin, River-croft, is probably represented by the modern Teanahaun, a farm at the mouth of the Conon.

Corrinagale, from its description as a ' yare,' appears to be from Ir. ' cora,' or ' coradh,' a weir across a river ; cf. the Irish Kincora and Tikincor, and, in Scotland, Achnacarry ; Norsemens' Weir ?

Dunvornie—Drumwarny 1456, Drumwerny 1458 ; Drumworny 1507 ; G. Dun-bhoirinidh ; ' drum ' and ' dun ' frequently interchange, in some cases at least because there was both a drum or ridge, and a dun or fort, and this is the case with Dunvornie. The name seems to be from Ir. ' boireann,'

a rock, or a stony, rocky district—'Stony Ridge,'
which would suit a locality where, as here, the
rock frequently appears above the surface.   In
Ireland we have Rathborney, Knockanemorney,
and many other names of the same origin.

Findon—Fyndoun 1456, Mekle Findon 1574, Little
Findon 1587 ; G. Fionndun, white fort.   We
have in 1608 " Baddrean and Teazet, pertinents
of Mekle Findon."   Baddrean, now Badrain,
thorny copse ; Teazet is a phonetic spelling of
Tigh 'gbeata, Gatehouse ; it is now obsolete, but
Knockgate is still part of Findon farm.   Another
pertinent of Findon, 1608, is Ballegyle, now
Balgoil, Stranger's town.

The Querrel, near the shore, appears 1503 ;
obviously G. An Coireall, the quarry.

Culbokie—Culboky 1456 and 1542 ; Eistir and
Westir Culboky 1563 ; G. Cuil-bhàicidh.   The
old form, retained in English, goes to prove that
the original Gaelic was Cuil-bhòcaidh, the modern
Gaelic showing the common change of ' o ' to ' a.'
This is confirmed by comparison with the less
know Cuil-bhòcaidh in Strathcarron, parish of
Kincardine.   The second part of the compound
appears to be from ' bòcan,' hobgoblin, Scottish
bogie, the meaning being ' the haunted nook.'
The name would, on this supposition, have been
originally applied to the hollow near the ancient
ruin, near the village, which is noted below, and
which could hardly fail to have had uncanny
associations.

Balgalkin — G. Bail' galcainn, from 'galc,' to thicken cloth, by a process akin to fulling— 'Fuller-town.'

Leanaig — G. Lìanaig, diminutive of 'lìana,' a meadow, swampy plain. This is a case of a feminine diminutive being formed from a masculine noun.

Cornton—G. Bail' an loch, Loch-town. West of it is

Cononbrae—G. Bog domhain, deep bog.

Ryefield—G. Ach an t-seagail.

Drummonreach—Speckled ridge.

Teandore—House of the grove; it was once a drinking place, but the name has no sinister implication.

Balnabeen—G. Bail' na binn; locally explained as Town of judgment, which is doubtless correct, seeing that near it is

Gallows Hill—G. Cnoc a' chrochaidh. Also

Crochair—G. Crochar, place of hanging; from 'croch,' gallows, modern 'croich.'

Teanagairn, House of the cairn, and Glascairn, G. Clais 'chàirn, are so called from the remarkable ruin in the wood about a quarter of a mile south of the west end of Culbokie. In Gaelic it is called Caisteal Cuil-bhàicidh, and also Caisteal Bhàicidh. It is circular, with two concentric walls, the inner of stone, and is surrounded by a ditch, now partly filled up. Some bones were found there about forty years ago, in the course of removing stones for dykes, since when it has remained untouched. Close by it is a small loch.

Duncanston—A quite modern name—its eponymus is still with us—the Gaelic of which is Bog a' mhiodair. Local tradition says that the place was so named from the loss of a mitre there by the Bishop of Ross as he was going from his residence of Castle Craig to Chanonry. But it is much more likely to come from 'miodar,' pasture ground, or, possibly, 'miodar,' a round vessel of wood.

Greenleonachs—G. Lìanagan a' Chuil-bhàicidh, wet meadows of Culbokie.

Baluachrach—G. Bail' uachdarach, Upper town.

Balmenach—G. Bail' meadhonach, Mid-town.

Baliachrach—G. Bail' iochdarach, Lower town.

Balachladaich—Shore town.

Badenerb—Roe-clump.

Tore—G. Tòrr, rounded hill.

Crask of Findon—Crasg, a crossing place. It includes Boggiewell, G. Bog an fhuail, palus urinae.

Balreillan—'Rèidhlean,' a green, or level plain; a derivative of 'rèidh,' level. Some graves were found in the neighbourhood.

Loch Sheriff—G. Loch an t-Siorra.

Bracklach—G. Breaclach, spotted place; cf. 'garbhlach,' rough place.

Knockandultaig — G. Cnoc an dialtaig, bat's hillock.

Balloan—G. Bail' an lòin; town of the low, damp meadow.

Coulnagour—Goats' nook.

Balavil—G. Bail' a' bhile, town on the brae-edge.

Cocked-Hat Wood—A small plantation, so named by the late Sir James Mackenzie.

Mossend—G. Ceann a' mhonaidh.

Sunny Brae—A euphemistic rendering of G. 'am braighead mosach,' nasty upland.

Cnoc na fanaig—G. Cnoc na' feannag; probably from 'feannag,' a 'lazy-bed,' but of course 'feannag,' a hoodie-crow, is quite possible.

Cnoc an araid, a mile or more west of Culbokie, most likely from 'anait,' linen, which in E. Ross becomes 'arad.'

Logieside, at the west end of the parish, preserves the old name of Logy.

Dùgaraidh, on Ord. Sur. map Dungary, near the border of Urray—Dubh-garaidh, black den or thicket; the lengthening of 'dubh' is owing to the stress of the accent; cf. Dùloch and dùlan, also, Dougrie in Arran.

Balvaird—Bail' a bhàird, Bard's town. Or it may be from 'bàrd,' a meadow, paddock; in Badenoch still used in the sense of 'meadow' in common speech.

Tigh na h-innse — Meadow-house—near Alcaig Ferry.

Cnoc 'chòis—Hill of the recess.

RESOLIS.

Resolis—G. Ruigh-sholuis, slope of light, or bright
slope. In 1662 the Commissioners for the
plantation of Kirks united the parishes of
Cullicudden and Kirkmichaell into one parish
church, to be called the Parish Church of Kirkmichael, and to be built at Reisolace. As the
site of the parish church has not been shifted
since, it is clear that the name Resolis originally
applied only to that slope on which the church
now stands, a spot with a bright south-easterly
exposure. The New Stat. Acc., written by Rev.
Donald Sage in 1836, records that Resolis rather
than Kirkmichael was then the name in popular
usage. It has now practically become the official
designation also.

Cullicudden included the western portion of
the united parish. In addition to the early
mention of it noted below, it appears as Cultudyn
in 1275 among the churches taxed by the Holy
See for relief of the Holy Land. The church was
dedicated to St Martin of Tours, and the name
of the parish in Gaelic was regularly Sgire
Mhartuinn. Hence such names as Kilmartin
(where the old church of Cullicudden stood, with
its burying-ground), Achmartin, St Martins. In

1641 Charles I. granted to Inverness the fair of
10th November, "quhilk was haldin of auld at
Sanct Martenis Kirk in Ardmannoche now lyand
waist."

Kirkmichael is the eastern portion of the united
parish. The church was known in Gaelic as Cill
Mhìcheil, and the parish itself as Sgire Mhìcheil.
The site of the church was at the east end of the
parish, close to the firth ; and Hugh Miller, in his
" Scenes and Legends," gives a wild legend
bearing on its churchyard. The same legend is
current with regard to the churchyards of Dala-
rossie and of Petty, in Inverness-shire.

Culbo — Eistir Culbo 1557, Eistir and Wastir
Culboll 1560 ; G. Cùrabol ; from Norse ' kúla,'
a ball or knob, and ' bol,' a farm-stead. Kula is
applied in place-names to a rounded hill ; cf.
de Kool o' Fladabister in Shetland (Jacobsen).
Gaelic ' r ' is due to dissimilation.

Balblair—Belblair 1551, Eistir Belblair 1557 ; G.
Bail' a bhlàir, town of the plain.

Kinbeachy—Kynbarch 1561-66, Kinbeachie 1565-
71 ; G. Cinn a' bheathchaidh, head of the birch
wood (beitheach). Cf. Kinveachy, Aviemore. It
is to be taken in connection with

Birkis 1551 ; G. a Bheithearnaich, still known as
' The Birks ' ; beith-ar-n-aich ; for the formation
cf. Muc-ar-n-aich, from ' muc,' pig ; preas-ar-n-ach,
from ' preas,' bush ; etc.

Drumcudden—Drumcudyn 1528 and 1546 ; Drumcudden 1458 ; G. Druimchudainn, also

Cullicudden—Culicuden 1227 ; G. Cùil a' chudainn, or, as a variant, according to the New. Stat. Acc., ' Coull a Chuddegin.' The N.S.A. makes it " the Cuddie Creek—that species of fish being formerly, though not now, caught in great abundance in a small creek on the shore of Cullicudden, and a little to the west of the old church." G. ' cudainn,' or ' cudaig,' a cuddy.

Braelangwell—Braelangwell 1577 ; a hybrid ; G. ' bràigh,' an up-land, and Norse ' langvöllr,' long-field. There is Langwell in Strathcarron ; also Langwell, Oykell.

Balliskilly—Bowskaly 1551, Ballaiskaillie 1580 ; G. Baile sgèulaidh, story-town, or town of the story-teller.

Brae—Brey 1533 ; town of Braire c. 1560 ; ' bràigh,' up-land.

Woodhead—The Wodheid c. 1560 ; near it is *am Bàrd Gobhlach*, the forked meadow.

Castle Craig—Craighouse c. 1560 ; G. Tigh na creige.

Tighninnich—Tawninich (Blaeu), east of Balblair ; G. Tigh 'n àonaich, town of the market ; there was a market at Jemimaville until recent times.

Badgrinan—Copse of the sunny hillock.

Chapelton—G. Bail' an t-seipeil.

Kirkton :

Drumdyre—G. Druim(a)doighr ; doubtful ; Daighre was an Irish personal name ; Maclruanaidh ua Daighre occurs in the Four Masters ; but it does not seem to occur in Scotland.

Bruichglass—Green brae.

Poyntzfield of old Ardoch, the high place.

Ballicherry—G. Bail' a' cheathraimh, town of the quarter (davach).

Cavin—Smooth pass.

Toberchurn—Well of the cairn.

Capernich—G. Ceaparnaich, or 'a' Cheaparnaich,' an extension of ' ceap,' a block, whence ' ceapach,' tillage plot ; cf. for formation 'a' Bheithearnaich ' above.

Fleucherries—G. Fliuchairidh, the wet place ; a locative of ' fliuch-ar-adh,' from ' fliuch,' wet. The ''s' is the English plural, as in Geanies, Pitnellies, &c.

Jamimaville : a modern name.

Am Bàrd Loisgte—The burnt meadow, near St Martins.

Burnside—G. Tigh an daimh, ox-house.

Camperdown—G. form not found ; named after the battle of 1797.

Obsolete are :—

Rostabrichty, situated, according to Blaeu's map, a little to the north-west of Braelangwell ; later Rosabrighty, 1740.

Auchnintyne 1580, a pendicle of ' Ballaskaillie.'

Wester Ballano 1580, mentioned in connection with the same.

Milltoun (Blaeu), on the ' burn of Milltoun,' apparently now Allt Dubhach (O.S.M.)

CROMARTY.

Cromarty—Crumbathyn 1263, Crumbauchtyn 1264, Crumbhartyn 1296, Crombathie 1349, Cromady and Crombathie 1349-1370, Cromardy 1398, Cromaty and Crumbaty 1479.[1] G. Cromba'. From an inspection of the old forms two things are clear —first, that the modern English form, Cromarty, is the descendant and representative of the ancient Crumbauchtyn (with accent on first syllable); and, secondly, that the second 'r' of Cromarty is not radical, but was developed at an early stage through sympathy with the 'r' of the first syllable; cf. Eng. bride-groom, from A.S. brid-guma, literally 'bride-man.' Further, these forms, as well as other considerations, negative the derivation Crom-bàgh, bent bay. The base is doubtless crom, bent; the question is whether we are to regard the *b* of Cromba' as radical or as developed. Developed *b* after *m* is seen in lombar, from lom; Ir. crompán, a sea inlet, from crom; and in the common Crombie applied to bent streams and to places at a bend, *e.g.*, Crombie in Fife; also Dal-crombie, G. Dul-chrombaidh, a place on a bend of

---

[1] Hugh Miller (Scenes and Legends," p. 49), mentions an ancient custom seal or cocket, supposed to belong to the reign of Robert II., and then in the Inverness Museum, bearing the legend 'Crombhte.'

L. Ruthven, Inverness. On this theory we have
(1) crom as base, (2) developed *b*, (3) terminations -ach, place of, and -dan or -tan, diminutive,
all meaning Little place of the bend ; cf. Loch
Saileach in Ireland, called by the Four Masters
Loch Sailcheadáin,[1] also Ardochdainn, Lochcarron.
On the other theory it would be possible to
suggest crom-bath, with extension, *bath* being.
an O. Ir. word glossed sàile and muir, sea.

Cromarty Firth—G. Caolas Chromba'.

Navity—Navitie 1578 ; G. Neamhaididh. The
lands of Navity formed the endowment of a
chapel in the Cathedral of Fortrose. Hence from
'neimhidh,' church-land ; Gaul. 'nemeton.' There
is another Nevity in Fife ; Nevody 1477, Navety
1531, which was also church-land.

Davidston—Dauidstoun 1529 and 1578 ; G. Baile
Dhà'idh.

Williamstoun appears on Pont's map east and north
of Davidston.

Peddieston—Peddistoun 1578 ; the proper name
Peddie occurs frequently in the session records.

Farness—Farnes 1576, Eistir Farnes and Litill
Farness 1578 ; G. Fearnais, place of alders ; from
'fearn,' with termination '-ais,' for which see Kinnettes in Fodderty. For the meaning cf. Allerton.
Cf. Glenferness, near Forres.

Udale—Vddall 1578 ; G. Uadal, from Norse ' y-dalr,
yew-dale.

---

[1] Joyce, *Irish Names of Places* II., 36.

The Souters—" Craiges callit the Sowteris" appears in an Act of Par., 1593; G. na Sùdraichean. Various theories have been offered in explanation of the name, the favourite being 'sutor,' a shoemaker. The Gaelic form favours a derivation from sùdaire, a tanner, which gives rise to many names in Ireland. Na Sùdraichean would thus mean the place of tanners, or the tanneries. "The Souter" is a hill in Strathglass, G. an t-ùtar, Mullach an ùtair, and there is Souter Head between Aberdeen and Cove.

Banans—The Gaelic is not forthcoming, but it is probably an English plural of 'beannan,' a hillock.

Ardevall—Height of the township.

" **Castlehill of Cromarty**, called the Mothill of the same," 1599.

Glen-Urquhart is supposed to have been so named by or from the Urquharts of Cromarty; but cf. the parish of Urquhart.

Rosefarm, originally Greenhill; so called after Mr Rose of Tarlogie.

Easter Ardmeanach, on the summit of the ridge, retains the old official name of the Black Isle— Mid-height.

English names for which no Gaelic has been found are :—Newton, Neilston, Allerton, Woodside, Muirtown, Whitebog, Lambton, Blackstand, Colony, Gallow hill.

Obsolete is

Arnoche 1644, ' place of sloes.'

Chaplainry of St Regule 1561 is located by Hugh Miller, as also the Chapel of St Bennet and St Duthus Well. He also mentions a curious spring called Sludach.

ROSEMARKIE.

Rosemarkie — Rosmarkensis Episcopus c. 1228; Rosmarky 1510. G. Ros-maircnidh or Ros-marcanaidh; also Ros-mharcanaidh; in Book of Clanranald Ros-mhaircni. Invermarky 1476 Reg. Mag. Sig. proves that we are dealing with a stream name; cf. Marknie Burn flowing into L. Killin, Whitebridge. Marcnaidh, or by regressive assimilation Maircnidh, is based on marc, horse, and might well be the old genitive of marcnach, place of horses; for formation cf. Muc-an-ach, place of swine; Clach-an-ach, place of stones. Here, however, it is better regarded as showing the -ie ending so common in stream names, *e.g.*, Feshie, Mashie, Tromie, representing an old -ios. Ros may mean (1) cape, point; (2) wood, but as Rosemarkie is situated at the base of Fortrose point, the whole name means Point of the horse-burn rather than wood of the same.[1]

Fortrose—Forterose 1455. G. a' Chananaich, the Chanonry, lit. Place of Canons, which has eclipsed the true Gaelic form of Fortrose just as that of Tain is eclipsed by Baile Dhubhthaich. The

---

[1] Dr Reeves (Culdees p. 45) quotes the Martyrology of Tamlacht— " 16 March : Curitan epscoip ocus abb Ruis mic bairend," and amends to Rosmbaircend, yielding " Curitan bishop and abbot of Rosmarky." The Martyrology of Donegal has Curitan of Ros-meinn.

strong accent on the first syllable of Fortrose
shows Fort to be prepositional or adjectival ; probably it is foter, a comparative of fo, under. The
second part may be ros, promontory ; and the
name may have been given to a part of the promontory in contradistinction to Rosemarky.

Balmungie—" The lands of Balmongie with the
mill of Rosmarky " 1567. G. Baile-Mhungaidh,
possibly Mungo's stead, but more probably from
mong, mongach, a plant name ; mongach measca
glosses " simprionica," and is rendered mugwort
by O'Reilly ; mong mhear is explained as
hemlock.[1]

Platcock—" Platcok within the bounds of the
college of the Chanonry " 1615 ; an obscure name
of which the Gaelic form cannot be recovered.
Plotcok appears in Kyle, and near Beauly is
Platchaig, G. Plat-chathaig, Jackdaw Flat. On
the West Coast Plàtach is fairly common.

Eathie—Ethie 1593 ; G. àthaidh ; a stream name,
applying here primarily to the Eathie Burn ; cf.
Inveraithie, Tain ; àthaidh represents a primitive
Celtic ātia or ātios, in root identical with àth, a
ford. The name, like other stream names in -ie,
is doubtless Pictish.

Learnie—Larny 1576 ; G. Leatharnaidh, locative
of leatharnach, from lethoir, side, meaning ' place
on the side of the slope.' Lernock, Stirling, may
be regarded as an accusative, Leatharnach, cf.
Dornie as against Dornoch and Dornock. Near

---

[1] Arch f. Celt. Lex. I. 3, pp. 336, 344.

Inverness is a farm Castle Heather, formerly
Castle Leather. *i.e.*, lethoir, Lordship of Leffare,
1460.

Kincurdy—Kincowrdrie 1591 ; chapel of Kincurdie
1615 and 1641 ; G. Cinn-chùrdaidh. With it
goes Cnoc-gille-chùrdaidh, Avoch, Englished
Hurdyhill, and probably Kincurdy on Speyside,
G. Cinn-chaordaidh, where the difference in vowel
sound may be dialectic. This very difficult word
might be compared with Cùrr in Duthil, G. cùrr,
corner or pit, Welsh cwr, corner, but for the fact
that the formation Cnoc-gille-chùrdaidh strongly
suggests some proper name.

Raddery—Ratherie and Wester Ratherie 1576 ;
G. Radharaidh from radhar ' an arable field not in
tillage ' (H.S.D.), pasture ground, with -ach
suffix, giving radharach, place of pasture, old
locative radharaigh. In Perthshire we have " na
radharaichean,' the places of pasture. ' Daimh
mhòr Radharaidh,' the big oxen of Raddery, is
part of a local saw, which may, however, be really
aimed at the people of Raddery.

Broomhill—' The Inche and Bromehill,' 1576.

Ardmeanach—Mid-height, *i.e.*, between the Cromarty and Moray Firths ; interesting as retaining
the old official designation of the Black Isle.

Boggiewell—G. Bog an fhuarain; there is a fine
spring just below the farmhouse.

Corslet—Probably Crois-leathad, cross-slope ; it is
by the road just above Rosemarkie, and may
commemorate the site of one of the sculptured
crosses.

Flowerburn—No Gaelic has been found for this modern name, but *Kinnock* of Blaeu and records appears to be now Flowerburn Mains.

No Gaelic has been found for Hillock, Feddenhill, The Gamrock, Berryhill, Ryeflat, Muiryden, Weston, Claypots ; while Pettyslanis or Petslaw of the records is obsolete ; its latest form is Piddslaw, and it seems to have been near Petconnoquhy, now Rosehaugh.

AVOCH.

Avoch—Baronia de Auach 1328 ; Auauch 1338
(Reg. Mor.) ; Alvach 1493 ; Awoch 1558 ; G.
Obh'ch (for Abhach with change of *a* to *o*), from
O. Ir. ab, later abh, a river, with -ach suffix :
River-place. Cf. Loch Awe, Gael. Loch Obha,
described by Adamnan as "stagnum fluminis
Abae," the loch of the river Aba.   The stream on
which Avoch stands is called in its upper reaches
the Gooseburn, G. Allt nan geadh, and appears in
1676 as "the Goossburn" in connection with
"the Goosswell of Killeane."

Rosehaugh—A name imposed by Sir George Mackenzie towards the end of the 17th century.   The
old name was Petconachy 1456, Petquhonochty
1458 ; Pettenochy 1526 ; Petconnoquhy 1527
(with a mill), *i.e.*, Pit Dhonnachaidh, Duncan's
stead.   The spot where the gardens of Rosehaugh
house now stand is still known as *Pàirc an
Leothaid*, Hill-side Park.

Castleton—Castletoun 1456 ; G. Bail' a' Chaisteil,
from Ormond Castle hard by.   The ruins of this
once great and important seat may still be seen
on Ormond Hill, also known as Ladyhill, from the
fact that there was a chapel on or near it dedicated to the Virgin Mary (Reg. Sec. Sig. 1528).

The Castle of Ormond appears to have belonged to the De Moravia or Moray family from thirteenth century times, but there is little mention of it in records subsequent to the middle of the fourteenth. Frequent mention, however, is found of the Moot-hill (mons) of Ormond, in connection with the titles of Earl, Marquis, and Duke of Ormond.

Muiralehouse—Muirailhouse 1611 explains itself.

Halloch—G. ? (S)halach ; doubtful.

Lochala—G. Loch-àla, an obscure name, but cf. Welsh ' alaw,' water-lily.

Bennetsfield — Bennatfeld 1456 ; Bennatisfelde 1458 ; Bannathfield 1527 ; Bannagefield 1541 ; Bennetisfield 1548 ; G. Baile Bhenneit, Town of Bennet, *i.e.*, St Benedict. Near it is *Clach Bhenneit*, Bennet's stone, immediately below which is the holy well called *Tobar Chragag*, well of the little rock, still frequented on the first Sabbath of May.

Ballone—G. Bail an lòin, town of the wet meadow.

Corrachie—G. Corrachaidh, from corrach, steep.

Arcandeith — Arkyndwycht 1586 ; Auchindeuch 1611 ; Arcanduth 1641 ; G. Arcan-duibh, Black Arcan ; cf. Arcan, Urray. Here ' duibh ' is obviously a translation of Arcan, the black place. On the place are the ruins of a small fortalice, whence the local explanation, àirc-Eoin-dhuibh, Black John's ark, or fortress. A Highland reaver, Black John has been evolved to lend colour to this piece of popular etymology, but the phonetics do not suit.

Newton—? Newton 1456 ; G. am baile nodha.

Insch—The Inch 1576 ; G. an ì's, the meadow (innis).

Rhives—G. given as (1) na Ruighean, the slopes ; (2) (ann an) Ruigheas. The latter may be a Gaelic pronunciation of the English form. Rhives in Kilmuir is ' na Ruigheannan ;' Rhives, Golspie, na Ruigheach.

Coulnagour—G. Cùil nan gobhar, goats' nook.

Killen—Kyllayn circ. 1338, Killan 1456 ; Killane 1524 ; G. Cill-Annaidh or Cill-Fhannaidh. The Gaélic form puts Cill-fhinn, White-church, or Church of St Fionn out of the question, and there seems to be no saint whose name will suit the dedication. St Anne, which would suit the phonetics, is hardly to be thought of on Celtic ground.

Near Killen is *Cnoc-an-teampuill*, Temple-hill.

Auchterflow — Ochtercloy 1456, Achtirflo 1560, Ochtercloy 1568 ; G. Uachdar-chlò. Clò is glossed by O'Mulconry ' gaoth,' wind. In the Psalms we have ' clò codail,' ' vapour ' of sleep. The word appears to be obsolete in spoken Gaelic, but ' windy upland' gives good sense.

> Buntàta proinnt' is bainne leo
> Biadh bodaich Uachdar-chlò !

Pookandraw—G. bog an t-strath, Strath-bog, in the Strath of Auchterflow.

Blairfoid (really pron. Blairwhyte) — Blairfoyde 1627; G. Blàr-choighde, Moor of Coit, with

which may be compared Erchite, Dores, G.
Airchoighd.' This spelling represents the Gaelic
pronunciation of this doubtless Pictish name,
which may, perhaps, be compared with Teutonic
hag, hedge.

Shawpark—G. Pàirc an t-sèadh ; doubtful.

Ordhill—G. Cnoc an ùird.

Templand—Tempilland 1586 ; no Gaelic found.

Geddeston—G. Baile na' geadas ; ? Town of the
tufty heads.

Pitfuir—Pethfouyr circ. 1338, Petfure 1456; Pet-
fuyr, with its mill called Denemylne, 1526 ; G.
Pit-fhùir, Pasture-stead, a Pictish name ; cf.
Dochfour, Balfour, Pitfure (Rogart), Inchfuir,
and Porin. The mill is now called the Mill of
Den.

Lochlaichley—G. Loch Ligh, spate-loch ; cf. Loch
Ligh in Contin. Achalee appears in 1458.

Bog of Shannon—Boigschangie 1586 ; G. Bog na'
seannan, ? seann àthan, bog of the old fords.

No Gaelic has been found for the following :—
Crosshill, Tourie-lum, Gracefield, Knockmuir,
Coldhome, Limekilns.

KNOCKBAIN.

Knockbain—G. An Cnoc-bàn, white-hill, is now
the name of the joint parishes of Kilmuir Wester
and Suddy (united 1756).

Kilmuir—Kilmowir 1561 ; G. Cill Mhoire, Mary's
Church. The old church stands near the sea-
shore. The graveyard contains many stones of
considerable antiquity, with late Celtic carving
similar to that seen on the stones in Killianan at
Abriachan and at Glenconvinth Chapel.

Suddy—Sudy 1227; Suthy 1476. G. Suidhe
(bheag is Suidhe mhòr), Seat ; the absence of the
article in Gaelic is noteworthy.

Kessock Ferry—Land and ferry of Estir Kessok
1437. G. Aiseig Cheiseig, generally connected
with St Kessock ; the Gaelic use, however, shows
no sign of Kessock being regarded here as a personal name.

Bellfield includes what is known in Gaelic as
Ceiseig uachdarach, Upper Kessock ; also partly
covers the old Do'ach Cheiseig, Davach of
Kessock. Near the firth is *Tigh a' mhuilinn*,
Mill-house.

Redfield—G. an raon dearg. *Broomhill*, G. an
cnoc bealaidh, is now part of it.

Arpafeelie—G. Arpa-phìlidh, also Arpa-phìlich, an
obscure name. The first part may be ' alp,' an

eminence. In it is included *Glaickmore*, G. a'
ghlaic mhòr, the big hollow.

Cotterton—G. Achadh nan coitear.

Allanbank—G. an Réim, ' the course '; O. Ir. réim
Near it is *Quarryfield*, G. Tigh an rothaid,
Road-house.

Teablair—G. Tigh a' bhlàir, House of the moor.
Near it is *Teawig*, G. Tigh a' bhuic, Buck-
house.

Teandore—G. Tigh an todhair, Bleaching-house.
There is another near Drynie.

Allangrange—Allangrange 1574. G. Alan (no
article); a Pictish name for which v. Alness.
Part of it is Bog Alain, the Bog of Allan.

Allanglack—G. Alan nan clach, Stony Allan.

Allanrich—G. Alan an fhraoich, Heathery Allan.

Whitegate—G. An geat bàn—modern name.

Belmaduthy — Balmaduthy 1456, Bowmalduthy
1538 ; G. Baile mac Duibh, Stead of Duff's sons ;
cf. Pitmaduthy. This disposes of the idea that
the old Church of Suddy was dedicated to
St Duthac of Tain, if, as the Editor of the Orig.
Paroch. states, " the sole ground for conjecturing
this is the local name Belmaduthy, interchanged
in old writs of Tain with Balleguith[1] or Baile-
dhuich."

Balnakyle—G. Baile na coille, Wood-town.

Balnaguie—G. Baile na gaoith, Windy town ; cf.
Ardgay, without the article—an older formation.

---

[1] Balleguith stands rather for Balkeith, q.v.

Muirends or **Muirtown**—? Merane 1456 ; Muren
1458 ; Meran 1478 ; G. Mòrdun, Great Fort ; the
strong accent on mòr has shortened dùn to dun ;
cf. Findon, G. Fionndun.   There is a stone circle
in a wood in this place.

Roskhill—G. An Roisgeil.

Belton—G. not known.

Shantullich—G. An t-seann tulaich, Old-hillock.

Braevil—G. Brèigh a' bhaile, Upland of the stead.

Drumderfit — Drumdafurde 1456 ; Drumdervate
1539 ; Drumdarwecht 1564 ; G. Druim(a)diar.
Locally explained as " ridge of tears." Its former
name was Druim dubh, but it became the scene of
a battle so sanguinary that of the beaten party
only one survived.   Hence it was said " Bu druim
dubh an dé thu, ach 's druima diar an diugh,"
Black ridge wert thou yesterday, but ridge of
tears to-day.[1] The legend as to the change of
name is significant in view of the double form in
Gaelic and English.   The probability is that we
are dealing with a word of Pictish origin, of which
the Gaelic speakers took the part that seemed to
them intelligible, dropping the rest which appears
in English as -fit, and in the records as -vate, etc.

Drynie—Dryne 1586 ; G. Droighnidh (no article),
place of thorns.   Above it is *Creagaidh thom*,
little rock of hillocks or humps.   Drynie includes

---

[1] With this may be compared the legend given in the Book of Deer as to
the origin of the name Deer : "tángator déara drostán arscartháin fri collum-
cille ; rolaboir columcille, bedéar áním óhúnn ímaic " ; Drostan's tears came
on parting with Columcille ; Columcille said : " Be Dear its name from
hence forth."

Ceann an achaidh, head of the cultivated field ;
Bail' a' bhlàir, Muirtown ; *Srath fhliuchaidh,*
strath of wetness ; *Tigh an t-sluic,* house of the
pit ; *An Lainnsear,* Englished Lancer, a doubtful
word perhaps, based on lainn, an enclosure.

Yairhead—G. a' cheir-éud, on Munlochy bay ; the
G. form, if it is not the English form taken over,
is beyond me.

Slagaharn—G. Slac a' chàrn, Hollow or Slack of the
cairn. Near it is *Muileann an t-sàil,* Salt-water
mill, once a tidal mill.

Drumsmittal—G. Druima-smiotail, probably by
dissimilation for Druim-spiteil, ridge of the Spital,
or hostelry. The Spittal wood is well to the west.
On the ridge are :—*An Carn Glas,* the grey
cairn ; also *Am Blàr Liath,* the hoary moor, with
many tumuli.

Isteane—G. I's-dian ; ' i's ' is the reduced form of
innis, haugh ; ' dian ' from the lie of the land
cannot mean ' steep '; it must, therefore, mean
' sheltered.'

Coldwells—G. am Bealaidh, the broom.

Charleston—G. baile Thearlaich, after Sir Charles
Mackenzie of Kilcoy. The first house here was
built 1812.

Craigbreck—G. a' chreag bhreac, the dappled rock.

Glaickarduich—G. a' ghlaic, the hollow ; also Glaic
ar dubhaig, hollow of the little black stream or
place, *ar* being a corruption of *an,* the article.
Cf. Glaic an dubhaig in Urray.

Croftnacreich—G. Creit nan Crioch, boundary croft.

Pitlundie—Petlundy 1456; G. Pit-lunndaidh, the
stead of Lundy. Lundy, G. Lunndaidh, adjoins,
and is very marshy. Also Loch Lundy, an ugly,
dark loch, reputed of great depth, and the haunt
of a 'tairbh uisge,' water bull, whose herd may be
heard in winter bellowing beneath the ice. For
meaning v. Maoil Lunndaidh, Contin.

Sligo—Slego 1579. G. Sligeach, (the) shelly place.
It is on the south shore of Munlochy Bay.

Bayfield, formerly Creit Seocaidh, Jockey's croft.

Craigiehow—G. creag a' chobh, rock of the cave.
Cobh is doubtless to be compared with the Ir.
diminutive cabhán, a hollow, Welsh cau, Lat. cavea.
In this cave lie the Feinn, awaiting the blowing of
the horn which is to rouse them from their sleep.
It is, or was, believed to extend to Loch Lundy.
A dropping well at the mouth of the cave was
resorted to until quite recently to cure deafness.
"Ged is mòr Creag a' Chobh, is beag a feum";
though big is Craigiehow, small is its use.

Arrie—G. an àirigh, the shieling, on the top of
Craigiehow.

Tigh na h-irich, locally connected with 'fireach,'
a hill, or steep declivity, which suits the place;
but this would require tigh an fhirich.

Teandore—G. Tigh an todhair, Bleaching-house.
Near it is *an Raoid'as*, an obscure name. Also
Creit a' chlobha, Tongs-croft; but perhaps clobha
(N. klofi) is here used in its primary meaning of
'fork.'

Paulfield—G. am Bard, the meadow.

Tullich—G. An Tulaich, the hillock.

Munlochy—Munlochy 1328, Mullochie 1605 ; G. Poll-lochaidh. Both the English and the Gaelic forms are corruptions of Bun-lochaidh, root or inner end of the loch, *i.e.*, Munlochy Bay, which in Gaelic is Ob Poll-lochaidh.

Hurdyhill—G. Cnoc-gille-chùrdaidh, cf. Kincurdy. This hillock is famous for fairies, and possesses a holy well once in great vogue and still visited.

James Temple—G. Cnoc-Seumas-Chaisteil, as if ' Hill of James of the Castle.' There is on it what may be the remains of a prehistoric fort.

Ord Hill—G. Cnoc an Uird, with remains of a large fort, with extensive vitrifaction.

Blar na Còi—G. Blàr na Cùinge, Field of the yoke, with tradition of a battle in which, as at Luncarty, the event was decided by a plough-yoke.

KILLEARNAN.

Killearnan—Kilernane 1561 ; G. Cill-iùrnain ; there
is also Càrn-iùrnain in this parish. In Kildonan,
Sutherland, is another Killearnan, the Gaelic form
of which is exactly the same. Iurnan is, of course,
the name of the saint who founded the ' cill,' or to
whom it was dedicated. Ernan, St Columba's
nephew, does not suit the Gaelic phonetics, but
we find exactly what we want in Iturnan, of whom
the Chronicle of the Scots records, under date
665, ' Iturnan et Corinda apud Pictones defuncti
sunt.' A fragment of Tighernac's Annals reads—
' 668 Itharnan et Corindu apud Pictores defuincti
sunt.' The name of Iturnan, who died among the
Picts circ. 665, will, with the regular aspiration of
intervocalic *t*, become I(th)urnan.

Càrn-iùrnain, Iurnan's cairn, suggests the possibility of the saint having been buried there. Local
tradition, as recorded in the new Stat. Acc., connects the name with Irenan, a supposed ' Danish
prince.'

Redcastle—G. an Caisteal ruadh. It is now agreed
that the modern Redcastle represents the ancient
castle of Edirdovar, founded by William the Lion
in 1179.[1] Edirdovar is from eadar, between,
and O.G. dobur, water, between the waters, from

---

[1] Or. Par. Scot. II. 2, Killearnan.

its position between the Beauly and Cromarty Firths.

Kilcoy—Culcolly 1294 and 1456, Culcowy 1479 and 1511 ; G. Cul-challaidh. Cul is perhaps cùil, nook, rather than cùl, back ; callaidh is to be compared with Bealach Collaidh, between Wyvis and Inchbae, both being based on coll, Welsh and O.I. for hazel, with -ach suffix, representing a primitive *Coslacon*. Kilcoy thus means nook (possibly back) of the hazel wood. 'The wood (bosco) of Culcolly' appears in record in 1294.

Drynie Park—Drynys 1579 ; G. Pairce Dhroighnidh, park of the thorn-place.

Muckernich—G. a' Mhucarnaich, the swine-place, common.

Tore—G. an Todhar, the bleaching spot ; cf. Balintore; at Tore is Cnoc-an-acrais, Hunger-hill, where a market used to be held called Féill Cnoc-an-acrais.

Croftcrunie—G. Creit a' Chrùnaidh ; can hardly mean Crowner's croft, though such appears on record somewhere between this and Avoch ; perhaps a Pictish word based on root seen in W. crwn, round, Ir. crón, a circular hollow. What appears to be the article *a'* may be only the common 'sporadic vowel,' as in Cill(e) Mhoire.

Drumnamarg—Drumnamarg 1456, Drumnamergy 1458, Drumnamarge 1511 ; G. Druim-nam-marg, merk-ridge, or ridge of the merk-lands.

Teanahuig—G. Tigh na h-ùige, House of the nook, a term often applied on the West Coast to a small inn or shebeen.

Ryefield—G. Ach an t-seagail.

Colington—G. Baile Chailein, after Sir Colin Mac·kenzie.

Whitewells—G. am Fuaran bàn, includes the small farm of *Allt-an-dìgeadair*, Dyker's burn.

Spittal—G. Spiteil, from hospital, a place of entertainment.

Garguston—Gargastoun 1456 ; G. Baile-ghargaidh. The form Gargastoun points to a personal name, or rather nickname, garg, fierce ; garg, however, seems to occur in genuine place-names ; cf. Lùb a' ghargain in Contin.

Blairdow—G. am Blàr dubh, the black moor.

Milton—G. Bail a' mhuilinn.

Fettes—Called after Sir William Fettes ; includes *An Clàran*, the little flat ; *Am Baile Nodha*, Newtown ; *A' Cheapaich*, the tillage plot ; *Burntown, Bunchairn, Barntown*, and *Drumore*, most of them holdings of fair size. Near it is *na Peit'chan*, an interesting formation from the Pictish pett, a stead, formed on the same principle as na Bothachan, Boath. The formation shows how thoroughly the Pictish *pett* became a Gaelic word.

Chapelton—G. Bail' an t-seipeil, now part of Fettes.

Parktown—G. Baile na pàirce.

Coulmore—Culmor 1394 ; G. A' Chùil-mhòr, the big nook, which describes it.

Balguneirie—G. Baile gun iarraidh, town without asking ; perhaps to be compared with the English Unthank, the name of three places in Cumberland and two in Northumberland, which, Canon Taylor says, denotes a piece of ground on which some squatter had settled ' without leave' of the lord.

Balgunloune—G. Baile gun lionn, town without beer ; perhaps modelled humorously on the preceding. There are local tales, too pointless to relate, as to the origin of both names.

Ploverfield—G. Blàr nam feadag.

Lettoch—Westir and Estir Haldach 1527, half the lands of Dawaucht 1530, lands of Haldacht with the kiln of the same called Toldegormok 1580, Wester Half Daokis 1586 ; Haddoch and Torgarnoche 1611, Leadanach and Torgormack 1639 ; G. An Leithda'ch, the half-davach. The record forms quoted show clearly the transition from the Gaelic Leith-dabhach to the hybrid Haddo. Part of Lettoch is *Bog na h-eileig* and *Loch na h-eileig;* eileag is doubtful, but may, perhaps, be a formation from ail, rock, used in the sense of eileach, a contrivance for catching fish ; cf. Allt Eileag. Seawards of this loch is Torgorm, green knoll, referred to in the record as Toldegormok, Torgarnoche, and Torgormack.

Corgrain—G. Coir' a' ghràin.

Wellhouse—G. Tigh an fhuarain.

Linnie—G. An linne, the pool ; also Linn' a' bhuic bhàin, pool of the white buck. *Linne Mac Vain* in old rental.

Gallowhill—G. Cnoc na croiche.

Cnoc-an-eireach—Hill of the assemblies or meetings (eireachd).

Artafaillie—Ardirfalie 1526, Arthirfairthlie 1584 ;
G. Airt-a-fàillidh.   From the old spellings and
the *t* of Airt in Gaelic it appears that a word
ending in *r* and beginning with *d*, or better *t*, has
been curtailed to *a* in the middle of the name,
thus giving Ard-tir-fàillidh or Ard-dor-fàillidh.
Fàillidh is probably genitive of fàlach, place of
sods, falaigh, with regressive assimilation.   The
whole word would thus mean ' High land of
the place of sods '; ' High water of,' &c., does
not suit the place.   With Fàillidh of Drochaid
Fàillidh, Faillie Bridge and farm of Faillie in
Daviot, and for meaning Fadoch in Kintail.

In 1456 appear on record the Smithy croft, the
Forestercroft, the Portarecroft, the Marecroft,
the Sergandcrofft, the Crownarecroft ; and in
1479 the Currourecroft—probably connected with
Redcastle.

CONTIN.

Contin—Conten 1227, Contan 1510 ; G. Cunndainn.
Contin is primarily the district at the confluence of the rivers Conon and Blackwater ;
from this the name has been extended to
cover the extensive Highland parish which
stretches from Contin proper to the neighbourhood of Kinlochewe. The Old Stat. Acc. suggests as a derivation ' con-tuinn,' from ' con,'
together, and ' tonn,' wave, meaning ' meeting
of the waves,' an explanation which satisfies the
phonetics ; cf. Contullich, from ' con ' and ' tulach.'
The question, however, is whether ' tonn ' would
be naturally applied to the water of a river, and
it will, I think, be agreed that such a usage would
be very difficult to parallel, ' tonn ' being, except
in the language of poetic metaphor, confined to
the waves of the sea. The first syllable is certainly ' con,' together, and the meaning is
doubtless something like ' confluence.' If we
turn to Gaul, we find that the stock name for a
confluence is Condate, represented in modern
French by Condé. This name appears often on
the map of ancient Gaul at the junction of streams,
and we find also Condatomagus, plain of the
confluence, as well as Condatisco. In ancient
Britain, Condate appears once, at the junction of

the ? Weaver (Cheshire) with a small stream.
The word is analysed into ' con,' and the root
' dhe,' set, a root familiar in Latin and Greek, the
etymological equivalent of Condate being in Greek
' syn-thesis,' and in late Latin ' con-ditio,' from
' condo,' a setting together.   It is tolerably certain
that in Contin we have the representative of some
such word as ' Condationn-,' an extension of Condate.   As a Scottish place-name, Contin, though
rare, is not unique.   Dr Macbain, in his Badenoch
Place-names, notes that Killiehuntly in Badenoch
is in Gaelic ' Coille Chunndainn,' the Wood of
Contin, and refers also to Contuinn in Ireland, on
the borders of Meath and Cavan.   There is also
Bohuntin in Glenroy, Gaelic Both-chunndainn.
Both these Scottish names apply to confluences.
Cf. also Confluentes, now Coblenz.

Achilty—Auchquhilye 1479, Hechely (Easter and
Wester) 1528, the two Achelies 1529, Auchelle
1539, Achillie 1681 ; G. Achillidh.   The ' t ' of
the English form is late and euphonic, and appears
also in Achiltybuy, in Coigach.   Achilty is a
Pictish name, of the same origin as Welsh ' uchel,'
high, seen in the Ochil Hills and in Oykel,
Ptolemy's High Bank.   The variation between
' o ' and ' a ' is common ; cf. Scone, old Gaelic
Scoan, genitive Scòine ; modern Gaelic Sgàin.

Coul—Cwyl 1476, alehouse of Coul 1576 ; Essy
Coull and the mill of the same 1586 ; Escoule
(Waterfall of Coull) 1669 ; G. a' Chùil, the corner,
recess.

Comrie—Cumre 1479, Cumerley 1528, Cumry 1529 ;
G. Comraidh, from 'comar,' confluence, meaning
Place of the confluence. The confluence is that
of the Conon from Lochluichart, and the Meig
from Strathconan. Cf. Comar in Strathglass,
Comrie in Perthshire, and elsewhere. It appears
also in Cumbernauld, *i.e.*, ' comar-nan-allt,' where
it has developed a 'b,' just like the English
'number' from Latin 'numerus.' There is a
Combaristum in Gaul, on a tributary of the
Liger.

Scatwell—Litill Scathole, Scathole Mekle 1479 ;
the two Scatellis 1529 ; G. Scatail beag and
Scatail mòr ; from Norse scat-völlr, *i.e.*, common
grazing land, the holders of which paid scat or
tax for the grazing privileges.

Strathconon — ? Strathconon 1309, Strquhonane
1479, Strachonane 1538 ; G. Srath-chonuinn.
The initial difficulty about Strathconon is that its
river, which by all analogy ought to be the
Conon, is the Meig. There is a local saying—

> Abhainn Mìg tre Srath-chonuinn,
> Abhainn Conuinn tre Srath-bhrainn,
> Abhainn Dubh-chuileagach tre Srath-ghairbh ;
> Tri abhnaichean gun tairbh iad sin.

> The River Meig through Strathconan,
> The River Conon through Strathbran,
> The River of black nooks[1] through Strathgarve ;
> Three rivers without profit these.

[1] Possibly ' River of black flies.'

The omission of the two last words of the fourth
line would be an improvement ; but I give it as I
got it, and it is a hard saying at best.   In the
first place, Strathbran has a river of its own, the
Bran, which, as is proper, gives its name to its
strath.   The head waters of the Bran come from
the watershed west of Loch Chroisg (Loch
Rosque), and the river is called Bran the moment
it leaves that loch.   Thence it flows through
Strathbran, widening out to form Loch Achanalt,
Loch a' Chuilinn, and finally Loch Luichart.
Issuing from Loch Luichart, it has a course of a
little over a mile before it joins the Meig above
Comrie, and it is in this last short stretch that it
is called the Conon.   Thenceforward the Conon
is the name of the joint stream.   The solution of
the difficulty that occurs to me is that the name
Conon applies properly only to the stream below
the junction with the Meig.   On this supposition
Strathconon would originally have been restricted
to the valley of the joint stream, but in time
extended to the valley of the Meig, of which it is
a continuation.   This would be natural enough,
and it would also be natural to extend the name
of Conon to the short stretch of river from Loch-
luichart, though, as this latter valley is a
continuation of Strathbran, the original name of
its stream most probably was the Bran, and the
name Strathbran would have covered the whole
valley down to the junction.   Such a change of
name would be helped by the size of Loch

Luichart, and the increased volume of water issuing from it.

A somewhat similar difficulty is presented by Stratherrick (Inverness) and the river Faragaig. The Faragaig ought to be in Stratherrick, G. Srath-fharagaig, but in point of fact it flows through a neighbouring glen.

As to derivation, it is natural to connect Strathconon with the personal name Conan. Conan was the name of a Fenian hero ; also of a Celtic missionary, whose name appears in Killachonan, Fortingall, Perth, and perhaps in the R. Conon, Uig, Skye, G. Abhainn Chonnain, where Connan is a diminutive of Conn, a proper name. There is, however, no authority for the connection of either hero or saint with Strathconon, nor will either Conan or Connan suit the phonetics of Srath-chonuinn. I should suggest that Conon represents a primitive Conona ; -ona is a good Gaulish river termination, and Endlicher's glossary (in a 9th century MS.) actually explains *onno* as *flumen*, river. For *con* we have three choices— con, together ; con from Gaulish kunos, high ; con, stem of cù, dog, giving respectively joint-stream, high-stream, dog-stream. If we could be certain that *onno* was a genuine Gaulish name, and not merely a termination raised to the standing of an independent word, it would be natural to render Conon as ' Joint-stream." This, however, is uncertain ; ' Dog-stream ' is unobjectionable ; ' High-stream ' does not suit the

physical requirements. The tidal part of the
Conon appears in the Dingwall charters as
Stavek, which may be N. staf-vík, staff-bay ; cf.
Stafá, Staff-river ; and Stafa-holt, Staffwood, in
Iceland ; Staffa, the isle, is N. Stàf-ey, Staff-isle,
from the columnar formation of its rocks.

Loch Beannacharan — Kenlochbenquharene 1479,
Kinlochbanquhare 1538, Kinlochbeancharan 1571 ;
G. Loch Beannacharan ; 'beann,' a top, horn, peak,
gives adjective 'beannach,' peaked, pinnacled ;
whence 'beannachar,' place of peaks, of which
'beannacharan' is a collective form. The classical
representative of 'beannach' is probably seen in
Lake Bēnacus, the 'horned lake,' in Cisalpine
Gaul, now Lago di Garda. Loch Beannach,
horned loch (from the shape), is a common Highland name. The best known Beannachar is
Bangor in Ireland, whence the Welsh Bangor.
Another well-known Irish form is Banagher. A
locative formation from 'beannachar' is seen in
Banchory Devenick and Banchory Ternan. Loch
Beannacharan, then (for which the Ord. Survey
Beannachan is a mistake) means 'the loch of the
place of the peaks,' a name appropriate and
descriptive. On the north side is *Allt an
Fhasaidh*, Burn of the dwelling, O.G. fasadh, at
a green place with signs of old habitation. On
the south side is *Allt na Faic'*, Burn of the lair or
hiding-place, half-way up the hillside from which
is *Bac an Airigh*, doubtful ; ? shieling. At the
west side is *Cnoc a' Mhinistir*, Parson's Hill, and

near it a small graveyard. A large rock on the
loch side is called *na Caidhean*, perhaps from
caid, a rock, summit (O'Reilly). At the outlet
of the loch is

Carnoch—G. a' Chàrnaich, from 'càrn,' a cairn,
place of cairns ; to be taken in connection with
Beannachar as far as meaning is concerned.

Invercoran—Innerquhonray 1479 and 1538, Inner-
chonray 1571, Inverchonran 1633 ; G. Inbhir
chòrainn (*o* nasal). The 'inver' is the confluence
of the stream flowing through Glencoran with
another small burn just before it reaches the
Meig. The old form shows 'n,' which has disappeared, but has left its influence on the nasal 'o.'
Còran is a stream name, and its old form, Quhon-
ray, or rather Conray, is paralleled by the stream
Conrie, flowing through Glenconrie in Strathdon,
Aberdeenshire, into the Don. Both are high-lying
streams, which suggests the first syllable to be
the Gaulish 'kunos,' high ; it can hardly be 'con,'
together. The second part may be the root seen
in 'drùdhadh,' oozing; cf. the stream Druie in
Strathspey ; Gaulish Druentia. This would give
'con-druent-,' which, with assimilation of 'd' to
'n,' would become 'connruent-,' resulting in 'còr-
rainn,' high oozing stream. Opposite Invercoran,
on the river, is *Creag Iucharaidh*, probably based
on iuchair, fish spawn, whence iucharach, place of
spawn.

Main and **Glenmeanie** — Meyn in Strquhonane
1479, Innermany 1479 and 1539, Meyn in

Strachonane 1538, Maneye 1543, Mainzie 1633 ;
Gaelic Gleann mèinnidh ; Leithdach Mèinn (half
davach of Main) ; from ' mèinn,' ore ; cf. Allt na
mèinn in Edderton, Lub na mèinn in Kincardine.
The term is applied usually where the water is
marked by the rust of oxidized iron.   Innermany
is the junction of the stream Mèinnidh flowing
through Glenmeanie with the Meig.   Opposite it,
and west of Baile na Creige, Rocktown, is *an
Annaid*, The Annat, or early church, a triangular
piece of ground.

Teanacallich—Old woman's house.

Craigdarroch—Oak rock ; there are still oaks.

Drumandarroch—Oak ridge.

Càrn na buaile—Cairn of the cattle fold.

Glascharn—Grey cairn ; commòn name.

Carn Sgolbaidh and **Loch Sgolbaidh**—Cairn and
loch of splinters ; showing old locative of sgolbach.

Curin—G. Caoruinn, place of rowans ; in Old Irish
we have Caerthend, dative Caerthiund, from
which latter comes our name Caoruinn.

Loch a' mhuilinn—Loch of the mill.

Allt na Fàinich—Burn of the flat place, from fàn ;
also *Poll na Fàinich*, in the river.   O.S.M. Allt
tuill an fhàire còise !

Càrn na cloiche mòr—Cairn of the big stone.

Loch na làrach blàire—Loch of the white-faced
mare.

Loch an uillt ghiuthais—Loch of the fir burn.

Balnault—G. Bail' 'n uillt, Burn-town.

Càrn na h-Annaid—Cairn of the Annat. Annat has been already explained. We have here also Allt na h-Annaid, Cladh na h-Annaid, Clach na h-Annaid, so that there is strong place-name evidence of an early Celtic religious settlement.

Glacour—G. a' Ghlaic odhar, dun hollow (among hills). There is another Glacour in Kilmuir·Easter.

Achlorachan—From the root seen in 'loirean,' a bedraggled or bemired person; 'loireachan' thus means a boggy or wet place, which applies exactly. Loireag means a water-sprite.

Drumanriach—Druimeinn riabhach, brindled Drummond, 'druimeinn' being the locative of 'drum,' ridge.

Cnaigean na leathrach—Leather knoll; a knoll east of the bridge over the Meig, not far from the U.F. Church of Strathconon. When the river is high, this knoll is surrounded by water, and it was used of old in connection with the process of tanning leather.

Dalnacroich—Hanging or gallows plain. There is also a llock called Cnoc na croiche, where malefactors are supposed to have been buried.

Cnoc na h-ùige—Hill of the recess, or retired place.

Cnoc na carrachan—Hill of wild liquorice.

Porin—G. Pòrainn. This is one of the best preserved examples in Scotland of the Pictish word so common in the aspirated form—'four,' *e.g.*, Pit-four, Doch-four. The root is that seen in the Welsh 'pori,' to graze, eat; and 'poriant,'

pasture. The Strathconon Porin is a flat piece of
land by the river side. *Cladh Phòrainn,* Porin
graveyard, was formerly *Cladh Mèinn,* Main
graveyard, and one good authority says that
he has heard it called Cladh Ceann-loch-
Beannacharan, but this is probably a confusion
with the graveyard at the west end of that loch,
noted above.

Milltown—G. Bail' a' mhuilinn ; close by is Allt a'
mhuilinn, Mill-burn.

Dalbreac—Speckled dale.

Crannich — G. a' Chrannaich, place of trees ;
common.

Blarnabee—G. Blàr na bìth ; 'bìth' means resin,
pitch ; the name having doubtless arisen from the
presence of fat fir-wood in olden times, either as
growing trees, or more probably as 'stocks' in the
moss.

Allt a' choir' àluinn—Burn of the beautiful corry.

Carn Uilleim—William's cairn ; Loch Gruamach,
gloomy loch ; Creag ghaineamhach, sandy rock ;
Loch an spardain, from 'spàrdan,' a roost, but
also, metaphorically, a level shelf or resting-place
in a hill-side ; cf. *suidhe* in this sense ; Meall
Giuthais, Fir-hill ; Corry sleuch and Allt coire na
sleaghaich, cf. Slioch, Gairloch.

Scardroy—G. Sgard-ruaidh. 'Sgard,' a scree, is
in common use, as is also its diminutive
sgardan. Scardroy means 'red scree.' Popular
etymology has explained it from a circumstance
connected with the over-driving of cattle by

Lochaber raiders, who had lifted a 'creach' from
the Strathconon direction, and were being hotly
pursued. The tale appears in Mr Dixon's
"Gairloch."

Corriewick—G. Coir' a' bhuic, buck's corry.

Glenuag, Gleniak, or **Glenevaig**—Gleneak (in
Kintail) 1542 ; G. Gleann fhiodhaig, glen of
the bird cherry tree. Cf. Loch fhiodhaig in
Lairg.

Meig—The Meig is the river of Strathconon. Its
source is at the head of Gleniak, and, after a
course of about ten miles, it widens out into
Loch Beannacharan. After the junction with
the stream from Loch Luichart, it is merged in
the Conon. The Gaelic is Mìg (*i* long and nasal).
The long vowel before 'g' points to compensatory
lengthening from the dropping of an original 'n,'
while the 'g' itself is reduced from an original 'c.'
This gives a primitive 'minc,' with which we may
compare the Mincius, the stream of Cisalpine Gaul
which flows by Virgil's birth-place, Mantus. It is
a curious coincidence that our Meig flows through
Loch Beannacharan, while the Mincius comes from
the lake Benacus. The root I take to be that seen
in Latin mingo, mic-turio ; Old English migan ;
Lithuanian miglà, mist ; Welsh, migen, a bog ;
the root in all cases being 'mic-,' and the notion
involved, that of 'pouring forth.' Cf. the Fife
Strathmiglo, with its river, the Miglo, known also
as the Eden ; perhaps also Loch Meiklie in Glen-
Urquhart, G. Loch Miachdlaidh ; Meigle in

Perthshire, which appears in the legend of St
Andrew as Migdele; and Maikle.

Sròn na Frianaich—Frianach occurs in *Loch na
Frianaich*, far up the R. Orrin, and in several
other places; meaning doubtful, but it may
possibly be friamhnach, place of roots. (In Ross
freumh is, of course, pronounced *friamh*).

Maoil Lunndaidh (3294)—'Maoil' as a hill name
is common, and is to be compared with G.
maol, bald, and Welsh moel, a conical hill. It
is applied to bare, rounded hills. Lunndaidh is
Englished Lundy, a name of very frequent occurrence, always in connection with lochs or bogs.
We have lochs of this name in Lochalsh, Applecross, Knockbain, Golspie, near Invergarry, and
in Forfarshire. There is also Lundin in the
parish of Largo, Fife, but these are sufficient to
show the frequency and area of its occurrence.
In certain parts there may still be heard in
common speech the word 'lunndan,' meaning
a green spot, but apparently primarily a
green wet place.[1] From all this it is clear
that Lunndaidh or Lundy means a wet place,
a boggy loch or stream. As to derivation,
it may be regarded as a nasalised form of 'lod,' a
puddle, the root of which is seen in Latin lutum,
mud. Hence, most probably, London, Latin
Londinium; and we may compare Lutetia
Parisiorum, the muddy town of the Parisii, now

---

[1] For this, as for much more information, I am indebted to the Rev.
Charles M. Robertson.

Paris, if, indeed, the reading Lutetia can be accepted as correct. South of Maoil Lunndaidh is **Maoil Choinnl'mas**—Candlemas Bare-hill, a very curious term.

Sgùrr nan Conbhair — Conbhair (1) dog-kennel (H.S. Dict.); (2) greedy person (E. Ross); (3) dog-man, attendant on dogs (W. Ross). ' Peak of the dog-men ' is most likely to be the meaning here. There are legends of Fingalian hunters attached.

Sgùrr a' Chaoruinn (3452 ft.)—' Sgùrr ' is locative of ' sgòr,' a sharp rock, and is applied to sharp-pointed rocky hills. ' Rowan Peak.'

Sgùrr nan ceannaichean—Merchants' Peak. I do not know the legend annexed, if there is one.

Càrn Eiteige—Quartz Cairn.

An Crom-allt—The bent burn at head of Gleniak.

Loch Coireag na' mang—Loch of the little corry of the fawns.

Cnoc an t-Sìthein—Hill of the sìthean, or small fairy mound.

Càrn Mhàrtuinn, Loch Carn Mhàrtuinn, and **Allt Carn Mhàrtuinn** — Cairn, loch, burn of Martin.

Leanaidh—Locative of lèanach, based on lèan, a swampy plain.

Càrn Chaoruinn—Rowan cairn; Allt na crìche, Boundary burn.

Camasie — G. Camaisidh, a stream name, also applied to the sheep farm ; from ' cam,' bent.

The stream is very winding. Cf. for ending
Lienassie, and for meaning Crombie.

Càiseachan—Apparently a collective from 'càiseach,'
abounding in cheese, a reminiscence of shieling
times.

Càrn na Fèith-rabhain—Rabhan is said to mean
refuse left by the tide or by a stream in flood ; cf.
Bad-a-rabhain, Dunrobin Glen.

Badanluchie — G. Bad-a-fhliuchaidh, clump of
wetness.

Achanalt—Auchnanald 1682 ; G. Ach'-an-allt, Field
of the burns.

Sgùrr a' ghlas-leathaid—Peak of the grey hill-side.

Sgùrr a' mhuilinn—Mill-peak.

Sgùrr ronnaich—' Ronnach,' of which ' ronnaich '
is locative, means ' abounding in saliva.' There is
a cliff over which there is a continual drip of
water.

Loch Rosque — G. Loch 'Chroisg, loch of the
crossing ; from ' crasg,' a crossing. The crossing
referred to is that from Kinlochewe through Glen
Docharty, and so on to the low lands. Around
Loch Rosque are the three following :—

Bad a' mhanaich—Monk's clump ; not so strange a
situation for a church-name when it is considered
that it lay in the regular track from Kinlochewe
to the east.

Lùib—Locative of lùb, a bend, ' loop '; distinguished
also as Lùb a' Ghargain, bend of the rough place.
The old inn of Luib was once a welcome stage

between Achnasheen and Kinlochewe, and thus
appears in song :—

'S e tigh-òsda Chailein
Dh' fhàg mo phòcaid falamh ;
'S ioma stòp is glainne
'Chuir mi 'n tarruing ann.

Lèanach—Place of swamp meadows, on the south
side of the loch.

Loch Crann, tree loch ; Lochan Sgeireach, skerry
lochlet.

Allt Ducharaidh—Cf. Cnoc Ducharaidh, Alness,
locative of dubh-chath'rach, a place of black
broken ground.

An Cabar—The antler.

Ledgowan—Leathad 'ghobhainn, hillside of the
smith ; also Loch Gowan.

Dosmuckaran—G. Dos-mhucarain, clump of the
place of swine ; mucaran is from mucar, place of
swine ; cf. Crochar, Beannachar.

Achnasheen—Auchownosein 1633 ; G. Ach-na-sìn',
field of storm ; sìan, stormy weather, gen. sìne.

Garve—G. Gairbh, rough (place); cf. R. Garry ;
probably here also a river name, since we have
Strathgarve. The river is now the Blackwater.
The N. Stat. Acc. says it was known as the Rasay,
but if that was so, the name has completely gone.
Yet the Life of St Cadroe mentions the river
Rosis in these parts, and it might well be Norse
hross-á, horse-river.

11

Garbat—Garrowbat 1633 ; rough clump — garbh bad.

Gorstan of Garve—G. Goirtean Gairbh, or simply 'an Goirtean,' the small corn-enclosure, from 'gort,' cognate with 'garth,' garden, hortus. The old ' in-town' of Garve.

Loch Garve—In G. Loch Maol-Fhinn, Loch of the shaveling or follower of St Fionn, to be connected with Killin, G. Cill-Fhinn, at the west end of the loch.   Taken together these names are conclusive as to the existence of a saint named Fionn, to whom the Garve Killin, and probably other places of the same name, were dedicated.   " Cill-Fhinn 's Cill-duinn, 's Cill-Donnain, na trì cilltean is sine an Albainn" ; Killin, Kildun, and Kildonan, the three oldest churches in Alba.

Dirriemore—G. An Dìridh mòr, 'the great ascent' ; the highest part of the road between Garve and Ullapool.   *Strath Terry*, Straintirie 1635 ; G. Srath an Dìridh, Strath of the ascent.

Tarvie—G. Tairbhidh, from ' tarbh,' bull ; ' place of bulls.'   Cf. Tarvie and Tarvie Burn in Glen Brerachan ; Tarvie Burn in Banff ; Tarves, Aberdeenshire.   Here may be noted the local saw : daoine beaga Roagaidh, 's crogaichean Thairbh-idh, buic Srath-Ghairbh, meanbhlach Srath-bhrainn, fithich dhubh Loch-Carrainn, 's clamhanan Loch Bhraoin ; the little men of Rogie, the crogs (*i.e.*, worn-out sheep) of Tarvie ; the bucks of Strathgarve ; the slender folk of Strathbran ; the black ravens of Lochcarron, and

the kites of Lochbroom : names descriptive of the
people of these districts.

Loch na cròic—Antler loch ; it is shaped like the
tine of an antler.

Achnaclerach, on the road from Garve to Ullapool,
Clerics' field, probably identical with Auchina-
glerach 1479 ; to be connected with Killin.

Loch an Droma—Ridge-loch, between Loch Garve
and Loch Achilty.

Am Fireach—'Fireach' is a mountain acclivity or
hill ground ; ' fireach an f'heidh,' hill of the deer.
This is the mountain-side along the left bank of
the stream from Loch Luichart.

Glenmarksie—G. Gleann-marcasaidh ; there are
also Sgùrr Marcasaidh and Sàil Marcasaidh, Peak
of Marxie and Heel of Marxie. Marcasaidh is
based on marc, horse ; cf. Rosemarky ; -asaidh is
difficult. It may be regarded as a double extension of the root, and compared with Lienassie,
G. Lianisidh, and Livisie, G. Lìbhisidh, Glen-
Urquhart, but might here be the locative of fasadh,
dwelling ; marc-fhasaidh, horse-stead. As coupled
with glen, we should expect it to be a stream
name, but Sàil Marcasaidh and Sgùrr Marcasaidh
rather point to its being primarily here the name
of a place.

Some easy names follow :—Strone, near Loch
Achilty ; Altnabreac, trout-burn ; Loch an eich
bhàin, Grey-horse loch ; Loch a' chlàrain, Loch of
the small flat place ; Loch ruigh a' phuill, Loch of
the marshy stretch ; Creag a' chaoruinn, Rowan

rock ; Cadha fliuch, wet pass ; Loch nan eilid,
hinds' loch ; Loch na' sgarbh, cormorant loch ;
Loch a' chairn dhuibh, black-cairn loch ; Loch a'
bhealaich (thrice), Loch of the gap ; Loch nan
dearcag, berry loch ; Loch a' choire léith, grey
corry loch ; Loch Bhaid ghaineamhaich, sandy-
clump loch ; Loch a' Chuilinn, Holly loch ;
Dubhchlais, black hollow ; Loch an alltain
bheithe, Loch of the birch burnlet ; Carn na Crè,
Clay cairn.

Lochluichart—Locative case of 'longphort,' an
encampment, or simply shieling, in which sense
it is used here. Longphort is primarily a harbour,
from 'long,' ship, and 'port,' harbour, but passes
into other derivative meanings. From it come
'lùchairt,' palace; and the place-names, Camus-
loncart on Loch Long, bay of the encampment ;
Lungard and Loch Lungard in Kintail ; Luncarty.

Ardachulish—G. Aird' a' chaolais, Height of the
Kyles, or narrows, where Loch Luichart contracts
at its lower end.

Cnoc na h-iolaire—Eagle hill, on north-east side of
Loch Luichart.

Corriemuillie—Mill-corry ; G. Coire mhuillidh, v.
Corriemulzie in Kincardine.

Dorrygorrie—Doire Goraidh, Godfrey's grove ;
Gorry, from God frid, God's peace, was a
favourite name among the Macdonalds (Macbain).

Strathvaich—Strathwaith 1635 ; from 'bàthach,'
cow-house, a frequent element in place-names.

Lubfearn—Alder bend, or angle.

Druimbuidhe—Yellow ridge; Lubriach, brindled bend; Sròn gorm, green point; Meall an torcain, hill of the young boar; Drumanguish, fir-ridge; Tombàn, white hillock; Coire nan laogh, Calves' corry; Meallan donn, brown hillock; Coir' a ghrianain, corry of the sunny hillock; Allt coir a' chliabhain, Corry of the little creel; Meall na glaic bàine, hill of the pale hollow; Allt beithe, birch burn; Allt a' ghlastuill mhòir, burn of the great green hollow; Creag Rainich, bracken rock; Creag mholach, shaggy rock; Càrn gormloch, green-loch cairn; Creag chlachach, stony rock; Toll-muic, sow hollow; Clach sgoilte, split stone (at the meeting point of three estates); Glenbeg, small glen.

Kirkan—G. na Cearcan, the hens; there are numerous boulders, whence apparently the name.

Glascarnoch — G. Clais-chàrnaich, cleft of the Carnach, or stony place.

Aultguish—G. an t-Allt giuthais, Fir burn.

Meall Mhic Iomhair—Maciver's Hill.

Strathbran and **River Bran**—'Bran' is an obsolete word meaning raven. As applied to a river, the reference is not very clear, but it may have been given simply from ravens having haunted some parts of it. It is possible to suppose the name to have been given from the black colour of the water; most probably, however, there is a mythological reference. The Ross-shire Bran must be carefully distinguished from the Perth-shire Bran, the Gaelic of which is Breamhainn.

Loch Fannich—G. Loch Fainich. In spite of its Gaelic ring, Fanaich is rather an obscure and difficult word. Assuming that the 'f' is radical and does not represent an aspirated 'p,' we may compare with Welsh 'gwaneg,' a surge, 'gwanegu,' to rise in waves, Welsh 'gw' corresponding to Gaelic 'f,' as in W. gwern, G. fearn, alder. Another step backward would lead us to an early Celtic 'van-' or 'ven-,' which suggests a comparison with the Gaulish Lacus Ven-etus, now Lake of Constance, and the two Gaulish tribes of Veneti, both maritime. But the name is one on which it is unsafe to be positive. In point of fact, when stormy winds from Strathcromble and from Cabuie meet at the nose of Beinn Ramh, the effect on the loch is said to be tremendous.

Grudie, G. Grùididh, is the river from Loch Fannich falling into the Bran half-way between Loch-a-Chuilinn and Loch Luichart. There is an Allt Grùididh on the south side of Loch Maree, and an Abhainn Grùididh in Durness, Sutherland, also Gruids, near Lairg, so named from Allt Grùididh from Loch na Caillich and Lochan na fuaralaich which flows at the back of it. I am not aware of any to be found further south, but the examples given above go to show that we are dealing with a river-name. The root is most likely ' ghru,' gritty, which is at the bottom of such words as ' grothlach,' a gravel pit; ' grùdair,' a brewer; ' grùid,' lees; ' grùthan,' the liver; allied with Eng. grit, Welsh grut, grit or fossil. The notion

involved may be either 'gravelly,' or 'full of
sediment.' Near the end of the wood on the
Fannich road is *Lèum Ruaraidh*, Rorie's leap,
close to a fine fall on the river. Further up is
an t-Eilean Crithinn, aspen isle, in the river, with
many aspen trees.

Eiginn—The Hill Difficulty, a hill with bare ribs of
rock at the north-east end of Loch Fannich.
Near its west end is *Beinn Ràmh*, hill of oars or
of rowing ; it is at a very stormy part of the loch.

An t-Alltan Mailis—The sweet burn, at Eiginn ;
its water is good ; mailis is a variant of meilis, the
usual Ross form of milis, sweet.

Aultdearg—G. an t-Allt Dearg, Redburn ; on the
way to Fannich.

Aultchonier—G. Allt a' Choin uidhir, burn of the
dun dog, *i.e.*, the otter ; Otterburn.

Nedd—G. an Nead, the nest ; the finest of the
magnificent corries of Fannich forest.[1] In it is
Comunn nan Caochan, meeting of the streamlets,
a point where five small burns meet. Other corries are *an Coire Mòr*, the big corry, with *Cadh'
a' Bhoicionn*, Path of the goat-skin, at its upper
end at the west ; *an Coire Riabhach*, the brindled
corry ; *an Coire Beag*, the little corry, with, at
its top, *Coire nam Mang*, Fawns' Corry. At the
east side of Coire Beag is *Gob a' Chùirn*, Beak

---

[1] In 1542 appear " the waste lands of *lie* Ned, between Lochboyne on the
north, Lochtresk on the south, *lie* Ballach on the west an l Dawelach on the
east." Lochboyne is either Lochivraoin (Lochaidh Bh aoin) or Loch Broom ;
Lochtresk (? Loch-cresk) is Loch Chroisg ; which Bealach or Gap is referred to
as the western boundary, is hard to say. Dawelach I cannot identify.

of the Cairn, a remarkable projecting mass, with
broad top almost perfectly flat and grassy.

Meall nam Peithirean—Lump (*i.e.* shapeless hill)
of the foresters; origin unknown; also *Cadh' a'*
Bhàillidh, the bailiff's path; both behind Fannich
Lodge.

Sgùrr nan Clach—Stony skerry; on its side, very
high up, is *éigintoll*, difficulty hole, a small corry
dangerous and difficult of access.

Sgùrr Mòr 3637—Great skerry; a peak from which
on a clear day may be seen practically all Scotland
north of the Grampians.

Fuartholl Mòr and **Fuartholl Beag**—Little and big
cold-hole; wild corries adjacent to each other.

Loch Ligh—Spate loch; above it is *Toll Ligh*,
spate-hole, a deep and narrow corry; from it
goes *Allt Gus-ligh*, probably for Giuthais, fir-wood
of Li.

A' Bhiacaich—The place of bellowing; also *Cadha*
na Biacaich, path of the same; a place where
stags roar.

An Coileachan 3015—'The cockerel'; the application is difficult, but we say 'tha an coileachan air
siubhal an diugh' of a fall when spray is seen
rising off it; 'tha coileachan math air a' ghaoith'
of a gale; 'tha coileachan air an loch' of waves.
On the other hand the name may mean literally
'Place of grouse cocks,' which is the accepted
meaning of Kyllachy, G. Coileachai(bh).

Meallan Raìrigidh—(O.S.M.) Is not known in
Fannich.

Cabuie—G. an Cadha Buidhe, the yellow path.
Behind Cabuie Lodge is *an Sgaoman*, the stack,
from its sharp conical shape.

Strathcromble—G. Srath chrombail, 'winding
strath.' 'Crom,' bent, here develops a 'b' before
the suffix, as it does in Aber-crombie, Dalcrombie.
Similarly from 'lom' we get Innis-lombaidh
(Rosskeen), and 'lombar,' a bare place. The last
example suggests that the form 'crombail' may
have arisen by dissimilation from 'crombair,'
parallel to 'lombar.' The Gaelic for Grantown-
on-Spey is the same.

Loch Droma—Ridge Loch; the ridge on which it
lies is the great ridge of Drumalban, which forms
the natural division between the east and west of
Scotland, running from Argyllshire northwards.

Loch a' Gharbharain—Loch of the rough place, is
the first of a series of five lochlets, connected by
a stream running almost due south. Into this,
the largest of the five, flows also Allt Mhucarnaich,
Burn of the place of swine.

Loch Coire Làir, north of the last mentioned loch.
Into it flows Allt Làir. Here làr is used in the
sense of 'low place,' or 'place at the foot"; *e.g.*, làr
a' ghlinn, lower part of the glen; cf. Lair, Lochcarron.

Loch na Still—Loch of the Spout; from 'steall,' a
spout of water, or long narrow strip of anything,
e.g., grass, ribbons.

Loch Prille, a curious word, suggesting comparison
with Welsh prill, a little brook or rill; cf. Lacus
Prilius in Etruria.

Loch Tuath—North Loch ; the most northerly of five small lochs.

Seann Bhràigh'—Old upland.

Fionn Bheinn (3060)—White Hill, south-west of Loch Fannich.

Airiecheirie and **Allt Airiecheiridh**—G. Airigh-chéiridh, waxen shieling, from céireach, waxen. The local explanation, which seems sensible enough, is that in summer, in walking through the grass, one's boots get a yellow waxen coating, testifying, as was thought, to the excellence of the pasture.

GLENSHIEL.

Glenshiel—Glenselle 1509, Innerselle 1571, Glen-
schall 1574 ; G. Gleann-seile, named, as usual,
after its river, Abhainn Seile. The Moidart Shiel,
which is the same word, appears in Adamnan's Life
of Columba as Sale, and again in the Dean of
Lismore's Book as 'selli.' The root is 'sal-,'
flow ; cf. 'seile,' saliva ; 'sil,' to drop ; 'seileach,'
willow ; and the Continental rivers Sala. Shiel
is doubtless a Pictish word.

Morvich—G. A mhor'oich (mormhoich), the sea
plain (Ir. 'mur-magh'); a very common name.
Cf. a Mhor'oich, the Gaelic of Lovat; the Mor-
richmore at Tain ; Mor'oich Cinn-déis, the Carse
of Bayfield. In Badenoch there is a moor called
'a Mhor'oich,' an instance of its use away from
the sea.

Eilean nan Gall—Lowlanders' isle.

Uchd an t-sabhail—Barn-knoll.

Achadh-ghiùrain — Auchewrane 1543, field of
giùran. The 'giùran' is a tall umbelliferous
plant closely resembling the wild hemlock, and
of the same family. It grows plentifully here,
and in E. Ross. O.S.M., Achadhinrain.

Torrluinnsich—Torlouisicht 1543, Torloiford (Blaeu),
lounging knoll, from 'luinnse,' a loafer, which comes
from the obsolete English word 'lungis,' lounger.

The natives say that it is a knoll where lazy people used to lie to the sun ; and it is very suitable for the purpose. O.S.M., Torrlaoighseach.

Ach-nan-gart — Achnangart, Auchnagart 1543, Achengart (Blaeu), field of the corn enclosures.

Ràtagan and **Bealach Ràtagain**—The Rateganis 1543. A diminutive of Ràtag, which again is diminutive of Ràt, *i.e.*, 'ràth,' with excrescent or strengthening 't.' In Badenoch we have Raitts, G. Ràt. The Irish 'ràth' was a fortified enclosure, usually circular ; cf. Màileagan, below. Along the south side of Loch Duich we have

Cill-Chaointeort — To be identified with Kilkinterne 1543, Kentigerna's cell. Kentigerna is in Irish 'Caintigerna,' kind lady (Cain, G. caoin), and the slight corruption at the end of the Gaelic form, Cill-chaointeort, is due to the strong accent on 'chaoin,' which caused the final part of the compound to be pronounced indistinctly. There is an old burying-ground here, now disused. The last burial took place some thirty years ago.

Eaglais Riabhachain — Church of the brindled place, is the parish church of Glenshiel, just west of the last-named.

Saraig—Norse Saur-vík, muddy bay.

Leacachan—Lakachane 1543, place of flagstones.

Letterfearn—Alder slope.

Ach na Taghart—Achniterd in rental of 1727 ; difficult ; taghart may be for 'taobh-ghart,' side-cornfield, which suits the place ; 'Field of the side-cornfields.'

Druideig—The little shut-in place ; G. druid, to close.

Totaig—G. an Tobhtaig ; also Coille na tobhtaig ; tobhta means the remains of a ruined house.

Aoinidh—Eunich (Blaeu), the steep place ; also Aoineadh, which is nom. or acc. case.

Ard an t-sabhail—Barn promontory.

Camus nan gall—Lowlanders' bay.

An Garbhan Còsach—The little rough place of caves or fissures.

The " five sisters " at the head of Loch Duich are given on the ground as—

Sgùrr na mor'oich (2870) (O.S.M., Sgùrr na mòraich)—Peak of Morvich.

Sgùrr nan saighead (2750)—Arrow peak.

Sgùrr U(dh)ran (3505)—? Oran's peak ; Oran, G. Odhran, from ' odhar, dun, is in the Dean of Lismore's Book written phonetically ' ooran.' Equally possible, however, is odharan, the plant cow-parsnip. The O.S.M. has Sgùrr Fhuaran, as if Well-peak, but the local pronunciation is quite against this.

Sgùrr nan càrnach—Peak of the stony places, or place of cairns ; not on O.S.M.

Sgùrr nan cisteachan dubh (3370)—Peak of the black kists. Under it, but not marked in O.S.M., is

Sgùrr na' Spainnteach—Peak of the Spaniards, just above the site of the battle of Glenshiel, 1719.

Beinn Fhada (3383), best known as Ben Attow, the long hill.

Sgùrr a' bhealaich dheirg (3378)—Peak of the red gap.

Càrn na Fuaralaich (3378)—Cairn of the cold place ; cf. Lochan na fuaralaich, Rosehall, Sutherland.

A' Chràileag (3673) (O.S.M., Garbh-leac), appears to be a variant of ' cròileag,' a circular place.

Sgùrr nan conbhairean (3634)—Peak of the dogmen ; *i.e.*, attendants of hunters ; this is the local explanation, which seems right. It may, however, mean ' Peak of the dog-kennels,' in allusion to some feature known to hunters.

Càrn Ghluasaid (3000)—Cairn of moving—from its screes.

Druim nan cnaimh—Hill of bones.

Na Paiteachan—The humps, on Loch Loyne.

Creag a' mhàim (3103)—Breast rock.

Aonadh air chrith (3342)—Shaking precipice ; ' airson gu bheil e cho biorach,' because it is so sharp-pointed and dangerous a ridge.

Maol cheann-dearg (3214) — Red-headed brow (accent on ' cheann ').

Sgùrr coire na Féinne—Peak of the Fenians' corry.

Sgùrr an lochain (3282)—Peak of the lochlet.

Sgùrr beag (2750)—Small peak ; Creag nan damh (3012), stag rock ; Sgùrr a Bhac Caolas, not known in Glenshiel ; Sgùrr na sgine (3098), knife peak, from its sharpness ; An Diollaid (3317), the saddle ; Sgùrr na creige (3082), rock

peak; Sgùrr leac nan each (3013), peak of the
flat rock of horses; Sgùrr a' ghairg gharaidh,
peak of the rough den.

Sgùrr 'ic Mharrais (O.S.M., Sgùrr Mhic Bharraich),
appears to mean peak of the son of Maurice. It is
near Shiel Inn.

Allt Undalain — Near Shiel; probably a Norse
compound involving dalr, ? with suffixed article.
The burn flows into the river Shiel through a
small flat. Opposite Shiel Schoolhouse is a
disused burying-ground, called *Cill Fhearchair*,
Farquhar's Cell or Church. St Ferchar does not
seem to be otherwise known.

Allt Coire Mhàileagain—Malegane 1543. We
have Coire Mhàileagan in the parish of Kincardine; Loch and Allt Valican in Glen Girnag,
Perth; Cnoc Malagan, Sleat. These again cannot
be separated from such names as the River Maillie
and Invermaillie, Kilmaillie in Inverness, Cul-
maillie in Sutherland, and Dalmally, Oban, all
of which have the '-maillie' alike 'màili' in
Gaelic. The root is 'màl,' probably identical with
Ir. 'mál,' noble (from a primitive 'mag-lo-s'), of
which Lhuyd has a feminine 'an mhal,' the queen.
This latter agrees well with the form 'màl-ag-an,'
meaning 'little queenly one'; cf. for meaning
Glen-elg, noble glen. Phonetically 'màl' could
come equally well from 'mad-lo,' wet, Latin
'mad-eo,' but though the root 'mad-' is found
in Celtic, we have no instance of it with this
particular suffix.

Allt Coire Làir into **Loch Cluanie**—Burn of the low corry ; possibly Mares' Corry, or Mid Corry. Near it, but in Inverness, is Loch Lundie.

Gleann Lic — Glenlik 1509 ; Glenlic 1633 ; from ' leac,' a flag-stone, not leac, a cheek ; the glen is narrow, with steep sides reaching a height of about 3000 feet. At its head is *Coire dhomhain*, deep corry. In Glenlik, at the foot of Ben Attow, is *Ach-a-dhachd*, where, according to local legend, Diarmid died. At his dying wish for water a well burst forth, which is still well known as *Tobar an Tuirc*, the Boar's Well. Diarmid was buried at Dùnan Diarmaid, near the manse of Kintail.

The stream through Glenlik is called *Abhainn a' Chrò*, from the *Crò* of Kintail at its mouth. The first deep pool is called *Fianntag*, heathberry. There is also *Innis a' chrò*, meadow of the *Crò*. The famous *Crò* of Kintail is a fine hillgirt circular flat.

Abhainn Conag—The river Conag joins the Crò river. The local account is that a man was drowned therein in presence of his wife, whence the river was called Conag—' airson gun do ghon bàs a fir i.' With this may be compared the derivation of Averon from ' ath bhròn.' The name is probably connected with ' con,' from ' cù,' dog. Just beyond the head of this glen is *Loch a' Bhealaich*, loch of the gap or pass, to wit, the well-known pass leading into Glen Affric, appearing in 1542 as ' lie ballach.' It is interesting to know that it is also known as *Cadha Dhubhthaich*,

St Duthac's pass, a name which implies that it was by the Bealach the saint travelled from Easter Ross to Loch Duich.

Dorusduan, at the junction of Connag and a burn called *Allt an leothaid ghaineamhaich*, burn of the sandy hillside. The Gaelic is Dorus-dubhain. Dubhain is very distinctly two syllables, and therefore may be regarded as from 'dubh-an,' black-water ; 'an,' genitive 'aine,' being an O. Ir. word for water. Dorusduan thus means Black-water door. There is here a ford over the Connag, in crossing which Donnachadh nam Pìos was drowned on a Friday.

Loch Loyne—G. Loch Loinn, Loch of shimmer or glitter ; this seems better than to take loinn as genitive of lann, an enclosure. Cf. Loch Neimhe in Applecross.

KINTAIL.

Kintail—Kyntale 1342, Kyntaill 1535 ; G. Cinn
t-sàile, 'head of the salt water.' The parish of
Tongue in Sutherland is Cinn t-sàile 'ic Aoidh.
Cinn t-sàile nam bodach 's nam bò ; Kintail of
carles and cows. Cf. Ir. Kinsale.

Lienassie — G. Lianisidh ; based on lèan, a
moist meadow ; for terminations cf. Caoilisidh,
Camaisidh.

Dùnan Diarmaid—Diarmid's little fort ; " Dounan
Diarmod, a circular stone building, 20 feet high
and 20 feet wide, near the manse of Kintail "
(O.S.A. 1790).

Ruarach—Roroch 1571 ; G. an Ruadhrach, the red
place, from the screes immediately behind the
farm house.   In 1727 divided into Mickle **Oxgate**,
Middle Oxgate and Culmuiln.

Tigh a' mholain—House of the little sea-beach (of
shingle), mol.

Loch nan Còrr—Loch of the cranes.

Achadh an droighean—Achadrein 1543, Achidren
1727, field of thorns ; where the manse is.   Behind
it is *Sgùrr an Airgid*, silver peak, otherwise
Tulach àrd or Ard-tulach, Artullich 1727, high
hillock.   " Tulach-àrd " was the rallying cry of
the Mackenzies.

Clachan Dubhthaich—St Duthac's Kirktown ; the old chapel and burying-ground.

Torr Chuilinn—Hazel Tore, above Kintail Church.

Inverinate — Innerenede 1571 ; G. In'ir-ìonaid, applied now to the district from west of Clachan Dubhthaich to the burn from Coire Dhuinnid, called in G. *Leitir Choill*, Hazel slope ; Letterchall 1509, Lettirchoull 1586, 1633. The only " inver " is that formed by the burn referred to, where it enters Loch Duich, and though the phonetics are not all that could be wished, In'ir-ìonaid can hardly be dissociated from Coire Dhuinnid, Corry of the ' Duinnid.' Duinnid might be the genitive of an abstract noun meaning ' brownness,' but it is better regarded as a river-name formed from donn, brown, after the model of the Irish river-names Dianaid,[1] dian, swift ; Buanid, buan, lasting. Part of the corry is *an Lethallt*, Half-burn ; cf. Lealty.

Keppoch—Water of Keppach 1509, Keppach 1571 ; G. a' Cheapaich, the tillage plot.

Carr—Creag Charr, Carr rock ; carr means a rocky shelf, or projecting part of a rock ; from the root *kars*, rough, seen in carraig, carrach. Near it is *Creag a' Chriabaill* (a nasal), Rock of the Garter.

Claonaboth—Climbo 1571, Clunabol, Blaeu ; Clinbow 1727, claon-both, awry or inclining booth ; the intervening a is the 'sporadic' vowel. *Claonabol* is also heard with *l* developed through sympathy.

---

[1] There is a stream Dèinaid in Strathardle.

Dornie—G. an Dòirnidh, the pebbly place, an old
locative of Dòrnach, pebbly, from dòrn, fist.
This will be found descriptive of all the places
of the name Dornie, Dornoch or Dornock, Durno.
Mr J. Macdonald (Place-names in Strathbogie,
p. 112), mentions Craigdornie, and near it
Beldornie ; Drumdurno, formerly Drumdornach ;
Mindurno, formerly Mondornach ; and Edindur-
nach, in all which dòrnach is adjectival, pebbly.
He thinks it is doirionnach, stormy. As applied
to the village, Dornie is modern. The old name
was Bun dà loch, foot of two lochs, to wit, Loch
Long and Loch Duich, but this is applied now
to the 'east end' of the village only. The original
Dornie was at Castle Donan, and applied primarily
to the passage from the shore to the castle, easily
fordable at low water, and strewn with rounded
stones. Between Dornie and Bundalloch is *Càrn
dubh*, black cairn, a part of the village. Beyond
Bundalloch is *Tollaidh*, place of the holes, at the
narrowest part of Loch Long.

Ellandonan — Alanedonane 1503 ; G. Eilean
Donnain, (? St) Donan's Isle. It is an island
only at high water. Ellandonan was a place of
strength from 13th century times, until its castle
was battered by cannon in 1719. But there are
clear indications that even before the days of
castles it was the site of a vitrified fort.

Cnoc an Tuairneil—Near Dornie, ? hill of dizziness.
Perhaps rather a variant of tuairnean, a mallet,
beetle ; mallet-hill. Cf. Ord.

Creag a' Chaisil—Rock of the bulwark or wall; cf Coill' a' mhùiridh in Applecross.

Camuslinnie—G. Camas luinge, Bight of L. Long.

Killilan—G. Cill Fhaolain, St Fillan's Church. Here is the site of a chapel, and a burying-ground still used, regarding which there is a tradition current that funerals come to it in threes. Some seven miles beyond is *Maol Buidhe*, yellow rounded hill.

Camaslongart — Bight of the encampment or shieling.

Fadoch—Nadoch, Blaeu; G. an Fhàdaich, place of fàd, turf or sod. In Ireland fód, sod, gives rise to many names. It applies to a smooth grassy place; cf. Swordale; Artafaillie.

Coille-righ—So spelled means King's wood; but it is really Coille-ruigh', Wood of the slope.

Glen Elchaig—G. Gleann Eilcheig, so named from its river Abhainn Eilcheig, a diminutive of eileach, meaning in modern G. a mill lade, but based on ail, rock or boulder, and therefore primarily rocky or place of rocks; cf. Craig-ellachie, the Irish Ailech, and Alesia, better Alixia, the Gaulish rock fortress. Thus Eilcheig is 'the little rocky one.' In its upper reaches it widens into *Loch na Leitreach*, loch of the hill slope, with *Carnach*, G. a' Chàrnaich, rough place, or place of cairns, at its head. It rises in Loch Muireagan.

Glòmach and **Allt na Glòmaich**, place of the chasm, from glòm, a gloomy hollow or chasm, gorge, applied in Lochcarron to the chasm or gorge of the river Taodal, which on a smaller scale resembles the terrific gorge of Glomach ; cf. the Gloume or Castle Gloom, Dollar ; now Castle Campbell.

Abhainn Gaorsaig, also **Loch Gaorsaig, Sgùrr Gaorsaig** ; doubtful ; ? gaorr, a thrill.

On the river is Loch thuill easaidh, loch of the waterfall hole ; easaidh being old genitive of easach ; cf. Essich, G. Easaich, near Inverness.

Gleann Shiaghaidh and **Abhainn Siaghaidh**— possibly from O. Ir. ségda, stately, handsome.

The river flows east into *Loch Lungard*, loch of the encampment or shieling, whose waters go to Maol-àrdaich (Loch Mullardoch).

Càrnan Cruithneachd 2386—The little cairn of the Cruithne, or Picts ; the meaning of wheat seems impossible. The article is prefixed, but that sometimes happens when the sense of the second part being a proper noun is lost, *e.g.*, an Fheill-Dubhthaich, St Duthac's Fair.

Riochan—G. Riabhachan, the brindled place ; deer-forest.

Càrn-éite 3877 — Cf. Carn-éit in Contin ; Allt-éiteachan in Kincardine parish ; Tobar na h-éiteachan in Nigg ; Loch-éite and Gleann-éite, Loch Etive and Glen Etive ; Allt Chill-éiteachan near Ullapool. Whether the base in all these cases is the same is doubtful. The éite of Gleann-éite applies no doubt primarily to the stream of that glen, and the accepted etymology is from the root seen in Lat. i-re, to go, with extensions, with which may perhaps be compared Gael. éite, éiteadh, stretching, extending. The connection in Càrn-éite is not clear.

Màm Sabhal 3862—Rounded hill of barns ; noted for grass.

> Càrn-éite nan gobhar, 's Màm-sabhal an fheòir.
> Càrn-éite of goats, and Màm-sabhal of grass.

Gleann Choilich and **Abhainn Coilich**—Glen and river of the rapid ; coileach is applied to the crests of broken water.

> Coileach is Siaghaidh is Bràigh Ghlinne-ghriabhaidh.

Màmag—The little màm, or rounded hill ; beyond Coille righ, opposite Carnoch.

Càrn na Breabaig—Beyond Carnoch ; ' cairn of the little kick or start ' ; the term ' breabag ' is applied to a hill in which there is a cleft such as might be supposed to have been caused by a sudden start ; cf. Breabag adjoining Ben More in Sutherland.

Ach-a-ghargain—Field of the rough place, near Kilillan ; cf. Gargastoun.

Lochaidh Mhuireagain — (O.S.M., Loch Muir-ichinn), Muireagan's Lochlet. The proper name Muireagan means ' mariner,' based on muir, the sea.

An Creachal Beag 2854 ; perhaps a variant of ' creachan,' a bare hill top.

River Ling—Abhainn Luinge, Ship's river.

Loch Long—Ship loch.

LOCHALSH.

Lochalsh — Lochalsche 1464 ; Lochalch 1472 ;
Lochelch 1510 ; Lochalse 1576 ; G. Loch-aillse or
Loch-ài'se (with *l* dropped before *s*, as usual) ;
undoubtedly the Volsas or Volas Bay of Ptolemy,
the geographer of the early part of the second
century.   The modern Gaelic favours an origin
from Volsas, and Dr A. Macbain would connect
with a root *vol*, to roll, as a wave ; Eng. *well*,
Lat. *volvo*.   Loch Alsh, in Sutherland, is the same
in Gaelic.

Ardnarff — Ardnanarf 1554 ; Ardenarra   1574 ;
Ardonarrow 1607 ; G. Ard-an-arbha, Promontory
of the corn.

Inchnairn—Inchenarne 1548, 1554, and 1607 ;
Inchnairnie 1574 ; G. Innis an fhearna, Alder-
haugh.

Fernaig—Fairnmoir and Fayrineagveg (big and
little Fearnaig) 1495 ; Fayrnagmore and Fayrin-
aegveg 1527 ; G. Fearnaig, place of alders.

Achmore—Achmoir 1495, 1527 ; Auchmoir 1548 ;
G. Acha-mór, Big Field ; with it went *Killochir*
1548, 1607, or *Cuylohir*, 1527 ? cùil odhar, dun
nook ; seemingly obsolete.

Achachonleich — Achechoynleith 1495 ; Achchon-
elyth 1527 ; Auchachondlig 1633 ; G. Ach-a-
chonalaich.   There is a confluence at the spot, and

the name seems to be based on coingeall, a whirlpool, 'Field of the place of the Whirlpool'; cf.
Connal Ferry.

Braeintra—Brayeintraye 1495 ; Brayeintrahe 1548;
Breaintread 1633 ; G. Braigh' an t-sratha : Upper
part of the strath.

Craig—Cragy et Harsa 1548 ; 1554 *lie* Craig ; Craig
et Harsa 1607 ; G. a' Chreag, the Rock ; with it
goes Duncraig, the old name of which was *am
Fasadh*, the dwelling, otherwise *am Fasadh
àluinn*, the lovely dwelling. Harsa seems obsolete.

Achandarach—Achenadariache 1495 ; Achendar-
iach 1527 ; Auchnadarrach 1548 ; G. Achadh nan
darach, Field of the oaks.

Achnahinich — Auchnahowgych 1548 ; Auchna-
henych 1554 ; Auchinnahynneych 1574 ; Auchna-
hinginche 1607 ; Auchnahenginche 1633 ; G.
Achadh na h-ìnich. Duncan Matheson, a
Matheson historian, spells it Acha na Shinich, and
he says that at *Achadh da Tearnaidh* (Field of
two descents) here, the Mathesons used to rally
as to a rendezvous when they took the field.
They drank of the sacred stream of *Alltan-
rabhraidh* (Burn of the murmuring) and started.
Achnahinich is for Achadh na h-iongnaich
(h-ìnich), Field of the Nail-place, *i.e.*, of the point ;
ionga, a nail, is common in Irish names in this
sense.

Balmacarra — Ballimacroy 1548 ; Ballamaccarra
1554, 1607, and 1653 ; Ballemakcarrane 1574 ;
G. Baile mac Carra, or possibly Baile mac Ara,

Township of the sons of Carra or Ara. MacAra
or MacCarra is a Perthshire name. For the
formation cf. Belmaduthy, G. Baile mac Duibh.

Auchtertyre—Wochterory 1495 ; Ochtertere 1527 :
Ochbertirie 1548 ; G. uchd-a-rìre, or Uachdar-
thìre, Upper part of the land ; cf. Iochdar-thìre
or Iochdar-rìre, Englished Eastertyre, in Strath-
tay.

Achtaytoralan—Auchtatorlyne 1548 ; Auchtator-
lane 1554 ; Auchridtidorillane 1574 ; Auchtator-
rellan 1607 ; G. Achadh-da-torralan ; a doubtful
word ; perhaps 'Field of two descents,' from
torluinn ; perhaps a derivative of torran, hillock,
from tòrr.   With Achtaytoralan went *Ardach*
1548, *Ardache* 1607, *Ardacht* 1574, High-field.

Nostie—Nostie 1548, 1574 ; Noyste 1554 ; Nostie
1607, 1633 ; G. Nòsdaidh for 'n òsd-thigh, the
inn, with the article in the dative or locative
prefixed as in Nonach.   There is tradition of an
inn here.

Ardelve—Ardelly 1548 ; Ardelf, 1554 ; Ardillie
1574 ; Ardelleive 1607 ; Ardelve 1633 ; Ardhill
1691 ; G. Ard-eilbh or Aird-il' (locally cf. 1691
spelling) ; Féill na h-àirde, Ardelve market ; most
probably for Aird-eilghidh, Height of the fallow
land.

Conchra—Connachry 1548 ; Concry 1554 ; Conchra
1574 and 1633 ; Conchara 1607 ; G. Conchra,
Place of Cruives, from con, together, and crà,
which is a variant of crò, fold, but specialised
in the sense of cruive.

Sallachy—Sallach 1548 ; Salche 1554; Sallachie 1574, 1633 ; G. Salachaidh, Place of Willows : O.G. sailech, willow, now seileach ; Scottish sauch for salch, O.E. salt ; cf. Sauchieburn for older Salchie (Stirling), where possibly the word is Scottish ; also Salachar, Applecross.

Port a' Chuilinn—Holly Port.

Plockton—G. am Ploc, the Lump, applied to the humpy promontory which ends in *Ruemore*, Gaelic Rudha-mór, Big-cape.

Duart—G. Dubh-aird, black point.

Strathy—G. an t-Srathaidh ; abhainn an t-Srathaidh, Strathy river ; these G. forms prove Srathaidh to be singular number, and I take it to be a diminutive, meaning Little Strath. It is very small for a strath.

Seann-chreag—Old rock.

Port-an-eòrna—Barley Port ; *Port-na-cloiche,* Port of the stone.

Badicaul—G. Bada-call, Hazel Clump.

Kyle of Lochalsh—G. an Caol, the narrow.

Glen Udalan—Udalan is a derivative of G. udail, to be unsteady, to rock; 'the rocker'; applied primarily to the stream. Udalan in common speech means a swivel or swingle-tree, with same notion. Cf. Ben Udlamain, east of Loch Ericht, a different formation from the same word ; and, for meaning, Aonadh air Chrith in Glenshiel.

Ullava—An islet near Duncraig ; N. úlf-ey, Wolf's Isle ; probably Ulf was a person's name. On the mainland is *Uaimh Ulabha,* Cave of Ulva ; cf. Ulva near Mull.

Duirinish—Durris 1548, Durness 1554, Dowrnes, Durinische 1607 ; N. dyra-nes, Deer's headland ; cf. Duirinish in Skye and Durness in Sutherland.

Erbusaig—Arbesak 1554, Erbissok 1633 ; G. Earbarsaig, with developed r, for which cf. Cromarty. It appears to mean Erp's bay, Erp being a personal name borrowed by the Norse from the Picts. The Gaelic form of Erp is Erc, e.g. Fergus MacErc, the first King of Dalriada.

Stromeferry—A hybrid ; ferry is English ; Strome, N. straumr, current, stream, common in the Orkneys and Norse regions generally ; G. Port an t-Sroim, where the presence of the article with Sroim shows it to have come to be felt a Gaelic word. The Castles of Strome and Ellandonan were of old the chief fortresses of the West Coast.

Pladaig—N. flatr, flat ; aig is either vík, bay, or possibly a G. diminutive terminative.

Scalpaidh—N. skálp-á, ship-river ; Scalpa, Skye, is Ship-isle, and in the Orkneys it is for Ship-isthmus (eið) ; G. Scalpa 'Chaoil, Scalpa of the Sound, i.e., Kyleakin.

Reraig—Rowrag 1548, Rerek 1554, Rerag 1607 ; G. Rèaraig, N. reyr-vík, Reed-bay. There is another Reraig in Lochcarron.

Avernish—Avernis 1495, Awnarnys 1527, Avarrynis 1548, Evernische 1607, Averneis 1633 ; G. Abhairnis ; probably N. afar-nes, Big or Bulky Ness.

Ceann-an-oba—G. Ceann an òib, head of the bay ; N. hóp, borrowed into Gaelic ; cf. Oban, Obbe in

Harris, Ben Hope in Sutherland. *Ob an duine,*
Man's bay, is in Plockton.

Palascaig—G. Palascaig, but Loch Fealascaig ;
N. fjalla-skiki, Hill-strip ; cf. Pládda from N. flatr.

Strathasgag—G. Srath-àsgaig, a hybrid; G. srath,
strath ; N. á-skiki, river-strip ; cf. Arscaig on
Loch Shin.

Lundie—Lunde 1495, Lundy 1527 ; G. Lunndaidh
v. Maoil Lunndaidh, Contin. There is also here
Loch Lundy. The name is Pictish. It is a
marshy place.

Kirkton—G. an Clachan Aillseach, the stone
church of Lochalsh ; dedicated to St Congan.
Near the burying-ground is *Cnoc nan Aingeal,*
Angels' knoll ; possibly knoll of beacon fires.

Kinnamoine—G. Ceann na mòine, Moss-head.

Eilean Tioram—Dry Island (a common name), at
the entrance to Loch Long. Between it and the
mainland is *an t-saothair,* where the rising tide
rushes with great speed.

Aultnasou—Auldinssie 1691 ; G. Allt nan subh,
Raspberry burn.

Nonach—G. 'Nònach ; Loch na h-ònaich, not far
off, shows that we have here the article *an* with
ònach; cf. Onich, near Ballachulish, from Omh-
anach (locative omhanaich), Place of foam.

Poll-an-tarie—G. Poll an tairbh, Bull's pool, where
a legendary battle between the Mathesons and
Sutherland men took place.

Patt—G. a' Phait Mhonarach, Hump of Monar.

Loch Calvie—G. Loch Cailbhidh, Loch of shoots ;
there is good grass here ; G. cailbh, shoot, twig ;
cf. Glencalvie.

Coire na sorna—Corry of the furnace, or furnace-
shaped gully, interesting as giving a fem. genitive
to G. sorn, but the word was both mas. and fem.
in early Irish.   We have the correct genitive in
Loch Hourn, G. Loch Shuirn, cf. the Dean of
Lismore's Book—

> Leggit derri di wurn
> eddir selli is sowyrrni
>
> an end of merriment is made
> between Shiel and Hourn.

i.e., in the Clan Ranald country.

Loch Monar—Monare 1542[1] ; G. Loch Mhonair ;
G. 'monar' means a trifle ; a trifling thing ;
but the place-name is probably quite different.   It
applies primarily to the place ; Loch Mhonair is
the Loch *of* Monar, and Monar may be a Pictish
name based on root of monadh, viz., *men*, high,
and meaning 'the High Land.'   Near it is
Innis-lòicheil : Ir. lochall or lochull is explained
as 'the plant called broomlime' ; the *o* in
the place-name is, however, long, and may be
the old adjective lòch, black, which would give
lòch-choille, Black-wood ; Blackwood-haugh.

----

[1] In 1542 appears : "the waste lands of Monare, between the water of
Gleneak on the north, the ridge of Laudovir on the south, the burn of
Towmik and Inchelochill on the east, and the water of Bernis running into
the water of Long on the west."   Gleneak is Gleann-fhiodhaig in Contin ;
Laudovir I cannot identify ; burn of Towmik is Allt-Toll-na muice, east of
Loch Monar ; the water of Bernis is still called Uisg' a' Bhearnais, water of
the Cleft.

Beinn Dronaig—Probably from the root seen in G. droineach, ragged ; for meaning cf. Beinn Féusaig.

Loch Cruoshie—G. Loch Cru'oisidh ; Loch of the hard place, based on cruaidh, hard, with the extensions seen in Caolisidh.

An Ruigh breac—The dappled reach (O.S.M. Carn an Réidh bhric).

Loch Anna—G. Loch an aini'.

Creag nan Garrag (= garradh)—Rock of the dens ; O.S.M. Creag na Cairge.

An Fhrith-ard—Freeard 1691, the small height ; G. frith, small.

Càrn nan Dobhran—Otter-cairn.

Drochaid Cnoc-a-chrochaire — Hangman's Hill Bridge.

Apparently obsolete are :—Fadamine 1495, Fynimain 1527, Fineman 1548, Acheache 1495, Acheachy 1527, and Auchcroy 1548, 1607, Auchnacroy 1611, mentioned in connection with Fernaigbeg. The two merklands of Culthnok, Achnacloich, Blaregarwe, and Acheae appear in 1495 and 1527. With Achtertyre goes Achich 1548, Achiche 1607. Fuday (a Teiroung) 1627, Idiu 1691, Innershinak 1691, Auchowlosk 1633, Auchanloisk, Auchinleisk 1669, Auchalloch 1699.

LOCHCARRON.

Lochcarron—Loghcarn 1275 (Theiner Vet. Mon.);
Lochcarryn 1474 ; G. Loch-carrann, from the
river Carron, which enters the sea loch after a
course through Glen-carron and Strath-carron.
There are in Scotland some half-dozen or more
rivers Carron, all with rough and rocky beds.
The root is ' kars-,' rough, seen also in ' carraig,' a
rock, and ' càrn,' a heap of stones. Ptolemy's
Carnonacæ, on the west coast of Ross, are the
' men of the cairns' or of ' the rough bounds.' On
the analogy of such Gaulish river names as
Matrona, the primitive form of Carron, which is
doubtless a Pictish word, would be Carsona ; cf.
Carseoli in Italy ; and for Gaelic ' rr ' arising from
' rs,' cf. Marr and the Italian tribe Marsi. But
cf. also the G. words barr and earr.[1] The old
graveyard at the old parish church is Cladh a'
Chlachain.

Kishorn—Kischernis 1464 ; Kissurine 1633 ; G.
Cis-orn, Norse ' keis-horn,' bulky cape. Blaeu's
Atlas put Combrich at the head of Loch Kishorn,
confusing with Applecross.

Tornapreas—G. Treabhar nam preas, bush-stead.
The English form is deceptive.

---

[1] A. Macbain's *Gaelic Dictionary.*

Courthill—Cnoc a' mhòid : the moot-hill in question
is close to the north side of the burying-ground
below Courthill House. Behind the house again
is *Cnoc na croiche*, Gallowhill. At the burying-
ground was a chapel called *Seipeil Donnain*,
St Donan's Chapel.

The Dun : quarter of Doun 1495, Doune 1633, near
Cnoc na croiche, was evidently once a township.
The hill-fort from which it took its name is still
traceable, though much broken. G. Lag an Dùin,
Hollow of the Fort.

Ach-a-bhànaidh—Auchvanie 1633 ; probably based
on bàn, white, yielding bànach, white place, or
untilled field. (Also Achbane 1548, Davach of
Achwanye 1583).

Seafield—G. An rudha, the point ; also Rudha
Nòis ; perhaps Rudha 'n òis, stream-mouth point ;
it is right opposite Russell Burn, on the other
side of the loch.

Sanachan—Tannachtan 1548 ; Safnachan, 1583 ;
G. Samhnachan ; G. samh, sorrel, with extensions ;
Little place of Sorrel.

Arddarroch—Oak-promontory ; south-east of it is
Ardochdainn, Little Highfield.

Achintraid — Auchnatrait 1623, shore-field ; cf.
Balintraid in Kilmuir Easter. The stream which
enters Loch Kishorn at this point is commonly
called the Kishorn river ; O.S.M., Amhainn
Cuag a' Ghlinne.

Goirtean na h-Airde—The small corn enclosure of
the point.

Camusdonn—Brown bay; *Meall na h-àirde*, hill of the promontory.

Loch Reraig—G. Rèaraig, Norse 'reyrr-vík,' reed bay. There is another Reraig in Lochalsh. Rerok 1583.

Eilean na beinne—Island of the peak. Beann is here used in its primary meaning.

Ardnaniaskin—G. Aird an fhiasgain, mussel promontory.

Strome—Strome Carranache 1495 ; Norse 'straumr,' a stream, current, race. There are Ström mór, Ström meadhonach, and Ström Carranach.

Bad a' chreamha—Clump of the wild garlic ; behind Strome Castle.

Slumbay—Slomba 1495 ; Slumba 1633 ; G. Slumba; probably Norse ' slaemr-vágr,' slim or small bay.

Lochcarron Village, or **Janetown**, formerly Torr nan clàr, Torr of the staves or boards. Referring to its change of name and improved houses, there is a local rhyme, ascribed to the Rev. Lachlan Mackenzie—

> Faire faire, Torr-nan-clàr !
> Baile Séin' th' ort an drast,
> Chan 'eil tigh air an teid fàd [air teine],
> Nach bi similear air no dhà.

> Out upon thee, Tornaclar !
> Town of Jane thou now art called ;
> Not a house on which goes sod,
> That has not chimneys one or two.

Behind Janetown is *An Teanga Fhiadhaich*, the wild tongue ; a very rugged piece of land.

Achintee—Achintee, 1633 ; Achnanty (Blaeu) ; G. Achd an t-sithidh, as if from sitheadh, force ; sith, an onset ; ? ' Field of the blast ' ; cf. Achnasheen.

Eas an teampuill—Temple waterfall, a very fine and wild double fall, fifteen minutes' walk from Strathcarron Station. The ' temple ' is said to have stood near it on the right bank of the burn, where there are some ruins. A further ecclesiastical trace is found in *Alltan an t-sagairt*, priest's burnlet, a little to the west, near Achintee. Both are no doubt to be connected with the Clachan at Lochcarron. Blaeu places Clachan Mulruy near Achintee, but west of it. The Temple fall is on the river of

Tao'udal, Englished Tweedle ; the birch and fir copses fringing its banks are called ' doire Thaoüdail,' copse of Taodail ; ? Norse haga-dalr, pasture-field, with the usual prefixed *t*. The dale is of course on the lower reaches of the stream.

Attadale—? N. at-dalr, fight dale ; the Norsemen were fond of horse-fights, *hesta-at*, and this fine level strath would have been a suitable place for that purpose ; cf. Attadale in Applecross.

Camallt—Bent burn.

Strathan—Little strath.

Immer—G. An t-iomaire, the rig, or ridge of land ; also Càrn an iomair, Cairn of the ridge.

Cnoc nam mult—Wedder hill.

Coulags—G. Na Cùileagan, the little nooks, or back places. *Sgardan nan Cùileag*, Scree of the little nooks, is a brae on the road near.

Balnacra—G. Beul àth nan crà, Ford-mouth of the cruives.

Arinackaig—Arimachlag 1543 ; G. Airigh-neacaig ; 'neacaig' looks like the genitive of Neachdag, feminine of Neachdan, Nectan.

Loch Dughall—L. Dowill (Blaeu) ; Dougald's loch.

Achnashelloch — Auchinsellach 1584 ; Auchna-shelloch 1633—Willowfield.

River Lair, Coire Làire, and **Farm of Lair** : from Làr in the sense of a low place, bottom.

Gorstan—G. an Goirtean fraoich, the small corn enclosure among the heather.

Lòn Coire Chrùbaidh—Moist flat of the bent corry.

Loch Sgamhain—' Sgamhan' means (1) lungs or lights, (2) corn or hay built up in a barn. Local authority connects the name of the loch with the former : when the water-horse devoured a man, the victim's lungs or liver usually floated to the shore. But the more peaceful alternative is preferable.

Beinn Féusaig—Beard-hill; it is bare on one side, and has long heather on the other.

Coulin,[1] **Loch Coulin, River Coulin** — Coullin 1633 ; G. Cùlainn (' u' strongly nasal). The word can hardly be other than a locative of ' con-lann,' meaning either ' high enclosure' (' kunos,' high), or ' collection of enclosures' (' con,

---

[1] " Coulin (or Connlin) is from Connlach, a Fingalian hero, who was buried on a promontory in the loch. The site of his grave is still pointed out "—Mr J. H. Dixon's *Gairloch*.

together). ' Lann,' enclosure, is found alone, as
An loinn, the enclosure ; and in composition as
An garbhlainn, near Loch Ruthven (Inverness),
which appears on the O.S. map as Caroline.
The Kinlochewe tenants of old had their shielings
where Coulin Lodge now stands. The old name
of the spot is still remembered, and appears in the
couplet—

> Cumain is snàthain is im'ideil [1]
> Ceithir thimchioll Lùb Theamradail.
>
> Milk pails and threads and coverings
> All round the bend of Temradal.

Teamradal, N. Timbr-dalr, timber-dale.

Torran cuilinn—Holly knoll ; at the east end of
Loch Coulin.

Loch Clair—G. Loch Clàir, loch of the level place.

Loch a' Bharranaich (O.S.M. Loch Maireannach),
Loch of ' barranach,' very long and strong grass
with broad leaves like corn, growing in lochs.
Fionnaltan, Whiteburns, is at its head ; Lochan
an iasgaich, lochlet of (good) fishing ; Lochan
gobhlach, forked lochlet (has a fork at either end).

Sgùrr Ruadh (3141)—Red peak ; Maol cheann
dearg (accented on ' cheann') (3060), red-headed
brow ; Ruadh stac (2919), red 'stack,' or steep
hill, are all of the red Torridon rock. Na cinn
liath, the grey heads, are quartzite. Càrn breac,
spotted cairn ; Fuar tholl, cold hole ; Cnoc na

---

[1] Im'ideal ; this was a vessel for carrying cream and milk home from the
shielings. Its mouth was covered with a piece of skin (called in the Reay
country *iolaman*), tied below the brim with thread (snàthan). The word is
doubtless *imbhuideal.—Rev. C. M. Robertson.*

h-àthan, kiln-hill ; Torr na h-iolaire, eagle torr ;
Glas bheinn, green hill.

Blaad—Bleyat, 1548 ; Blaad 1633 ; G. Blathaid ;
O. Ir. bla, glossed faithche, a green ; blà, a
place, glossed baile (both apparently the same
word) ; with the suffix seen in Bial-id, Caol-id, &c.
'Place of the green.' The place is noted for its
pasture.

New Kelso—G. Eadar dha Charrainn, between two
Carrons. The river Carron makes a large bend
round it. Edira-carrain, Blaeu.

Dail Mhàrtuinn—Delmartyne 1633 ; Martin's dale,
marching with Balnacra.

Dail Charmaig—Cormac's dale.

Revochan—Where the smithy is, a mile west of
New Kelso. Ruboachane 1546 ; G. Ruigh-
Bhuadhchain ; near it is Abhainn Bhuadhchaig
(O.S.M. Abhainn Bhuidheach) ; also Buadhchaig ;
Buadhchain is genitive of Buadhchan, probably
Buadh-ach-an, place of victory, or place of virtue
(*i.e.*, efficacy) ; Buadhchaig is merely a variant
with feminine termination. The ' virtue ' may
have been in the place itself, *i.e.*, in producing
herbs of worth ; or in the water of its river.
Abhainn Bhuadhchaig, however, means ' River of
Buadhchag,' the inference being that Buadhchag
is primarily the name of the place, not of the
river. Cf. however Ir. river name Buaidnech.

Tullich—G. an Tulaich, the hillock ; but of old
an Tulchainn.

Brecklach—G. a' Bhraclach, the dappled place.

Coire Fionnarach—May be a formation from
fionnar, cool (Ir. fionn-fhuar, white-cold), or it
may come directly from fionn, white; cf. ruadh'-
rach, from ruadh, red ; ' Cool Corry,' or ' Corry of
the white places (or white water).' The river
from *Loch Coire Fionnaraich* is *Fionn Abhainn*,
white river, from the clearness of its water.
About midway between the loch and Allt nan
Ceapairean is *Clach nan Con Fionn*, Stone of the
White Dogs ; a tapering stone about 10 feet high,
to which local legend says the hero Fionn used to
fasten his dogs. It is all worn by their chains.
Probably a trysting place for hunters and their
dog-men.

Allt an ruigh' shleaghaich—(O.S M. Allt reidh
sleighich). Cf. Slioch in Gairloch. It rises in
Mòin' a' Chrèathair, sieve moss.

Allt Doir-ithigean—West of Cnoc na h-àthan ;
obscure ; perhaps contains a proper name.

Allt a' Chonais—Burn of Coneas ; G. an Conais ;
this was a homestead by the burn. For Coneas
cf. Coneas in Kiltearn, and na Coineasan, in
English 'the Rockies,' a series of pools and falls in
the Gruinard River.

Coire Liridh—Liridh is doubtless connected with
G. Lìrean, meaning the green slimy stuff that
forms in quiet water ; cf. the Liris, a river of
Italy ; Liriope, a fountain nymph. Liridh is
probably a Pictish stream name, primitive Lirios ;
root *li*, smooth, polished, seen in Lat. limo, polish;
G. liobh ; cf. Glenlyon, G. Li'un, primitive Livona.

Sgùrr nam Feartag—'Peak of the sea-pinks,' which grow there (O.S.M. Sgùrr na Fiantag). From it comes *Coire Bhànaidh*, cf. Achvanie.

Eagon (2260)—A hill ; probably a formation from *eag*, a notch ; ' Place of the Notch, or, of Notches."

Moruisg (3026)—G. Mórusg ; first part is mór, great, the strong accent on which has reduced the second part to obscurity.

Poll Druineachain— On the stream that twice crosses the Dingwall road, near the junction with it of the road from Strathcarron Station. The more easterly of the bridges is *Drochaid Poll Druineachain* ; the other is *Drochaid na h-Uamhach*, Cave-Bridge. Between that and the head of the loch is *Cladh nan Druineach*, Burial-place of the ? Druids, where cists are said to have been found.

Peitneane 1563—Now obsolete, shows Pictish influence. There is still *Pitalmit* in Glenelg, G. Bail' an Ailm.

APPLECROSS.

Applecross—"Malruba fundavit ecclesiam Apor-crosan 673" (Tighernac's Annals). This is also the form which occurs in the Aberdeen Breviary ; but Ablecross 1275 (Theiner Vet. Mon.). The old forms show the meaning to be ' estuary of the Crosan,' and the best native authority available to me gave the name of the Applecross river as Abhainn Crosan. There is also a field by the river side known as Crosan, and entered under that name in the valuation roll. Crosan may be a genuine old river name, Crosona, with which cf. the River Crosa, now Creuse, a tributary of the Vienne, which again is a tributary of the Loire.[1] The parish, how-ever, in Gaelic, is always spoken of as ' a' Chomraich,' the girth, from the right of sanctuary, extending, it is said, for six miles in all directions, possessed by the monastery founded by Malruba. ' In Applecross ' is idiomatically ' air [not anns] a' Chomraich." The minister of Applecross is, however, not ' Ministir na Comraich," but, logi-cally enough, ' Ministir a' Chlachain ' (Minister of the Clachan), and the hill behind the church and

[1] The usual explanation of Crosan is "Place of Crosses." This would, of course, imply that the name was given subsequent to the arrival of the Christian settlers, a rather difficult supposition in view of the Pictish ' aber.' The word is more likely to be Pictish throughout.

manse is Beinn a' Chlachain, the 'clachan' denoting primarily the cell or the church of stone used by the early missionaries. Ecclesiastically there is no spot in Ross, nor, indeed, with the exception of Iona, in Scotland, more venerable than the churchyard of Applecross, which contains, according to Dr Reeves, the site of that monastic settlement which was founded by Malruba, and from which he laboured as the Apostle of the North. Malruba's grave is still pointed out, marked by two low round pillar stones, and within a yard or two of the spot so marked there was excavated, in the incumbency of the late minister, what appears from the present indications to have been a cist burial. Nor has the belief, mentioned by Dr Reeves, died out, that the possession of some earth from the saint's tomb ensures safety in travelling, and a return to Applecross. The sculptured stone on the left as one enters the graveyard, known as 'Clach Ruairidh mhóir Mhic Caoigean,' has been described by Dr Reeves; but he did not see the beautifully carved fragments of a cross shaft which are built into the wall of the small chapel-like building at the east side, showing spiral, fret, and interlaced ornament.

It is said that when the present church was built several carved stones were buried under the gravel path near the south wall.

The Strath of Applecross is 'Srath Maol-chaluim'—Strath of Malcolm. This, which is

the name given by the oldest inhabitants, is
being corrupted into 'Srath Maor-chaluim,' or,
worse still, 'Cul-chaluim.'

The holy well by the roadside, west of Applecross House, is unfortunately nameless. Near it
are the four trees in the form of an oblong, which,
with a (supposed) crab-apple tree in the centre,
were absurdly propounded as the origin of the
name Applecross. This is the supposed site of
Malruba's cell, and is called *Lagan na Comraich*,
the little hollow of the sanctuary.

Rudha nan Uamhag--Promontory of the hollows,
or the small caves, the most southerly point of
Applecross ; named from

Uags—G. Na h-Uamhagan, the hollows. It is a
tiny township.

Toscaig—Toskag 1662 ; G. Toghscaig (close o);
't-hauga-skiki,' how-strip ; 'hauga,' a cairn, bar-
row, how. There is also Abhainn Thoghscaig,
the river of Toscaig, and Loch Thoghscaig, the
loch of Toscaig.

Coillegillie—G. Coille-ghillidh, Gilli's wood.

An Airde Bhàn—The white promontory ; also *Sròn
na h-àirde bhàn*, nose of the same.

Culduie—G. Cùil-duibh (locative), the black nook.

Am Poll Creadhaich (O.S.M. Poll creadha)—Clay
pool.

Camusterach — G. Camas-teirach ; *am Macan
earach*, north of it, on the shore, is a rock
column. Probably Camas(t)-earach, Easter bay,
with develcped *t* ; cf. an dràst for an tràth-s'.

Camusteel—G. Camas-teile ; ? Linden Bay, from
G. teile, borrowed from Latin *tilia*, a linden
tree.

Milton — G. Bail' a' mhuilinn ; also *Loch a'
mhuilinn.*

An Fhaoilinn—The beach-field, opposite the manse
of Applecross.   Behind it is Cadha na Faoilinn,
pass of the ' faoilinn.'

Applecross Mains—Of old Borrodale, from N.
borgr, a burg or stronghold, and dalr, a dale ;
' Fort-dale '; Gaelic curiously accents the second
syllable,   which   suggests   that   some   third
element, *e.g. á*, river, has to be reckoned with.
Near   this   appears   to   have   been   *Sardale*,
muddy dale.   A third Norse name in dale is
Coire Sgamadail, Corry of Scamadale, from
N. Skam-dalr, Short-dale.   It is west from *Coire
nan àradh*, Ladder Corry.   *Langwell*, Longfield.

Hartfield—G. Coille-mhùiridh, wood of the bulwark ; mùrach, place of the mùr, or rampart,
bulwark, which here would serve to keep the
river to its channel.   A local song has ' Coille-
mhùiridh da thaobh na h-aibhn''—on both sides
of the river.   DrRee ves takes it to be ' Coille
Mhourie,' Malruba's wood, but accent and quantity
combine   to   make   this   impossible.   Near   the
keeper's house is a pool called *Poll a' bhior* or
a' Bhior-pholl ; bior is an old Ir. word glossed
' water ' and ' well'; ' Well-pool.'

An t-allt Mòr, big burn, comes down opposite.   Its
head branches are *Allt a' chùirn dheirg,* from Carn

Dearg, Red Cairn (2119), and *An t-allt grànda,*
ugly burn.

Maol an uillt mhòir—Bare hill of the big burn.

Coire Attadale—Corry of Attadale. Attadale
seems to have been the Norse name of what is
now called Srath-Mhaol-Chaluim. It is a very
wild corry, branching off at right angles from the
head of Srath-Maol-Chaluim. G. Coire Atadail;
cf. Attadale, in Lochcarron.

An Crua'ruigh—Hard slope, west of the manse.

Rudha na guaille—Shoulder-promontory; also Allt
na guaille.

Allt na mucarachd—Burn of the piggery.

Allt Tausamhaig (O.S.M. Allt sabhsach)—Norse
't-hausa-vík,' skull bay.

Cruinn-leum, the round leap, is a narrow, rounded
bay; cf. the common Cuing-leum, narrow leap, in
English Coylum.

Sand—G. 'sannd,' Norse 'sand.' Behind it is

Am meall gaineamhach—Sandy hill.

Salachar (final 'a' open), on a small burn; an
extension of 'sailech,' willow; with meaning
'place of willows'; cf. Croch-ar, place of the
gallows; also the common Sallachy. There are,
I am told, no willows now.

Ard na claise mòire—Point of the big gully.

Lonban—G. An Lòn bàn, white damp meadow;
near it are *Rudha na mòine,* peat point; and
Allt na mòine, peat burn. Near Lonban is a
cave on the sea shore called *an Eiginn (é),*
perhaps meaning 'the place of resort in danger.'

Calnakil—Culnakle 1662—Harbour of the cell; an old church name. G. Cal na cille.

Chuaig—Norse 'kúa-vik,' cow bay; the bay is now 'òb Chùaig.' There are, besides the bay and township, rudha Chùaig, abhainn Chùaig (the latter from Loch gaineamhach), and eilean Chùaig.

Rudha na fearna—Alder point.

Ob na h-Uamha — Cave bay; also *Creag na h-Uamha*, rock of the cave. The cave in question is on the east side of the headland, facing the north-eastern bight of Ob na h-Uamha, and is called *an Uaimh Shiannta*, the charmed or tabooed cave. The most northerly point of Applecross, *Sròn an Iarruinn*, Iron point, wrongly given on the O.S.M. as *Rudha na h-Uamha*, which latter name belongs to the headland that projects north-westward into Ob na h-Uamha.

Fearnmore and **Fearnbeg**—"The Farnacks Litill and Meikil" (Ret.): big and little Fearn; from 'fearna,' alder. The two places are commonly called *na Fearnan*.

Faingmore, and **Roinn an fhaing mhòir**—Big fank and big fank point.

Rudh' a' chamais ruaidh—Red bay point.

Sgeir an eòin (O.S.M., Sgeir neonach)—Bird skerry.

Airigh nan Cruineachd (O.S.M., Arrin-a-chruin-ach)—'Cruineachd,' wheat, as the writer of the Old. Stat. Acc. saw, is out of the question; and we can hardly escape the conclusion that here we have to do with the Cruithne, the Gaelic name of

the Picts. Cf. An Carnan Cruineachd, in Kintail.
The Old Stat. Acc. says "Arenacrionuic, literally,
sheiling of wheat, is clearly a corruption of
'arenan Druinich,' of the Druids," which is still
the popular notion. There is another place of
this name near Scourie.

Camas an eilein—Island bay ; the island is *An
garbh eilean*, the rough island, called in O.S.M.
Eilean mór. Further on is *Glas sgeir*, grey
skerry.

Kenmore—G. a' Cheannmhor ; ceannmhor (Ir.
cend-mór or cendmár) means 'big-headed'; cf.
ceanndearg, red-headed. This adjective seems to
be here used as a noun fem. The G. of Kenmore
in Perthshire is the same, and both are accented
on the first syllable. *Sròn na Ceannmhoir*, Kenmore Point.

Loch Cràiceach, or **Loch a' chràicich** (O.S.M.,
Loch Creageach)—'Cràiceach' or 'cròiceach'
means (1) rising into foam ; (2) full of cast sea-
weed (H.S.D.) ; and the latter meaning suits
very well here. At the head of the loch is an
Cràiceach, the place where the sea-weed collects.

Ardheslaig—? Ardestag 1662 ; G. Ard-heisleag ;
Norse 'hesla-vík,' hazel bay ; thus, with Gaelic
'àrd' prefixed, meaning point of the hazel bay.

Sròn a' mhàis—Point of the buttock ; màs Aird-
heisleig and màs Diabaig or màs na h-Araird
opposite it, two great ice-smoothed and rounded
rocky promontories, are known as *An dà mhàs*,
the two buttocks.

Ob na h-acairseid—Bay of the anchorage; a narrow cleft in the eastern side of Ardheslaig.

Inverbane—G. an In'ir-bàn, white estuary ; the outlet of the Abhainn Dhubh from Loch Lundie.

Rhuròin—Seal point.

Doire-aonar—Lonely copse ; and *Ceann locha,* loch head, at head of Loch Shieldaig.

Shieldaig—G. Sìldeag, Norse ' sìld-vík,' herring bay ; the herrings are not now as numerous as they were. There is another Shieldaig in Gairloch. In Shieldaig Bay is *Eilean Shildeig,* with Clach na h-Annaid, Stone of the mother-church. facing the village, the name of a mass of rock which fell from the cliff above, and said to be modern. Behind the village is *Gascan,* G. an Gasgan, the little tail, extremity ; applied to a place where a plateau ends in an acute angle and narrows down to the vanishing point ; cf. Gask. On the north side of Ben Shieldaig is *Creag Challdris,* or rather *Challdarais,* rock of the gloomy hazel wood ; G. call, hazel, and dubhras, a dark wood. *An Corran,* the Point.

Bail' a' Mhinistir—Minister's town ; *Camas an leum,* Bay of the leap ; *Camas ruadh,* Red bay ; all on east side of Loch Shieldaig.

Badcall—Hazel-chump ; inside the narrows (O.S.M., Badcallda).

Casaig—On east side of Loch Shieldaig, is a perpendicular rock ; from cas, steep, ' the little steep one.'

Eilean a' chaoil—Strait-isle, at entrance to Loch Torridon.

Doir' a' chlaiginn—Skull copse ; the 'claigionn' is an ice-rounded hill.

Ob 'mheallaidh—Deceitful bay ; it is dangerous owing to large boulders. Its south-west angle is Camas dà Phàidein, Bay of two Patons or Patricks.

Camas a' chlàrsair—Harper's bay.

Balgy—Balgy 1624 ; G. Balgaidh ; a township near the mouth of the river Balgy, from Loch Damh ; ' bubbly stream.' Cf. Strathbogy, G. Srath-bhalgaidh. Balgy is a fairly common stream name.

Badan Vugie (Mhùgaidh)—As the article is not prefixed, the second part is probably a proper name ; perhaps Mungo's little clump.

Ob gorm beag and **Ob gorm mor**—Little and big green bay ; two pretty inlets, near *Dubh-airde* (Duart), black point.

Camas Drol—Rather Camas Trol ; the burn falling into it rises in *Coire Rol*, and is called *Allt Coire Rol;* G. rol, a roaring noise ; the burn runs a very steep course over numerous boulders. The name of the bay, Camas Trol, probably contains the same word with *t* developed between *s* and *r*.

Annat—G. an Annaid, 'the mother church,' with an ancient grave-yard and chapel ; dedication unknown. Behind it is *Beinn na h-Eaglaise*, Church-hill.

An t-Ath Darach—The oak ford ; below Annat Bridge.

14

Loch Neimhe—(O.S.M. Loch nam Fiadh) ; from its
situation can hardly be connected with neimhidh,
seen in Dalnavie, &c.   Lhuyd gives neimh,
brightness (*dealradh*), which would give good
sense : ' Gleaming Loch ' ; cf. Loch Loyne.   From
it comes

Abhainn Tràill— Cf. Poll Tràill, Monar ; this rather
obscure name may be from traill, a trough
(Lhuyd), a loan from Lat. trulla.   ' Trough pool '
is good sense, nor is ' Trough river ' inappropriate.

Torridon—Torvirtayne 1464 ; Torrerdone 1584 ;
G. Toir(bh)eartan ; cf. Ir. tairbhert, to transfer,
carry over, the infinitive of tairbrim ; this would
give the meaning of ' Place of transference,' with
reference to the portage from the head of Loch
Torridon through Glen Torridon to Loch Maree.
It can hardly come direct from G. tairbeart, a
portage, as the *b* of ' tairbeart ' never aspirates.
The name applies specially to the strip of land at
the head of the loch.

Liathach (3456), pronounced Liathghach, the *gh*
developing naturally ; ' the hoary place.'   The
name is more appropriate to Beinn Eighe, which,
except for the deep gash separating the two, is a
continuation of Liathach towards Kinlochewe,
and, enveloped in hoary gray screes, forms a
striking contrast to the ruddy tiers and buttresses
of its neighbour.   A common derivation is
Liaghach, place of the ladle or ladles, but this
seems merely absurd.   *An Rathan*, ' the pulley,'
designates two jagged stumps of rock near the

top of the mountain, and seen from the sky-line
from the head of Loch Torridon. 'Rathan' is
the local name for the grooved pulley at the end
of the spindle of a spinning wheel which receives
the driving cord. Another place-name at Torridon
contains the word. The ridge falling eastwards
from the highest point of Ben Alligin is deeply
notched three times, so that it presents a serrated
outline of three peaks and notches, and these are
named *na Rathanan*, 'the pulleys.'

> Liathach 's a mac air a muin.
> Liathach with her son on her back.

Spidean a' Choire Léith, Pinnacle of the gray
corry, is the highest peak of Liathach.

Sgorr a' Chadail—Sleep scaur.

Fasag—G. Am fasag, a hardened form of the
O. Gael. 'fasadh,' a dwelling; cf. An Crom-
fhasag (Cromasag), near Kinlochewe; Fasnakyle,
Fassiefern, Dochanassie, the Perthshire Foss,
Teanassie, etc.

Am ploc, or **Ploc an Doire**—The lump, or lump of
the grove, a small rounded projection with narrow
neck extending into the loch. It has an arrangement of stone seats, once used for open air
services. Cf. Plockton.

Coire mhic Cròmuil, also **Coire mhic Nòbuill**.
Corrivicromble 1793; Corrivicknobill 1633, 1672,
Corrivicknoble 1668, 1672, 1741; these forms go
to prove Coire mhic Nòbuill to be the older form
of the name. MacNoble was a common surname,
though now only Noble.

Beinn Dearg (2995)—Red Hill; west of which is
Beinn Ailiginn (3232)—Ben of Alligin; there is
also the township of Alligin and
Inveralligin — G. Inbhir-àiliginn, which proves
Alligin to be a stream name. It is usually
connected with àilleag, a jewel, a pretty woman,
which may possibly be correct; but the single *l* in
àiliginn is a serious difficulty.
An t-Alltan Labhar—The loud little burn, from
Loch na Béiste, the Monster's Loch.   O.S.M. Allt
Lair.
An Lagaidh dhubh (O.S.M., Lagan dubh)—The
black hollow, a patch of land among the rocks,
facing seawards.   North of it is
Port Làire—Port of Lair; Lair is the name of the
place, meaning probably here 'low place.'
An Araird—The Fore-headland; G. air, àird; cf.
Urard at Killiecrankie, at the junction of Tummel
and Garry.
Creag nan caolan—Gut-rock, between Araird and
Port Lair, so called from pegmatite veins in it.
Diabaig — Norse 'djúp-vík,' deep bay; cf. the
numerous Dibidales.   The bay itself is deep, and
is surrounded by hills.   Its remoteness and
security are indicated by the saying—" 'S fhada
bho 'n lagh Diabaig, 's fhaide na sin sios
Mealabhaig "—Far from the law is Diabaig, yet
farther is Melvaig.   " A far cry to Lochow."

   We shall now take the principal names of the
interior of Applecross, which have not yet been
mentioned.

A' Bhinn Bhàn (2936)—The white hill ; the highest
in Applecross proper.

The corries on the north side of A' Bhinn Bhàn
are—*Coire Each*, Horse corry ; *Coire na Feòla*,
Flesh corry ; *Coire na Poite*, Caldron corry ;
Coire an Fhamhair, Giant's corry ; all magnificent
corries.

Sgùrr a' Chaorachain (2539)—(O.S.M., Sgorr na
Caorach). Based on ' caoir,' a blaze of fire, with
the secondary meaning of torrent. The mountain
is extremely steep on the Kishorn side.

Meall Aoghaireachaidh (O.S.M., Meall an fhir-
eachan)—' Hill of shepherding.' It is N.E. of
Beinn a' Chlachain, and marks the spot where
the green plain of Srath Maol-chaluim changes
into the bleak uplands of Applecross. Near it is
Meall nan doireachan, hill of the copses.

Eas nan cuinneag—Waterfall of the buckets, in a
dangerous gorge beside the path at the head of
Applecross Glen. The buckets are pot-holes.
Cf. Carn Cuinneag, in Rosskeen.

Fuaid, or **an Fhuaid** (O.S.M. Meall na h-uaidne)—
' Fuat ' appears in the Lecan glossary as ' bier.'
There is a Sliabh Fuait in Ireland.

At its foot, not far from the path, is Uamh an
righ, the king's cave.

Cròic bheinn—Antler-hill.

Staonag—The bent or crooked hill, E. of Loch
Lundie ; a fem. diminutive from staon, bent.

Loch Lundie—G. Loch Lunndaidh, a Pictish name ;
v. Maoil Lunndaidh, Contin.

Loch Gobach (O.S.M. Loch Ceòpach)—Snouted loch.

Loch na maola fraochaich (O.S.M. Loch Meall an fhraoich)—Loch of the heathery brow.

Loch na h-oidhche (O.S.M. Loch na h-eangaich)—Night loch. The name is common, and is applied to lochs that fish best at night. It is near the bigger of the two lochs Gaineamheach.

Coire nan àradh ('dh' hardened to 'g')—O.S.M. Coire nam faràdh; ladder corry. Through it there was once, before the Bealach road was formed, a ladder-like path ascending by tiers of steps in the rocky face.

Bealach an t-suidhe—Pass of sitting or resting; the route of pedestrians between Applecross and Shieldaig.

Am Bealach—The gap or pass, or Bealach nam Bò, Pass of Kine, is the name of that remarkable road, rising among barren rocks and frowning precipices to a height of 2054 feet, which affords the only means of entrance to Applecross by land.

Loch an lòin—Loch of the damp meadow. It is really part of the larger

Loch Coultrie—G. Loch Caoltraidh, Loch of the narrow place, an extension of 'caol,' narrow, with developed 't'; 'caolt-ar-adh.' Cf. 'bog-ar-adh,'; Kildary. *Caoltraidh* is at the south end of the loch.

Loch Damh and **Beinn Damh**—Stag loch and hill. Beinn Damh gives its name to the deer forest. Also Doire Damh, Stag thicket.

Srath a' Bhàthaich—Byre-strath, opening on to
Loch Damh. Cf. Strathvaich, in Contin. *Na
Mulcanan*, innumerable hillocks filling part of
Strathvaich, exactly resembling the *Coire Ceud
Chnoc* formation in Glen Torridon. Mulcan is
used in common speech as equivalent to bucaid,
a pustule ; hence *na mulcanan* means the little
mounds.

Loch Dùghall—Dougald's Loch, in Glen Shieldaig.

Sgùrr na bana-mhorair—The Lady's scaur ; the
lady was placed on the top of it by her cruel lord.
and fed with shell-fish. The shells may still be
seen !

Loch Uaill—Proud loch ; above it is *Meall Loch
Uaill*, in O.S.M. Meall a' Ghuail, Coal or Charcoal
hill—a very natural mistake, which is corrected
with certainty only from the name of the loch.

Na Botagan and **Creag nam Botag**—There are
three little flats, terraced one above the other, at
the foot of the rock (creag). The natives assert
the meaning to be 'the little flats'; but *bota*
locally means a wet or soft channel in a peat
moss. Cf. Bottacks at Achterneed.

Loch na(m) Frianach—Loch of the place of roots ;
also *Cadha na' Frianach*, Path of the same ; cf.
Sròn na Frianaich in Contin.

Airigh nan Druineach—Shieling of the ? Druids ;
cf. Càrn nan seachd Druineachan in Glenfintaig,
and Poll Druineachan, etc., in Lochcarron.

Loch an Turaraich—(O.S.M., Loch an Treudaich),
also *Creag an Turaraich*, Loch and Rock of the
rumbling or rattling noise.

Rassal—Rassor 1583 ; Rassoll 1633 ; G. Rasal; N. hross-völlr, Horse-field ; cf. Rossal in Sutherland.

Russel —Ressor 1583 ; G. Riseail; N. hryssa-völlr, Mare-field.

Aridrishaig — G. an àirigh dhriseach, thorny shieling.

Crowlin Islands—G. Crólaig, but also Crólainn ; *An Linne Chrólaigeach*, the pool of Crowlin, between these islands and Scalpay.

Coire Ceud Chnoc—Corry of a hundred knolls, on the road between Kinlochewe and Torridon. The corry is literally packed with small rounded hillocks, a formation seen often elsewhere in the Highlands, but nowhere perhaps in such perfection. Cf. Na Mulcanan.

Allt nan Corp—A tributary of Abhainn Tràill ; Burn of the Bodies, to wit, bodies of clay, placed there for evil purposes of magic.

Cadha nan Sgadan—The part of the path leading to Strathcarron on the slopes of Meall Loch Uaill. "Path of the herrings"; cf. Creachann nan Sgadan.

Sgeir an t-Salainn—Skerry of the salt. A rock, uncovered at low water only, where formerly, it is said, the fat of seals and porpoises used to be melted down.

Port an t-Saoir—Wright's haven.

Torr Fhionnlaidh—Finlay's rock, where a Kintail man, Finlay Macrae, who hanged himself, is buried.

Creag Raonailt—Rachel's rock ; N. Ragnhildr,

Còs Dubh Bean a' Ghranndaich—The black nook of Grant's wife ; where the original owner of the famed Annat skull drowned herself.

Càrn an t-Suidhe—Cairn of the sitting, about half a mile west of Ben Damph Lodge, said by local tradition to have been a resting-place of Malruba's body on its way to Applecross.

Port 'ic-ghille-Chaluim Ràrsaidh—The landing place of Macgilliecallum of Raasay. This is the little bay where the Hon. Capt. Lionel F. King-Noel's boathouse is. There seems to have been a skirmish here once with the Raasay men. An Annat man, whose son and house had been burnt by the Raasay band, is said to have performed some destructive archery practice from Sgeir na Saighid, killing a whole boat-load by himself !

Am Mol Mòr—The great shingle bank, between Annat and mouth of Torridon river. Also called Faoilinn na h-Annaite, sea beach of Annat.

Na Campaichean—The Camps ; two narrow dells running from *Port an t-Seobhaic*, Hawk's port, and *Ob na Caillich*, Old Woman's Bay (or Nun's Bay). This bay is also called *an t-òb Làghaich*, the muddy bay (for *làthaich*).

Cadha na Mine, path of the meal, is to be taken along with *Glac dhubh a' Chàis*, the dark hollow of the cheese, and *Bac nan Cisteachan*, the ridge of the chests, all just above Annat. After the Rebellion of 1745 a Government vessel entered Loch Torridon, and the people, though they are said to have been neutral, thought it wise to

remove themselves and their gear from harm's
way.   Hence these names.

Airigh nam Bàrd—Shieling of the Bards, possibly
of the meadows ; but it is high up.

Tunna Beag—The little cask, a small rock on
Sàil na Beinne Bige, a spur of Ben Damh, from
which a spring rises, making a noise as of water
working about in a cask.

Garaidh nam Broc—The badgers' den.

Toll nam Biast—Hole of the monsters, also Spìdean
and Stùc Toll nam Biast on Ben Damh.

Allt an Turaraich — This burn makes a great
rumbling noise.

Creag an Dath—The dyeing rock.

Criathrach Buidhe — The yellow marsh, from
criathar, a sieve ; hence a boggy place.

Gob nan Uisgeachan—The point (beak) between
the waters ; a confluence.

Achadh Cul-a-mhill—The flat field at the back of
the hill ; at Lochan Neimhe ; the reputed scene of
a battle between the Macleods and the Mackenzies.

Spuic nighean Thormaid—The peak of Norman's
daughter.

Meall Gorm or **Green Dasses**—A steep green pass
on Ruadh-stac.   The latter name, which is regularly used, was given by Lowland shepherds ; dass
means a hayrick.

Loch na Cabhaig—Loch of the hurry ; it lies in a
hollow where the wind is always unsteady, and
blows the water from side to side.

Leathad an aon Bhothain—The slope of the one bothy.

Meall na Teanga Fhiadhaich—The hill of the wild point.

The Stirrup Mark—A peculiar mark on the S.E. slope of Ben Damh below the high top, and a well-known landmark.

Doire-mhaol-laothaich—Under Liathach by the roadside ; also called *Doirbhe-la(gh)aich*, popularly said to be for *Doire Bheul Bhaothaich*. A curiosity of uncertainty.

Doire nam Fuaran—Derrinafoiran 1668 ; Spring-copse.

An Doirneag—'The little pebbly one,' a field containing many rounded pebbles, at the N.W. end of *an Fhaoilinn*, the beach-field, which latter is next the shore between Torridon Mains and the 'Ploc.'

Mormhoich a' Choire—Sea plain of the Corry, west of mouth of Corry River.

GAIRLOCH.

Gairloch—Gerloth 1275, Garloch 1574 ; G. an Gearr-loch, the Short Loch ; cf. Gareloch. A well by the roadside at the mouth of *Abhainn Ghlas*, Gray River, is affirmed to have been the original Gairloch.

Dibaig—Debak 1638 ; G. Diabaig ; N. djúp-vík, deep bay. *Oirthir Dhiabaig*, Coast of Dibaig.

Craig—G. a' Chreag, or Creag Ruigh Mhorgain ; the Rock, or the Rock of Morgan's slope.   Morgan is a Pictish name ; Old British, Morcant, ' sea-bright ;' Gaulish Moricantos.   The Craig river runs through *Bràigh-Thaithisgil*, upper part of Taisgil.   In Taithisgil the latter part is N. gil, a ravine ; the first part is perhaps genitive of haf, sea, with prefixed *t*, giving t-hafs-gil, sea-ravine.

Allt, Meall and **Loch na h-Uamhach**—Burn, Hill and Loch of the Cave.   Between the burn and *Allt na Crìche*, Boundary Burn, is a stone pillar called *An Nighean Liath*, the gray girl.   Near the mouth of the little burn is *Oirthir an Rudha*, Coast of the point, off which is *Sgeir an Trithinn*, Trinity Skerry, a rock in the sea with three humps.

Allt Saraig—Burn of Saraig ; N. saur-vík, mud-bay.

Red Point—G. an Rudha dearg ; but sometimes called an Rudha lachdunn, the dun or swarthy point.

Port an Fhaithir Mhòir—Harbour of the great
shelving slope. Faithir, a sharp slope with a flat
place at top, is in very common use in Gairloch
and Lochbroom ; ? Ir. fachair, a shelf in a cliff; cf.
Foyers, Inverness, G. Foithir, the same word.[1]
On the West Coast *faithir* is applied typically to
the steep slope between the old raised beach,
about 30 feet high, and the present shore.
The north-west point of this peninsula is *a'*
Chreag Luathann, Rock of Ashes, with a peculiar
genitive form, seen also in Cnoc na h-àthan
(single *n*) in Lochcarron ; Tom na h-àthainn,
Strathnairn ; Mullach na h-Eagann (*eag*, a notch),
the highest point of Ben Alligin.

Bailesios—G. am Baile Shìos, the Lower township,
as opposed to *am Baile Shuas*, the Upper township.

Allt a' Chaol-doire—Burn of the narrow copse.

An Tarbh—The Bull, primarily the name of a
knoll, but extended to designate the coastland
from Bailesios to Erradale.

South Erradale — Erredell 1638 ; G. Eàrradal
Shuas or Eàrradal a Deas ; N. eyrar-dalr, gravel-
beach dale. Great banks of gravel extend from
here to Bailesios.

Allt Uamh a' Chléibh—Burn of the Creel-cave ;
also *Creag Uamh a' Chléibh* and *Achadh Uamh*
a' Chléibh, Rock and Field of the same.

An t-Seòlaid—A skerry north of the mouth of
Abhainn Ruadh, Red river. There is another

---

[1] Foyers is the name of the place ; the famous fall is in G. Eas na
Smùid, Fall of Smoke, *i.e.*, spray.

Seòlaid near Fearnmore, Applecross. Based on
seòl, sail, with extension as in Bial-id ; Place of
sailing, *i.e.*, requiring careful navigation ; or,
Sailing mark. On the shore adjacent are *am
Faithir Mór* and *am Faithir Beag*, the big and
the little shelving declivities.

Openham—G. na h-òbainean, the little bays ; G.
òb, borrowed from N. hóp.

Creagan na Mi-chomhairle—Little rock of bad
counsel. Two men quarrelled and fought here.
One wished to stop fighting, but the other would
not, and both were killed.

Cnoc nan Carrachan—Hill of wild liquorice.

Sròin a' Charr—Nose of the projecting rock ;
cf. Carr Rock in Kintail.

Camas nam Ploc—Bay of the lumpish promontories.

Uamh Fhreacadain—Cave of the watch.

An Camas Raintich—Fern Bay ; by-form of
raineach.

An Sgùman—The stack ; the northernmost point
west of Port Henderson.

Port Henderson—Called by natives Portigil, N.
port-gil, gate-gully ; by others Port an Sgùmain,
Haven of the Stack.

A' Chathair Dhubh—The black fairy knoll ;
between the above and *Loch nan Eun*, Bird Loch.
N.E. of Port Henderson is *Cnoc an Sgàth*, Hill of
the fright.

Sròn nam Mult—Nose or point of the wedders ;
Na Muilt, the wedders, are three skerries that
appear at ebb off the coast.

Badantionail—G. Bad an Inneil; Clump of the tackle, or instrument.

Badachro—G. Bad a' Chròtha, Clump of the Fold. Also Caolas, Meall, Abhainn, Eas and Loch Bad a' Chròtha, Sound, Hill, River, Waterfall, and Loch of the same.

An Uidh—The outlet to the sea of *Loch Bad na h-Achlaise*, Loch of the arm-pit; achlais is very common in place-names.

An Caochan Fearna—The alder brooklet; caochan, from caoch, blind, denotes a stream so small as to be almost covered by the heather. It is common in Gairloch.

Loch nam Breac-Athar—Loch of the sky-trout, *i.e.*, trout that were supposed to have fallen in a shower; cf. Creachann nan Sgadan. (O.S.M., Loch nam Breac Odhar).

Badaidh nan Ràmh—Little clump of the oars. Badaidh, which must be a diminutive of bad, is common. Ràmh, a root (Arran), long root as of a tree (Perthshire); not so used in Ross.

Loch Clàir—Loch of the flat.

Loch Sguata Beag and **Loch Sguata Mor**; cf. Sguataig.

Glac na Senshesen, which appears on some maps, is Glac nan seani(nn)sean, hollow of the old haughs or inches; cf. Loch na Shanish, Inverness.

Doir' an Eala—Swan copse; also Lòn Dhoir' an Eala, Marsh of the same, and Abhainn Dhoir' an Eala.

An t-Allt Giuthas—Fir burn ; the formation is the
regular one on the west coast here.

Doireachan nan Gad—The copses of withes.

Bràigh Thòiriosdal—Upper part of Horrisdale, *i.e.*,
N. Thorir's dale.   Also Loch and River of the
same.

Beinn Bhric—Dappled hill.

Bus-bheinn—G. Badhais-bhinn (or baoghais-bhinn,
ao short).   The phonetics do not admit the popular explanation ' Forehead Hill,' G. *bathais*.   The
name is probably a hybrid of the same type as
Suilven, Blaven, Goatfell, G. Gaota-bheinn, where
Norse *fell*, a wild hill, has been translated into G.
beinn, the first part being left untranslated.   The
G. of Loch Boisdale is Loch Bhaoghasdail, or, Loch
Baoghasdail.

Nead an Eòin—Bird's nest ; a safe anchorage.

Camas na h-Eirbhe—Bay of the fence or wall.
Eirbhe is in O. Ir. airbe, meaning (1) ribs (2)
fence.   It occurs often in Ross and Sutherland,
e.g., Altnaharra is G. Allt na h-Eirbhe, burn of the
wall.   Further examples will occur later.   On
examination it will be found that wherever this
name occurs there are traces of an old wall
stretching through the moor ; some of these walls
are of great length.

Leac nan Saighead—Flat rock of the arrows.   The
story of the destructive archery practice made
from it is to be found in Mr Dixon's ' Gairloch.'

Camasaidh—The little bay ; cf. badaidh above.

An Cobhan—The little recess ; it is a sea nook ; cf.
Cavan, in Ireland.

Shieldaig—G. Sìldeag; N. Síld-vík, herring-bay; cf. Shieldaig, in Applecross. Also the hybrid name Aird-shìldeig, Promontory of Shieldaig.

Kerry River—River Kerrie 1638 ; G. Abhainn Chearraidh, N. kjarr-á, copse river, still as descriptive as ever. Also Inverkerry, G. Inbhir-Chearraidh, and Loch Kerry. But Kerrysdale is in G. a' Chathair Bheag, the little fairy knoll or seat.

Loch Bad na' Sgalag—Loch of the clump of the farm-workers.

Loch na h-Oidhche—Night loch, with large trout which take only at night.

Beinn an Eòin—Bird-hill ; common.

An Uidh Phlubach— The ' plumping channel,' between Loch Bad na Sgalag and Feur-Loch, grassy loch.

Loch nam Buaineachan (also **Buannachan**), Loch of the Reapers.

Meall Aundrary—G. Meall Andrairigh ; a Norse formation ; possibly Andrew's shieling, Andres-erg (erg borrowed from Gaelic àirigh). But this should give Andrasairigh.

Charlestown—G. Baile Thearlaich.

Ob Cheann an t-Sàile—Kintail Bay. This Kintail is a tiny estuary, and at the bridge there was formerly a change-house.

Flowerdale—G. am Baile Mór, Big-stead.

Flowerdale House—The old house of Gairloch was called an Tigh Dìge, Moat House, from its having been surrounded by a ditch. The present house

15

is called Tigh Dìge nan Gorm Leac, Moat House
of the blue flags, *i.e.*, slates. Dialectically *Tigh
Gìge.*

Port na h-éile ; éile is most probably éibhle,
genitive of éibheal, a live coal; ' Port of the
Ember ;' the reference is lost.

An Dùn—The Fort ; there are traces of such.

Caisteil na Cloinne—The Children's Castle ; a
rock full of holes in which children play.

An Crasg—The crossing ; a ridge crossed by the
road.

Gairloch Hotel—Its site is in G. Achadh Déuthasdal, Field of Déuthasdal, an obscure N. word.

An Cachaileath Dearg—The red gate.

Creagan nan Cudaigean—Cuddies' Rock.

Achtercairn — Auchitcairne 1638 ; G. Achd-a'-
chàrn, Field of the Cairn ; with hardening of -adh
to -ag in achadh, and contraction.

Leac Roithridh—Ryrie's flag-stone ; in the bay.
Roithridh is a personal name still in use, and
stories are told of Coinneach mac-Roithridh.
Cf. Creag-Roithridh and Toll-Roithridh.[1]   The
MacRyries were a sept of the Macdonalds.

Poll an Doirbh—Pool of the hand line ; a deep
pool at the mouth of the stream here.   N. dorg.

Loch Airidh Mhic Criadh—G. Loch Airigh Mac-
Griadh, Loch of the shieling of the sons of Griadh.

Strath—G. an Srath.

Mial—Meall 1566 ; Meoll with the mill 1638 ; G.
Miall (two syllables) ; Norse mjo-völlr, narrow

---

[1] These have been wrongly explained at p. 12.

field. It is the higher ground of which Strath is the lower ; cf. Miavaig, Lewis.

Smithstown—G. Bail' a' ghobha.

Lonemore — G. an Lòn Mór, the great damp meadow.

Big Sand and **Little Sand**—The two Sandis 1638 ; G. Sannda Mhor agus Sannda Bheag ; N. Sand ; cf. the common Shandwick or Sandaig. Near Big Sand is *Cathair a' Phuirt*, Fairy Knoll of the harbour.

Longa Island—Lunga (Blaeu) ; N. lung-ey, ship-isle. The passage between it and the mainland is *An Caol Beag*, the little narrow.

North Erradale—G. Eàrradal Shios or Eàrradal a Tuath. For the usage of sios, cf. Bailesios above, and for meaning, South Erradale.

Na Feannagan Glasa—The Green Rigs. Feannag, from G. feann, flay, was a ' lazy-bed.' (O.S.M., Fannachain glas).

Senabhaile—G. an Sean-bhaile, old-town.

Peterburn—G. Alltan Phàdraig.

Camas nan Sanndag—Sand-eel Bay.

A' Chipeanoch—The name of the shore lands from Peterburn (or perhaps from N. Erradale) to Altgreshan ; a derivative of G. Ceap, a block, a piece of ground.

Altgreshan—Auldgressan 1638 ; G. Allt Ghrìsean, *i.e.*, grìsionn, or grìs-fhionn ; ' Brindled Burn ;' cf. Inverbreakie.

Melvaig — Malefage 1566 ; G. Mealabhaig ; N. melar-vík ; melr denotes bent grass, or a sandy

hillock overgrown with bent grass ; vík, bay.
From melr we get the G. Mealbhan, sandy dunes
with bent grass, common on the west.   In Port-
mahomack 'mealbhan' means bent grass.   Also
G. mealach, full of bent grass ; cf. Loch'an
Mealaich between Strathy and Armadale, in
Sutherland.

Port nan Amall—Harbour of the yokes.

An Rudha Réidh—The smooth point ; the north-
westerly point of the peninsula.

An t-Seann Sgeir—Old Skerry, is the north point
of Rudha Réidh.   The sound of the sea on this
rock is sometimes heard, it is said, in Glen
Docharty, Kinlochewe.

Camustrolvaig—A hybrid ; N. troll-vík, goblin
bay, with G. Camas, a bay, prefixed.   It is still
counted a most uncanny place.

Abhainn nan Leumannan—River of the leaps.
Abhainn, river, is often applied to quite a small
stream if its course is comparatively smooth.

Locha Dring—(O.S.M. Loch an Draing) ; *Tobar
Dringaig*, at its south end, points to the name
being Gaelic ; perhaps a personal name or nick-
name.

Achadh nan Uirighean—Field of the couches or
beds.   There is, I think, a Fingalian tale
attached.

Bac an Leith-choin—Moss of the Lurcher.

Fura Island — G. Eilean Futhara ; Fùra also
heard ; final -*a* is Norse ey, island ; first part
obscure.

Sgeir Mhaoil-Mhoire—Myles' skerry.

Am Bodha Ruadh—The red sunken rock, a very dangerous shoal skerry.

Rudha an t-Sàsain—A wild promontory just as one enters the Minch. Sàsan is from sàs, a hold or grip, and means metaphorically 'a place or thing that grips,' *i.e.*, a point difficult to get past ; or, where lines get entangled.

Cove—G. an Uaghaidh ; the north part of Cove is Achadh na h-Uaghach, meaning ' Place of the Cave ' and Field of the Cave respectively.

Smiùthaig—N. Smuga-vík, Cave bay. *Am Faithir Mór* and *am Faithir Beag*, the big and little shelving declivity ; also *Gaineamhach Smiùthaig*, Sands of Smiùthaig.

An t-Eilean Tioram—Dry Island, off the latter.

Creag Bean an Tighe—Housewife's Rock ; a good place for fishing.

Sguataig—To be connected with Loch Sguata, which is inland from it. There are three lochs of this name in Gairloch, all of which have tail-like ends or promontories, which suggests N. Skùti, to project. Sguataig is Sguat-bay.

A' Chathair Ruadh—The red fairy knoll.

Stirkhill—G. Meallan a' ghamhna, the Stirk ; an Gamhainn is a rock.

Inverasdale — Inveraspidill 1566 ; Inverassedall 1569 ; Inveraspedell 1638 ; Inner-absdill (Blaeu) ; G. Inbhir-àsdal, a hybrid ; G. inbhir, estuary ; N. aspi-dalr, Aspen-dale, from ösp, the aspen tree. The old forms, together with the independent authority of Blaeu, prove that the modern Gaelic is a contraction with compensatory lengthening of the vowel *a*.

Coast—G. an t-Eirthire.

Faithir an Ròin—Shelving declivity of the seal.

Féith Chuilisg—Bog of Cuilisg. Cuilisg was a witch who ran off with the kettle of the Féinne. Caoilte caught her here, and the kettle spilled in the struggle, causing the ' féith.' The Fenian ' coire ' was kept in the *Feadan mór*, the big runnel.

Brae—A' Bhruthaich ; behind it is *an Leith-chreig*, half-rock ; also *Creag Chòmhaidh*.

Loch a' Bhadaidh Shamhraidh—Loch of the little summer clump. *An Gead Dubh*, the black rig, is near Brae ; also *Gead a' Chòis*, Rig of the nook.

Naast—The Nastis 1638 ; G. Nàst ; doubtful. We may compare the Irish Naas, derived from nás, a fair ; *t* would easily develop. Norse naust, a boat-place, would land in G. nòst, hardly nàst, unless we could suppose a change from *o* to *a*. Also *Plàtach Nàst*, the flat place of Naast ; and *Dùn Nàst*, Fort of Naast.

Boor—G. Bùra ; N. búr-á, bower-stream. Also *Loch Bhùra*, from which comes *Allt a' Chuingleim*, Burn of the narrow leap (Coylum) ; *Sgeir Bhùra*, Boor skerry. *Torran na Clè*, ? Hillock of the Hurdle ; it is haunted. Above Boor is *Torr a' Bhiod*, Torr of the Point.

Poolewe—G. Poll-iù ; the village is called by the natives *Abhainn Iù*, Ewe River. That Loch

Maree was formeily called Loch Ewe is clear from
the facts that the River Ewe issues from it, that
Kinlochewe stands at its upper end, and Letter-
ewe on its north side. Blaeu's map makes it
Loch Ew, yet Lochmaroy 1638. Iù is difficult,
but may be Ir. eó, Welsh yw, a yew tree; cf.
Tobar na h-iù in Nigg.

Tollie—Tolly 1638; G. Tollaidh, Place of the Holes;
there are the farm, bay, rock, burn, and loch of
Tolly. Common; this Tolly is a place of knolls
and hollows.

Slattadale—G. Sléiteadal; N. Slóttr-dalr, Even-
dale.

Talladale — Alydyll 1494; Allawdill 1566;
Telbadell 1638; G. Tealladal; N. hjalli-dalr,
ledge-dale; hjalli is a shelf or ledge in a
mountain side.

Beinn a' Chearcaill—Hill of the circle, from the
lines of stratification running round it like hoops.

Grudie River—G. Abhainn Grùididh; cf. Grudie,
in Contin.

Ru Noa—G. Rudh' 'n Fhomhair, Giant's point.

Tagan—Taag 1633; G. na Tathagan; Fear nan
Tathag, the goodman of Tagan. The singular
nom. is thus Tathag, as in the 1633 spelling, a
diminutive in form, which I take to be a loan
from N. taði, fem., an in-field, homefield. Tathag
thus means the small in-field; na Tathagan, the
small in-fields.

Anancaun—G. àth-nan-ceann, ford of the heads.

Cromasag — G. an Cromasag for Crom-fhasadh,
bent or crooked dwelling.

Beinn Eighe—File peak, from its serrated outline
as seen from Kinlochewe. The upstanding rocks
which form the teeth of the file are called
Bodaich Dhubh Binn Eighe, the black Carls of
Ben Eay. The sides of this wild mountain are
one mass of shingly screes, ever slipping, whence
it was said

> 'S i mo rùn Beinn Eighe,
> Dh'fhalbhadh i leam is dh'fhalbhainn leatha.
>
> My love is Ben Eay,
> She with me and I with her would go.

A' Ghairbhe—The Garry; the river from Loch
Coulin; G. gairbhe, roughness, which describes
it. The Inverness Garry is in Gaelic Garadh.

An Giuthas mòr—The great fir wood; a relic of
the indigenous forest. Also *Màm a' Ghiuthais*,
Breast or round Hill of the Fir-wood.

Bruachaig—Little bank, locative of bruachag. Also
Abhainn Bruachaig, Bruachaig River. Opposite
Bruachaig is *Cruchoille*, Horse-shoe wood, where
the stream makes a complete bend like a horse-
shoe. Also *Cathair Chruchoille*, Fairy knoll of
the same.

Eilean a' Ghobhainn—The Smith's isle, with a
burying-ground. Adjacent is the farm of *Culin-
ellan*, Back of the Island.

Am Preas Mor—The big thicket; here preas, which
usually means ' bush,' must mean ' thicket.' It is
a loan from Pictish, and in Welsh means brushwood, covert.

Beinn a' Mhùinidh—So called from a waterfall in its face, called Steall a' Mhùinidh ; cf. the Continental Piss-vache.

Fasag—G. am Fasag for fasadh, the dwelling. Also *Abhainn an Fhasaidh*, River of the dwelling. Site of old ironworks.

Claona—G. an claon-ath, the wry ford ; the vowel of àth is shortened by the strong accent on the prefixed adjective.

Beinn Làir—To be taken in connection with Ardlàir ; there are two rocks near this promontory in L. Maree called *an Làir*, the mare, and *an Searrach*, the foal. The meaning is thus Marehill, and Mare-promontory.

Slioch—G. an Sleaghach ; the adjective ' sleaghach ' is common, in conjunction with ' coire,' a corry ; and ' ruigh,' a sloping stretch. Here ' sleaghach ' is a noun. The base can hardly be other than sleagh, a spear, but the application is far from clear. Slioch is a truncated cone, almost void of vegetation, with many water-worn gullies on its steep slopes.

Smiorasair—So in G., where a final *-igh* has been dropped ; Blaeu writes Smirsary, and cf. Smearisary, Moidart. *Smior* is the N. smjör, butter ; *ary* is N. erg, shieling, borrowed from G. àirigh at an early stage. The *as* after *smior* is all that remains of some Norse word, which can only be guessed at. Norse compounds of this type (with three parts) are specially liable to " telescoping" in Gaelic.

Rigollachy—G. Ruigh-ghobhlachaidh, sloping reach of the forked field.

Coppachy—G. Copachaidh ; cop means knob, foam ; probably ' foam-field,' as it is on the shore of Loch Maree.

Furness—G. an Fhùirneis, the Furnace.   There were extensive smelting works here.   Also *Abhainn na Fùirneis*, River of the Furnace.

Folais—For fo-ghlais, sub-stream, small stream; also *Allt Fólais*, Burn of Fowlis, a reduplication or tautology which shows that the name Fólais has long ceased to be significant.   Cf. Fowlis.

Inishglass—G. an Innis-ghlas, the green haugh.

Meall Bheithinnidh—Probably based on G. beithe, birch ; also *Bealach Bheithinnidh*, Gap of the Birch-place.

Binn Airigh a' Charr—Pronounced quickly with accent on first and last syllables, and shortening of *à* of àirigh ; hill of the shieling of the pro-jecting rock or rock shelf.

Ardlair—G. Ard-làir v. Beinn Làir above.

Poll Uidhe a' Chrò—Pool of the water-isthmus of the fold ; joined to Loch Kernsary by a narrow neck.

Kernsary—Kernsery 1548 ; G. Cearnai'sar ; of same formation as Smiorasair, above.   The last part is N. erg, shieling, borrowed from Gaelic ; the first part may be kjarni, kernel, denoting also ' the best part of the land ;' or it may be kjarr, copse. In the former case the *s* has to be explained as in Smiorasair ; the latter theory leaves *nas* to be accounted for.

Innisabhaird—G. Innis a' bhàird, the poet's mead.
The poet in question was the ' Bàrd Sasunnach,'
a descendant of one of the English-speaking iron-
workers on Loch Maree side.

Loch Ghiùragairtaidh also **Achadh-ghiùragair-
tidh**—Probably from giùran, a plant resembling
the wild hemlock, and gart, an enclosure ; cf.
Achadh-ghiùrain in Glenshiel.

Inveran — G. Inbhirean, the little ' inver,' or
estuary, where the water of Loch Kernsary falls
into the lower end of Loch Maree. It does not
seem to have the article prefixed in Gaelic, and
this is the case also with the Sutherland Inveran,
on R. Shin.

A' Phlucaird—The Lump-promontory, a locative
of ploc-àird. Inverewe House, which stands in
its lee, is called *Tigh na Plucaird.*

Loch nan Dailthean—Loch of the Dales.

Coille-éagascaig — Wood of Eagascaig, which is
Norse eikir-skiki or eiki-skiki, oak-strip. *A'
Ghlac Dharach*, the oak dell, is in it, or at least
very near it.

Tuirnaig—Towrnek 1548 ; G. Tùrnaig; a difficult
name ; -*aig* looks like N. *vik*, bay ; but Tùrnaig
in Strath Oykell, far inland, is seriously against
it ; and the first part *tùrn* is not readily explained
from N. sources. Perhaps locative of G. *tuairneag*,
a rounded thing ; boss, hillock ; which would suit
the places. *Plàtach Thùirneig*, flat of Tuirnaig, is
the stretch of moor between *Sùil Mill a' Chròtha*,
Bog-eye of the hill of the fold, and *Loch a'*

Bhaid Luachraich, Loch of the Rush-clump. There are also Loch, Burn, and Point of Tuirnaig.

Còis Mhic 'Ille Riabhaich—Nook or recess of the son of the brindled lad. Also, *Eileach* of the same. Eileach, which usually means a mill-lade, is used in the west in the sense of an artificial narrowing of a stream for the purpose of catching fish by means of the 'cabhuil,' a sort of creel. There are legends with regard to the worthy referred to in these and other Gairloch names which may be found in Mr Dixon's " Gairloch."

An Slugan Domhain—The little deep pit.

Aultbea—In G. an Fhàin, the gentle slope, locative case of am Fàn. The real Aultbea, G. Allt-Beithe, Birch burn, is some little distance from the village. The Aultbea Coast is in G. *an t-Eirthire Donn*, the brown coast.

Badfearn—G. am Bad-fearna, the alder clump.

Tighnafiline—G. Tigh na Faoilinn, House of the Shore-field.

Croc nan Culaidhean—Hill of the Boats (O.S.M. Cnoc nan Columan).

Culchonich—G. a' Chuil-chóinnich, mossy nook.

Ormiscaig—G. Ormascaig ; N. orma-skiki, snake strip ; possibly Ormr, a proper name meaning ' snake.'

Buailnaluib—Fold of the bend.

Mellon Charles—G. Meallan Thearlaich, Charles's little hill.

Camas nan Dòrnag—Bay of the rounded pebbles ; cf. Dornie.

An Fhaithche—Pronounced *an Fhothaigh*, almost one syllable; the green; also *Allt na Faithche*, burn of the green; cf. Foy Lodge, Lochbroom.

Slaggan—In G. *an Slagan odhar*, the dun rounded hollow. Slaggan is the name for the hollow of a kiln; for sense cf. Loch Hourn, G. Loch Shuirn, Kiln-loch. Slaggan is noted as the residence of the Big Bard of Slaggan, Bàrd Mór an t-Slagain.

Sian na h-Eileig—Sian for sìthean, a fairy hillock. Eileag, I think, was a V-shaped arrangement, open at both ends, into the wide end of which deer were driven and shot with arrows as they came out at the narrow end.

Greenstone Point—Row na Clach-moin (Blaeu); G. Rudha na Cloiche uaine.

Obbenin—G. na h-Obainean, the little bays; cf. Oban. Near it is *an Fheodhail*, a shallow estuary, a dialectic form of an Fhaodhail, meaning 'an extensive beach'; cf. na Feodhlaichean, in Lochbroom.

An Carr Mòr—The great rocky shelf; also *an Carr Beag* and *Camas a' Charr*, Bay of the rocky shelf, or projecting rock.

Fèith Rabhain—Pronounced, as usual, Rawain; rabhan is a very common element in names, often coupled with fèith, a bog-stream; also with bad, a clump, *e.g.*, Allt Bad-a-rabhain in Dunrobin Glen. It has been explained as wrack left by a spate or tide. But *rabhagach* means 'certain weeds at the bottom of a lake or stream,' also, 'water lily,' and rabhan is doubtless practically the same word.

Udrigle—? Udroll 1638 ; G. Udrigill (ù) : N. útarr-
gil, outer cleft or gully.   Also *Meallan Udrigle,*
little hill of Udrigle.

Am Fiaclachan—The little place of teeth ; sharp
jagged rocks on the shore ; cf. an Fhiaclaich, Coire
na Fiaclaich.

Laid—An Leathad, the broad slope ; Laid House,
G. Tigh an Leathaid ; cf. Laid in Sutherland.

Allt Ormaidh—N. orm-á, snake stream ; also *Bad
Ormaidh,* copse of Ormy.

Loch na Cathrach Duibhe—Loch of the Black
Fairy Knoll.

Sand—G. Sannda, N. sand-á, sand-stream, as is
proved by the presence of Inbhir-Shannda, estuary
of Sandburn.   The burial place is *Cladh Inbhir-
shannda.*

Am Pollachar Mòr—The big place of pools or holes ;
also *am Pollachar Beag,* and *Cois na Pollach-
arach,* foot of the place of pools ; for Pollachar
from poll, cf. *Beannachar* from beann.   Here is
an t-Saothair, a common term on the west,
applied to a bank between an island and the
shore which is bare at low tide, or to a spit of
land projecting into the sea, covered at high tide
and bare at low tide.   Probably for saobh-thìr,
false-land, *i.e.,* land that is not real dry land.

First Coast—G. an t-Eirthire or an t-Eirthire shios.

Second Coast—G. an t-Eirthire donn, or an t-
Eirthire bhos.

Loch Maoil na h-Eileig—Loch of the round bare hill of the 'eileag' (O.S.M. Loch Mòine Sheilg).

Strathanmore—G. an Srathan mór, Big Little-strath; a curious but not uncommon name.

Am Fionn Loch—The white loch.

An Dùbh Loch—The black loch; vowel of *dubh* lengthened by accent. Also *am Fuar Loch*, the cold loch.

A' Mhaighdean—The maiden; a hill.

Loch Maree—Lochmaroy 1638; Loch Ew, Blaeu; G. Loch-Ma-rui(bh), Loch of St Malruba; v. Poolewe. In it is *Isle Maree*, G. Eilean Ma-rui' with a holy well and ancient burying-ground, whence, doubtless, the change of name in the case of the Loch. On the north side is *Ach' ruigh 'n fheadhail*, Field of the sloping reach by the shallow water. An old name for the Loch itself was *Loch Feadhal feas*,[1] but what feas means is uncertain.

Loch na Fideil—Loch of the 'Fideal,' a certain dangerous water monster. Near Loch Maree Hotel.

Glen Docharty—G. Gleann Dochartaich, from the negative prefix *do* and *cartach*, scoury, or place of scouring; 'Glen of evil (*i.e.*, excessive) scouring,' which describes it well. Cf. the Rivers Cart.

Loch Doire na h-Eirbhe—Loch of the copse of the fence. An old wall is stated to run from Loch Maree to Loch Torridon, but I have not ascer-

---

[1] Heard by O. H. Mackenzie, Esq. of Inverewe, in his boyhood from an old man.

tained whether it runs near this loch, which is
near the south-west side of Loch Maree.

Cliff—Clive 1638 ; G. a' Chliubh ; *Cliff House*, G
Tigh na Cliubha ; there are also *Meall na Cliubha*
and *Bruthach na Cliubha*, all at Poolewe. A
very steep rocky hill rises just behind. N. *klif*,
a cliff, would answer as to meaning, but it appears
in G. as *cliof* (H.S.D.), which is exactly parallel
to N. *rif*, a reef ; G. Riof in Coigach.

LOCHBROOM.

Lochbroom — Lochbraon 1227 ; Inverasfran et Loghbren 1275 (Thein Vet. Mon.) ; G. Lochbhraoin. In the uplands is *Lochaidh Bhraoin,* where lochaidh can scarcely be other than a diminutive of Loch ; cf. Lochaidh Nid. From it flows the river Broom, Abhainn Bhraoin, through Glenbroom, famed in William Ross's song, " Bruthaichean Ghlinn Braoin." The name Broom, G. Braoin, thus primarily applies to the river ; G. braon, O. Ir. bróen, a drop, shower, water. There are also R. Broom and Loch Broom, G. Loch Braoin, in Perthshire ; cf. Brin, G. Braoin, Inverness ; Fairburn, G. Farabraoin ; Braonag, a spot by the river side beyond Kildermorie.

At the head of Lochbroom is *Clachan Loch-Bhraoin,* the stone Church of Lochbroom, still the site of the Parish Church ; dedication unknown.

Gruinnardgarve — G. Gruinneard garbh, rough Gruineard.

Beinn a' Chàisgein—There are two hills so called, Little and Big. Also *Fèith Chàisgein.*

Inveriavenie River—Inverivanie 1669 ; G. Inbhir-riamhainnidh, also Allt Inbhir-riamhainnidh out

16

of *an Gleanna garbh*, the rough glen ; riam-
hainnidh is probably based on the root seen in
G. riamh, riadh, a course, running (in modern G.
' a drill '). The suffixes may be compared with
Ptolemy's Lib-nios. A Pictish name.

Fisherfield—G. Innis an Iasgaich, of which the
English is a rough translation.

Gruinard River—Flows into Gruinard Bay ; N.
grunna-fjörðr, shallow firth. *Dabhach Ghruin-
neard*, the davoch land of Gruineard, is still
heard. On the river is *Na Coineasan*, the joint-
falls, from con, together, and eas, a fall, a series of
pools and rapids ; cf. Coneas, Allt a' Chonais.

Lochan Giuthais—Fir lochlet, behind *Creag nam
Bord*, Rock of the flats.

Guisachan — G. Giùthsachan, place of fir-wood.
Creag Ghiùthsachan, Rock of Guisachan. Cf.
Guisachan in Inverness-shire.

Lochan na Bearta—Lochlet of the deed. Near it
are said to be *uamhagan* (little caves, holes), that
would hold twenty persons. This seems like a
description of earth-houses. Unfortunately the
place is remote, and those who knew the
uamhagan in their youth are too aged to guide
one to the spot.

Glenmuick—G. Gleann na Muice, glen of the sow ;
Abhainn Gleann na Muice, River of Glenmuick.

Larachantivore—G. Làrach an Tigh-mhóir, site of
the big house ; once a large farm-house.

Lochan a' Bhràghad—Lochlet of the upper part.

Suidheachan Fhinn—Finn's Seat ; a place like a long seat, in the north side of Beinn Tarsuinn, Cross-hill.

Beinn a' Chlaidheimh—Hill of the Sword.

Loch na Sealg—Loch of the hunts ; *Srath na Sealg,* and *Abhainn Srath na Sealg,* Strath and River of the Hunts ; cf. Srath na Sealg, Sutherland.

Lochaidh Nid—Lochlet of the nest ; from its situation ; cf. the Nest in Fannich. There is a farm of Ned, situated in a hollow, near St Andrews.

Achnegie—Auchanewy 1574, Auchinevie 1633 ; G. Achd an fhiodhaidh, Field of the place of wood ; G. fiodh, fiodhach. It is, or was within living memory, full of alder and birch.

Eilean nan Ceap—Island of the blocks or tree stumps.

Shenavall—G. an Sean-bhaile, the Old-town ; above it is *Bac an Aorigh* (*ao* short) ; cf. *Bac an Airidh,* near Loch Benncharan.

An t-Sàil Liath (3000)—The Gray Heel.

Sgurra Fiona (3474)—? Wine peak.

An Teallach (3484)—The Forge ; either from its smoke-like mists, or from some supposed resemblance to a forge. The whole group of Bens is called *an Teallaich,* locative.

Spidean a' Ghlas-tuill—Pinnacle of the green hole (O.S.M. Bidein a' Ghlas-Thuill).

An Sgurra Ruadh (2493)—The red skerry ; Lochan Ruadh of O.S.M. is *Lochan an Diabhaidh,* Lochlet of Shrinking or drying.

Càrn na Béiste—Cairn of the Monster. By it is *Càrn a' Choiridh,* Cairn of the little corry.

Loch na Cléire—Loch of the Clergy.   It flows into
Loch Badcall.

Lochan na Caoirilt—Lochlet of the Quarry, or
quarry-like face (O.S.M. Lochan na Cairill).

Loch an Eilich—Loch of the *eileach*, which usually
means a mill-lade, but here a short, shallow,
narrow channel.

Inchina—G. Innis an àth, Haugh or water meadow
of the ford.   Below it is *Torra Càdaidh*, probably Knoll of Adie's son, Adie being a diminutive
of Adam.   Mac-àdaidh is an Easter Ross surname or an alternative surname for Munro in
certain families.   Cf. Eas Càdaidh in Coirevalagan,
Kincardine.

Am Bad Rabhain — Waterweed clump, or water
lily clump; *Allt a' Bhaid Rabhain* enters the
sea N. of Gruinard House; cf. Fèith Rabhain in
Gairloch.

Cladh Phris—Burial-place of the bush or copse; a
disused burying-ground on Isle Gruinard, at the
landing-place S.E.   *Camas an Fhiodh*, wood-bay,
is also on the Isle.

An Eilid—The Hind, a small hill on Isle Gruinard;
Na Gamhnaichean, the Stirks, are rocks; *An
t-Seanachreag*, the old rock, a common name.

Miotag—G. Mèideag; the terminal part is N. vík,
bay, which describes the place; *mèid* is difficult,
and as there seems to be no single Norse word
which would yield this in Gaelic, it appears to be
the result of " telescoping " with compensatory
lengthening of *e*.   Cf. Inverasdale.

Mungasdale—Mungasdill 1633 ; G. Mungasdal ;
N. Múnks-dalr, Monk's dale. *Faithir Mungas-
dail*, the shelving slope of M., and *Mealbhan
Mungasdail*, the links on the shore at the farm ;
N. melr. *Sròn an Fhaithir Mhóir*, Point of the
great shelving slope, is on the coast further north.
Faithir Mungasdail runs from Stattic nearly to
Rudha na Mòine, Moss Point.

Stattic Point—G. Stàdaig ; -aig is N. vík, bay ;
the only N. word that would result in Gaelic
stàd is *stát*, prudishness, which gives no sense ; cf.
Miqtag, above.

Little Loch Broom—G. an Loch Beag. Blaeu has
it as Loch Carlin ; but this name, if it ever
existed, is quite gone.

Badluachrach—G. am Bad luachrach, the clump of
rushes.

Durnamuck—Derymuk 1548, Derynomwik 1574,
Dirinamuck 1633 ; G. Doire nam muc, Swine
copse.

Badcall—G. am Bad-call, the Hazel Clump. *Allt
a' Bhaid choill*, Burn of Badcall, flows through
Badcall, but does not rise in Loch Badcall.

Badbea—G. am Bad beithe, the Birch Clump.

Ardessie—G. Aird-easaidh, Promontory of Essie,
which latter is perhaps best regarded as a stream
name, meaning Fall-stream. There is a very fine
waterfall on the Ardessie Burn ; rises in Lochan
an Diabhaidh above.

Camasnagaul—G. Camas nan Gall, Lowlanders'
Bay.

Mac 'us Mathair 2293 — Son and Mother; a
fanciful name for two adjacent hills.

Strathbeg—G. an Srath beag, the Little Strath,
as distinguished from Strathmore at the head of
Lochbroom proper.

Auchtascailt — Auchadaskild 1548; Achadrach-
skalie 1574; Achtaskeald 1633; G. Acha dà
sgaillt, Field of two bald (places); G. sgallta,
bald, bare.

Allt Toll an Lochain—Burn of the hollow of the
lochlet; the upper part of *Allt a' Mhuilinn*,
Mill-burn.

Corryhallie—Corrinsallie; G, Coire-shaillidh, Corry
of Fatness, from its good pasture.

Gleann Coire Chaorachain—Glen of the corry of
the place of mountain torrents; cf. Sgùrr nan
Caorachan in Applecross.

Càrn a' Bhreabadair—The Weaver's Cairn.

An Cumhag—The narrow; ravine and waterfall;
cf. Coag; G. An Cumhag in Kilmuir Easter.

A' Chathair Dhubh—The Black Fairy Knoll;
where the public road crosses the Strathbeg
River.

Meall an t-Sithidh—O.S.M. Meall an t-Sìthe; cf.
Achintee.

Na Lochan Fraoich—The Heather Lochs; two
lochs joined by a short, narrow, shallow channel,
of which it is said ' tha *eileach* eatorra.'

Allt Eiginn—Burn of Difficulty; éiginn is applied
to places very rough and difficult of access; also
Loch Eiginn.

Fain—G. na Fèithean, the bog channels.

Càrn a' Bhiorain—Cairn of the little sharp point.

Loch an Airceil—Probably Ir. aircel, a hiding-place ; loch of the hiding-place. *An Airceal* was the name of a croft ; and there is a spot on Loch-broom Glebe called *An Airceal*.

Maoil an Tiompain—The bare round hill of the ' tiompan.' A ' tiompan' is a one-sided hillock. *A' Chathair bhàn*, the white fairy knoll.

Creag na Corcurach—O.S.M. Creag Corcurach ; based on root of Ir. corcach, a bog ; rock of the boggy places. *Torr na Cathrach*, Mound of the fairy knoll ; *Bruthach na Gearr(a)choille*, Brae of the short wood ; cf. a' Ghearrachoille, near Ardgay.

Dundonnell—Auchnadonill 1548, Auchtadonill 1633, Auchterdoull 1649 ; G. Acha dà Dòmhnaill, Field of two Donalds. This is the current G. for Dun-donnell ; but *Dùn Dòmhnaill* also exists as the name of a spot near the farm-house. The spot where the lodge stands is *an t-Eilean Daraich*, the Oak Isle.

Preas nam Bodach—Bush or copse of the spectres ; it is haunted. *Am Preas Mór*, the big clump ; once an alder clump, now a green island with fringe of alder trees on north side. Both near Dundonnell House.

Loch na Lagaidh—Loch of the pace of the hollow. Lagaidh, when it occurs on the west coast, is fem., and is used with the article ; the

E. Ross Lagaidh, Logie, has not got the article
prefixed.

Cladh a' Bhord Bhuidhe—Graveyard of the yellow
flat ; *Pàirc a' Bhord Bhuidhe*, Park of the same.

Keppoch—G. a' Cheapaich, the tillage plot ; com-
mon.   Also *Raon na Ceapaich* and *Creag na
Ceapaich*, Field and Rock of Keppoch.   *Sròn na
Ceapaich*, Point of Keppoch, also called *a' Chlach
Cheannli*, for Cheann-liath, gray-headed stone ;
cf. Maoil Cheanndearg.

Kildonan—G. Cill Donnain, St Donan's Church.
Corran Chill Donnain, Kildonan Point.   Corran
is very common along the west coast in this sense,
and is usually found at the horn of a small bay.
Cladh Chill Donnain, Kildonan graveyard.

Na Faithrichean—The shelving slopes.

Badrallach—G. am Bad-ràilleach, the oak clump ;
Ir. rál, oak.   Birch and hazel still grow here.   A
poisonous plant used to be found here called
' am boinne mear ;' Ir. benn mer, henbane.
Corran a' Bhaid-ràilleach, Badrallach Point.

Allt an Leth Ghlinne—Burn of the half-glen.

Loch na h-Uidhe—Loch of the water-isthmus.

Loch na Coireig—Loch of the little corry.

A' Bheinn Ghobhlach — The forked hill ; Bin
Cowloch, Blaeu.

Allt an Uisge Mhath—Burn of the good water.

Rhireavach—G. Ruigh' riabhach, dappled hill-
reach.

An Càrnach—The stony place, which describes it.

Sgoraig—N. sgor-vík, rift-bay, from a narrow gully at the place.

> Sgoraig sgreagach, 's dona beag i,
> Aite gun dion gun fhasgadh, gun phreas na coille.
> Scraggy Scoraig, bad and little ;
> A place without protection or shelter, bush or wood.

Mol Sgoraig, Shingle beach of Scoraig. *Càrn na Fir Fréig* (for *bhreug*), Cairn of the false men ; fir-bréig are stones on the sky-line, which might be taken for men ; behind Scoraig.

Cailleach Head—G Sròn na Caillich, nun's point ; in O.S.A. Rudha Shanndraig. *A' Chailleach*, the nun, and *Bodach a' Chléirich*, the parson's carl, are points facing one another.

Camas nan Ruadhag—Crab Bay.

Meall a' Chaoruinn—Rowan Lump, otherwise *Stac Chaoruinn*, Rowan Stack ; an island.

Càrnasgeir—Cairn-skerry ; for formation cf. Eigintol and Plucaird. There are a cairn and a skerry, joined at low water.

An Leac Dhonn—The brown flat rock ; a basking-place of seals.

Annat—G. an Annait, the mother-church. *Cladh na h-Annait*, Annat graveyard. Annat Bay is G. Linne na h-Annait, or am Polla Mór.

Glaic an Righ Chonanaich—Hollow of the ? Strathconon King. This *may* be Torquil Conanach, son of Rory Macleod of the Lewis, so called because he was brought up in Strathconon. This Torquil, who was rightful heir to the Lewis, flourished in

the latter half of the 16th century, and might
have been styled 'king' by the people of the west.

An Talla—The Hall ; a point with site of a tower
occupied by *Righ. an Talla Dheirg*, the king of
the red hall.

Achmore—G. an Acha' Mór, big field.

Badacrain—G. Bad nan Cnàimhean, Clump of the
Bones ; otherwise *Badaidh* nan Cnàimhean.
Near it is *Stall an t-Sagairt*, Priest's Rock, about
which there is a tradition that a certain stone is
to fall on a priest passing in a boat.

Camas a' Mhaoraich — Shell-fish bay ; Cammez
Murie, Blaeu.

Altnaharrie — G. Allt na h-Airbhe (or Eirbhe),
Burn of the wall or fence ; it comes from *Loch na
h-Airbhe*, Loch of the Fence.   The fence or wall
in question runs along by the north end of the
loch, and so on towards *Maoil na h-Eirbhe*, Hill
of the Fence.   It is a very old wall, composed of
sods and stones.   G. Airbhe or eirbhe is O. Ir.
airbe, meaning (1) ribs (2) fence ; and is not
uncommon in northern place-names ; cf. Camas
na h-Eirbhe and Loch Doire na h-Eirbhe in Gairloch ;   Loch Doire na h-Eirbhe in Coigach ;
Altnaharra, G. Allt na h-Eirbhe, in Sutherland.
At all these places similar old walls exist, and
their antiquity may be gauged from their appearance, as well as from the fact that the word *eirbhe*
is quite obsolete in the north, and that there is
no tradition as to the purpose of them.

Logie—Logy 1548 ; G. an Lagaidh, the place of the hollow. Here is *Dùn na Lagaidh*, Fort of Logie, a broch in a very ruinous condition. The current in the narrows here is called *Sruth na Lagaidh.*

Blarnalevoch — G. Blàr na Leitheoch, Plain or moor of the half-place, *i.e.*, place between hill and loch. But I have got also Blàr-na-leamhach, Elmwood plain ; cf. an Leithead Leamhach in Kincardine.

Rhiroy—G. an Ruigh Ruadh, the red hill-reach. Here is *Dùn an Ruigh Ruaidh*, Fort of the red slope (O.S.M. Dùn an Righ Ruaidh), a broch of about 40 feet internal diameter, with its first storey gallery in very fair preservation. Very large stones have been used in it all round. Its north side is on the very edge of a precipitous rock, and it stands between two burns, each less than 100 yards distant from it.

Ardindrean—G. Ard an Dreaghainn, Thorn-point.

Letters—G. an Leitir, the hill-side slope.

Strathmore—G. an Srath mór, the big Strath, at the head of Lochbroom. This is the Strathmore of the well-known Gaelic chorus which ends—

> Gur bòidheach an comunn
> 'Th' aig coinneamh 'u t-Srath-mhóir.

The words of this chorus, which are best known through the famous song beginning ' Gur gile mo leannan,' were composed by Mrs Mackenzie of *Ballone*, now Inverbroom ; G. Bail' an Lóin, Stead of the damp meadow.

Croftown—G. Bail' na Croit.

Achlunachan—Aglonoquhan 1548, Achnaglowna-
chane 1574, Auchlownachan 1633, Auchalunachan
1669, Achaglounachan, Blaeu ; G. Ach-ghlùinea-
chain and Acha-lùinneachain, of which the former
is the better form ; G. glùineach, kneed, jointed,
applied to grasses with jointed stalks ; Field of
the jointed grass.

Garvan—G. an Garbhan, the rough place.

Achindrean—Auchquhedrane 1543, Auchindrewyne
1574, Auchindrein 1633 ; Thorn-field.

Meall a' Chrasgaidh 3062—Hill of the crossing.

A' Chailleach 3276—The Nun, or the old woman.

Abhainn Dhroma—From Loch Droma, Ridge Loch,
on the watershed.   Otherwise *Dubhag*.

Corryhalloch—G. Coire-shalach, Ugly Corry, the
tremendous chasm near Braemore House.   The
fine waterfall at the bridge which spans the
ravine is *Easan na Miasaich*, the waterfalls of
the place of platters ; the 'platters' are the great
pot-holes worn by the action of the water.   (Falls
of Measach).

Meall Leacachain—Hill of the place of flagstones ;
also *Leathad Leacachain*, Hillside of Leacachan.
There is a tale attached to it which is too long to
repeat.[1]

Dirriemore—G. an Dìridh Mór, the great ascent.

Beinn Eunacleit — O.S.M. Beinn Aonaclair ; N.
Enni-klettr, Brow-cliff ; cf. Enaclete.

Braemore—G. am Bràigh' Mór, the big upper part.

---

[1] V. Guide to Ullapool and Lochbroom.

Fasagrianach — G. an Fhasadh-chrionaich ; na Fasadh-chrionaich (genitive) ; Rotten-tree Stead ; the compound takes the gender of the latter part crionaich, feminine ; fasadh is masculine. The formation is common, especially in the West ; cf. an Lòn-roid, an t-Allt-giuthais.

Diollaid a' Mhill Bhric—Saddle of the speckled hill (meall).

Glackour—G. a' Ghlaic odhar, the dun hollow.

Inverbroom Lodge or **Foy Lodge**—G. an Fhothaith ; Tigh na Fothai', a weakened form of faithche, a green, a lawn ; cf. Baile na Foitheachan, Stead of the green places or lawns (wrongly explained *supra*, p. 25).

Inverlael — Innerlauell 1608 ; Inner laall, Blaeu ; G. Inbhir Làthail ; N. Lág-hol, Low hollow, with G. Inbhir, confluence ; near the place where R. Lael enters Lochbroom.

Gleann na Sguaib — Known locally as Gleann Mhic-an-Aba, Macnab's Glen. The O.S.M. name I have not been able to verify.

Sgùrr Eideadh nan Clach Geala — Garment-of-white-stones Peak ; sgùrr is defined by the whole following phrase, to which it stands in apposition.

Ard nan Long — Promontory of the ships ; the anchorage at the head of Lochbroom.

Ardcharnaich—Ardhernich 1666 ; G. Ard-Cheatharnaich, Champion's Promontory. *Corran Ardcheatharnaich*, Ardcharnaich Point.

Raonachroisg—G. Raon a' chroisg, Field of the crossing.

Leckmelm—Lachmaline 1548; Lochmalyne 1574; Lekmaline 1633; Leach Maillinim, Blaeu. G. Leac Mailm; leac, a flag-stone, a flat stone over a grave; Mailm, the old forms of which all show *n*, is probably the name of a man who was buried here; cf. " the battle of Liacc Maelain," Ann. of Ulster, 677 A.D.

Beinn Eildeach—Hill of hinds; eildeach contracted for eilideach. Under it is *Leac Mhór na Clè*.

Corry—G. an Coiridh, the little corry; it is a little hollow. Also Corry Point.

Braes of Ullapool—G. Bruthaichean Ullabuil.

Gadcaisceig—G. Gead-càisceig, narrow rig or lazy-bed of Caisceig.

Ullapool—Ullabill (Bleau); G. Ullabul, N. Ulli-bólstȧr, Ulli's stead.

Calascaig—N. Kali-skiki, Kali's strip; at the foot of Loch Achall. *Maol Chalascaig*, Bare hill of Calascaig, about a mile east of Ullapool. *Leathad Chalascaig*, broad hill-side of Calascaig, on south side of Loch Achall. Blaeu has *Avon Challas-caig* flowing into the loch.

Loch Achall—G. Loch Ach-challa, also Loch Ach-a-challa, Loch of the field of hazel, G. call. Also *Gleann Loch-Achalla*, Glen of Achall.

Poll-da-ruigh—Hollow of two hill-slopes; near Ullapool. One slope rises up to *Cnoc na Croiche*, Gallows Hill.

Rhidorroch—G. an Ruigh dhorcha, the dark hill-slope.

Allt Chill-éiteachan, behind Ullapool, in the Rhidorroch direction. The name implies an ancient chapel. Cf. Carn-éite, Kintail.

Meall na Mocheirigh—Hill of the early rising; or perhaps rather of the achievement that comes of early rising.

Douchary—G. Duchairidh for dubh-chàtharaigh, place of black broken moor ; common. Also Glen Douchary and River Douchary.

Glastullich—So Blaeu ; Green hillock.

Morefield—G. a' Mhór-choille, the great wood. Morefield Cottage is *an Ceanna-chruinn*, the round head.

Allt an t-srathain—Burn of the little strath ; O.S.M. Allatyrne Burn.

Rudh' Ard a' Chadail—Point of Ardachadail, which again means Sleep-promontory.

Cùil a' Bhodha—Nook of the reef ; a good fishing bank. O.S.M. Cùl Bò.

Ard na h-Eigheamh—Promontory of shouting (for the ferry-boat).

Isle Martin—G. Eilean Mhartainn ; a burial place in it is *Cladh Eilein Mhartainn*.

Ardmair—G. Ard Mhèara, Finger promontory ; with fine beaches. The spit of land projecting into the sea and covered at high tide is called *an Saothair*.

Keanchilish—G. Ceann a' Chaolais, Head of the Narrows or Kyle ; at entrance to Loch Kanaird. South of it is *Glutan*, ' throat'—a gorge.

Loch Kanaird—L. Cannord, Blaeu ; G. Loch Cainneart ; N. kann-fjörðr, Can-firth ; the Can was doubtless the broch, now ruinous, near the entrance to the loch on its western side, called still *Dùn Canna.* Its can-like shape struck the Norsemen,[1] as did the can-like peak of the chief hill in Raasay, also called in Gaelic Dùn Canna, in English Dun Can.

Pollachoire—G. Poll a' Choire, Cauldron pool.

Duasdale—G. Dubh-astail, black dwelling ; also Burn of Duasdale.

Loch a' Chroisg—Loch of the crossing.

Rapag—Noisy place ; *Allt Rapag,* Noisy Burn.

Meall a' Bhùirich—Hill of bellowing (of stags).

Langwell—N. lang-völlr, long-field.

Ach nan Cairidhean—Field of the tidal weirs ; O.S.M. Achnacarnean.

Drienach—G. an Droighneach, place of thorns.

Achendrean—G. Ach' an Dreaghainn, Field of thorns.

Blughasary — G. Blaoghasairigh (*ao* short), or Bladhasairigh ; to be divided Blaogh (or Bladh)-as-airigh ; for *airigh* cf. Kernsary, Smiorasair, Meall Andraraidh ; *as* may well stand for N. hús, a house ; the first syllable is doubtful ; it requires a N. blag- or bleig-, which is not forthcoming.

Drumrunie—G. Druima Raonaidh, also *Abhainn Raonaidh.* Raonaidh is probably the stream name ; 'River of the upland plain.'

---

[1] This goes to prove, if additional proof were needed, that the brochs are pre-Norse.

Loch Lurgainn—Shank Loch ; there is a Fingalian tale attached explanatory of the name. Fionn and his mother came to blows with some giants in the Garve direction, and as he was getting the worst of it he seized his mother by the legs, threw her over his shoulder, and fled westwards. He stopped at this loch, and on taking the old lady down, found he had only the shanks of her, which he threw into the loch. A more rationalistic explanation may be found in the fact that the loch has an outlet at both ends.

Loch a' Chlaiginn—Skull loch ; claigeann is commonly applied to a knob-shaped hill.

Loch Eadar dà Bheinn—Loch between two hills.

Na Beannanan Beaga—The little hillocks.

Coigeach—Cogeach 1502 ; Ladocchogith 1508 ; Coidgeach, 1538 ; Coygach, Blaeu ; G. a' Chóigeach, Place of fifths ; for which use of cóig cf. the five Coig's in Strathdearn, Cóig na Fearna, &c. Division of land into fifths is a common and ancient Gaelic practice, the best known fifths being the five fifths of Erin—cóig cóigimh na h-Eirinn.[1] Tradition makes the five-fifths of Coigach to have been Achnahaird, Achlochan, Acheninver, Achabhraighe, and Achduart—the five Ach's, ' na cóig achaidhean,' and this is the local derivation of the name.

---

[1] A Gaelic saying has it, "Tha cóig cóigimh an Eirinn, agus tha cóig cóigimh an Srath-éirinn ; ach 's fearr aon coigeamh na h-Eirinn ; na cóig cóigimh Srath-éirinn ;" there are five-fifths in Erin and five-fifths in Stratherin ; but better is one fifth of Erin than the five fifths of Stratherin (Strathdearn).

Creag Mhòr na Coigich — The great rock of Coigach ; In it is *Allt nan Coisichean*, Burn of the walkers, a resting place on the way to Ullapool

Coulnacraig—G. Cùl na Creige, Back of the Rock.

Achduart—G. Achadh Dubhard, Black-point Field. Duart is a common name. *Rudha Dubh-ard*, Duart Point.

Iolla Bheag—The little fishing rock ; also *An Iolla Mhór*.

Horse Sound—G. Caolas Eilean nan Each.

Horse Island—G. Eilean nan Each.

Acheninver—G. Achd an Inbhir, Field of the estuary.

Achabhraigh—G. Achd a' Bhràighe, Field of the Upper part.

Badenscallie — Badskalbay 1617 ; Badinscally, Blaeu ; G. Bad-a-Sgàlaidh, Clump of the place of spectres ; Ir. Scál, spectre.   Cf. Bothan Bad-sgàlaidh beyond Kildermorie, a place notoriously haunted.   Local tradition derives the name from Sgàl, one of the three brothers who first settled Coigach.   The second was ' an Gille Buidhe,' the Yellow Lad, who settled at Achiltybuie.   The name of the third I failed to learn.   They used to meet at a great stone in the moor about equidistant from the three, called *Clach na Comhalach*, Trysting-Stone.

Polglass—G. am Poll glas, the green hollow.

Achlochan—G. Achd an Lochain, Field of the little pool.

Rudh' an Dùnain—Point of the little fort.

Achiltibuie—Badincarbatakilvy 1617 (read *t* for *c*);
Achamuilbuy, Blaeu. The Gaelic is heard as
Achd-ille-bhuidhe, Aichilidh bhuidhe, Achill
bhuidhe. Local tradition derives as 'Field of
the yellow lad,' or 'Cave *(faic)* of the yellow
lad," and there are tales of the Gille Buidhe.
But this is probably mere popular etymology,
and it is to be feared that the first of the three
Gaelic forms is a popular corruption to suit the
story. The other two are similar to Achiltý
in Contin G. Achillidh, and may show the same
root as Welsh uchel, high ; cf. Oykell, Ochil.

Badentarbet — Badintarbat 1617 ; G. Bad an
Tairbeirt, Clump of the Portage ; the lochs
behind it are separated by a narrow neck, across
which boats would be hauled.

Polbain—G. am Poll bàn, the white hollow.

Dorney—Dorny 1617 ; G. an Dòirnidh, the place
of rounded pebbles. The real old Dorney, G. an
t-Seann Dòirnidh, is opposite Isle Ristol, to which
it stands in the same relation as the Kintail Dornie
to Ellandonan. There are here also rounded
pebbles, and *Meall na Sgriodain*, Hill of the
Scree, comes down to the water's edge ; v. Dornie
in Kintail.

Summer Isles—G. na h-Eileanan Samhraidh. The
chief of these follow, the last being Isle Ristol.

Tanera—G. Tannara (Tawnnara) ; N. h·fnar-ey,
with usual prefixed *t*, Harbour-isle. The anchorage, G. an acarsaid, on the eastern side of Tanera,
is well known on the west for its security. There

is another Tanera on the east of Lewis, near the Birken Isles.

Ardnagoine—G. Ard nan Gaimhne, Promontory of the Stirks ; from its good pasture.

Caolas a' Mhuill Ghairbh—Narrow of the rough Mull or promontory ; N. múli, a jutting crag ; cf. Mull of Kintyre.

Sgeir Ribhinn—Lady Skerry ; O.S.M. Sgeir Revan.

Sgeir Neo-ghluasadach—Immovable skerry ; Fast-skerry.

Na Feadh'laichean—The shallow sandy channels between *na Sgeirean glasa*, the green skerries, and *Càrn Deas*, South Cairn, and between the latter and *Càrn Iar*, West Cairn ; pl. of feadhail, a variant of faodhail, an extensive beach.

Bottle Island—G. Eilean a' Bhotuil ; otherwise *Eilean Druim-briste*, Broken-backed Isle ; there is a depression in the middle.

Priest Island—G. an Cléireach ; the Cleric (never Eilean a' Chléirich).

A' Mhullagraich—? The place of bumps, or knolls.[1]

Isle Ristol—G. Eilean Ruisteil ; on the mainland opposite is *Allt Ruisteil*, Ristol Burn, which suggests that the original Ristol was on the mainland ; N. hryss-dalr, Mare dale.

Altandow—G. an t-Alltan dubh, the little black burn ; name of a township.

Reiff—Reiff 1617 ; G. an Rif (as Eng. *riff*), the reef; N. rif, a reef. The reef here is called *Bogha a' Bhùraich*, Reef of the bellowing.

---

[1] *Mullagrach* occurs as an adjective, meaning, apparently, 'full of pro-tuberances,' in the Poems of Egan O'Rahilly (*Irish Texts Society*, Vol. III.).

Loch na Totaig—Loch of the ruined homestead.

Faochag—G. an Fhaochag, 'the wilk,' a quaint name. *Camas na Faochaige*, Faochag Bay.

Rudha na Coigich—Coigach Point.

Camas Coille—Wood bay.

Achnahaird — Auchnahard 1617 ; G. Achadh na h-Aird, Field of the Aird. The Aird, or promontory, of Coigach, is a large district.

Loch Raa—L. Rha, Blaeu ; G. Loch Ra, Red Loch ; N. rauðr, red.

Loch Battachan—G. Loch nam Badachan, Loch of the copses.

Garvie Bay—G. Garbhaidh, seems to be the name of the stream from Loch Osgaig which enters the sea here ; Rough River ; cf. Garry. There is also Loch Garvie, a widening of the stream before it reaches the sea.

Loch Osgaig (ó)—N. óss-skiki, Outlet-strip. O.S.M. Loch Owskeich.

Loch Bad a' Ghaill—Lowlander's-clump Loch.

Aird of Coigach—Dauachnahard 1617 (Dabhach na h-Airde) ; G. àirde na Cóigich, Promontory of Coigach.

Loch na Sàile—Loch of the Heel ; from its shape.

Beinn an Eòin—Hill of the bird.

River Polly—G. Abhainn Phollaidh ; also *Srath Phollaidh*, Strathpolly ; *Inbhir-Phollaidh*, Inverpolly. Pollaidh is a river name, with the common river termination : River of Pools, or Holes.

Loch Sianascaig — N. sjónar-skiki, Observation strip. O.S.M. Loch Skinaskink.

Cuthaill Mhòr and **Cuthaill Bheag**—The latter
part is N. fjall, a hill ; first part obscure. The
names recur in the parish of Urray, where I have
doubtfully suggested kúa-fjall, Cow-fell. More
probably kví-fjall, Pen-fell, Fold-fell ; cf. Cuidha-
shader, p. 270.

Ruighgrianach—G. Ruigh-ghrianach, Sunny slope.

River Kirkaig—Abhainn Chircaig ; also Loch
Kirkaig and Inverkirkaig ; N. kirku-vík, Church-
bay.

Cùil na Bioraich—(O.S.M. Cùil na Beathrach) ;
nook of the dog-fish (possibly of the heifer).

Loch Veyatie — L. Meaty (Blaeu) ; G. Loch
Mheathadaidh ; for the first part may be compared the numerous Lewis names in *meatha-*,
from N. mjó, narrow ; terminal *-aidh* is probably
N. á, river, *d* being all that remains of the noun
qualified by mjó ; ' the river of the narrow —— ? '
The loch would naturally be called after the
river.

Loch Doire na h-Airbhe—Loch of the copse of the
wall.   An old wall runs near the loch ; cf. Altnaharrie.   O.S.M. Loch na Doire Seirbhe.

Loch an Arbhair—Loch of the Corn ; O.S.M. Loch
na Darubh.   This loch and Loch a' Choin, Dog-
loch, have got transposed on the one-inch O.S.M.

Loch Call nan Uidhean — Hazel-loch of the
isthmuses ; there are four isthmuses round it.
O.S.M. Loch Call an Uigean.

LEWIS.

The name of **Lewis** or **Lews**, Gaelic *Leòdhas*, or popularly *Leòdh's*, appears in the Norse sagas as Ljóðhús[1] and Ljóðus[2]; and the contemporary Gaelic form Leódús is found in an Irish MS. of 1150.[3] Only another instance of the name occurs, and this was the name of a town not far from Gothenburg, in Sweden, latterly known as Lödöse. This fact shows that the name is not special to either island or town. The attempts to derive it from Gaelic sources, such as Martin's (1700) *leog*, a marsh, have naturally failed. The latter part of the name is plainly Norse *hús*, a house, but—and this is very unusual—there is quite a plethora of root and stem forms available to explain the phonetics of the first part. Professor Munch favoured "the sounding house" (*hljóð*, sound) : "people's house" (ljóð-) is just possible ; the real meaning seems best found in Ljóða-hús, "house of songs or lays," in short a *céilidh* house. A farm-house or such devoted to more or less public entertainment, first must have given its name to a district and then to the whole island. Norse-Gaelic phonetics will not suit the favourite derivation of the Lewis scholars, viz.,

---

[1] Magnus (c. 1100 A.D.) and Orkney Sagas.   [2] Hacon Saga.
[3] Book of Leinster.

Ljót-hús, " Leod's House," because the *t* of Ljót regularly becomes hard *d*. Its " higher parts" were called Hin Haerri, and later made into the Gaelic form of Na Hearradh, Englished Harris.

We shall first take in alphabetical order the chief Norse words that enter into the composition of names in Lewis.

á, river : the River *Creed* or Greeta ; G. Grìde ; grjót-á, shingly, gritty river ; *Torray*, Thor-á, Thori's water ; *Laxay*, Lax-á, salmon river ; *Gisla*, G. Gìosla, gísl-á, ? hostage river, but Gísl is also a proper name ; *Avik*, á-vík, river bay, at the mouth of the Galson river ; *Eirera*, eyrar-á, beach river.

bær, stead, town—very rare; *Eoropie*, G. Eòrrabaidh, beach-town ; *Crumby*, G. Crumbaidh, Krum's town.

Bakki, a bank ; G. bac ; hence the district of *Back* ; *Tabac*, G. Tàbac, t-há-bakki, High Bank ; *Bacavat*, N. bakka-vatn, Ridge-loch.

Bekkr, brook—*Bec-amir*, bekk-hamarr, the rock by the stream.

Beit, pasture land—*Beid-ic*, pasture bay ; *Beid-icean*, pasture bays, at Càbag, Lochs.

Bólstaðr, a homestead, appears in *Bosta*, Bernera. It is very common as *-bost*, at the end of names. *Garrabost* for Geira-bólstaðr, comes most probably from *geiri*, a goar or triangular strip of land. *Shawbost*, G. Sìabost, sjá-bólstaðr, Sea-stead ; *Melbost*, G. Mealabost ; melr, bent grass, or a sandhill grown over with bent ; Link-stead ;

Swanibost, G. Suaineabost, Sweyn's stead ; *Leur-bost*, G. Liurbost, clayey stead (leir, clay) ; *Cross-bost*, Cross-stead, Rood-stead ; *Calabost*, from kald, cold, possibly from Kali, a proper name ; *Habost*, high stead ; also as *Tabost*.

Borg, a fort—*Borve* or Borgh is in Barvas ; *Boranish* in Uig, borgar-nes, fort-ness ; *Boreray*, borgar-ey, fort-isle ; *Dun-bhuirgh*, a hybrid where *dun* is tautological.

Búð, a booth, genitive búðar—*Putharol*, búðar-hol, hill of the booth, at Roineval ; *Tom Phutharol* at Gisla ; in the Flannan Isles is *Màs Phutharol*, buttock of Puarol ; *Gearraidh Phutharol* is east of Eristadh in Uig. *Putharam*, búðar-holm, island of the booth, in Loch Roag. (Cleite) *Putharamarr*, buðar-hamarr, the rock of the bothy. These examples all agree in the change from *b* to *p*.

Dalr, a dale—*Dell*, G. Dail, the dale, with its divisions, Dail o' dheas, South Dell, and Dail o' thuath, North Dell ; *Laxdale*, G. Lacasdail, lax-ár-dalr, salmon-river dale ; *Dibidale*, G. Dìobadail, deep dale ; *Raonadail*, reyni-dalr, rowan-dale ; *Swordale*, G. Suardail, from svörðr, sward, grassy dale ; *Suaineagadail*, from Sveinki, a derivative of Sveinn, Sweynki's dale ; *Bruadale*, brú-á-dalr, bridge-river dale ; *Eoradale*, G. Eòrradal, eyrar-dalr, beach-dale, cf. Erradale ; *Lundale*, G. Lun-dal, hlunn-dalr, roller-dale (hlunnr was a roller for launching ships ; also, a piece of wood put under a ship when beached in winter) ; *Capadal*,

kappa-dalr, champion's dale ; *Ulladale*, Ulli's
dale ; *Langadale*, long dale.

Egg, an edge, ridge—*Eig bheag* and *Eig mhór*,
little ridge and big ridge at Bragar moor ; *Druim
na h-Eige*, back of the ridge (a tautology), at
Galson.   Apt to be confused with G. eag, a notch.

Ey, an island—appears terminally as -*a*, -*ay*, G.
-*aidh*.   *Orasay* (a common name) is Orfris-ey,
ebb-isle, an island which is joined to the mainland
at low tides ; the Gaelic equivalent is Eilean
Tioram, Dry Island ; *Bernera*, Björn's isle ;
Vatersay, vatns-ey, water-isle ; *Berisay*, bergs-ey,
precipice-island ; Captain Thomas' byrgis-ey does
not suit the phonetics.   It was on the rock of
Berisay that Neil Macleod made his three years'
stand (1610-1613), before he was ultimately
captured and executed.[1]   *Risay*, hrís-ey, brushwood isle ; *Rosaidh*, hross-ey, horse-isle ; *Eilean
Thorraidh*, Thori's isle ; *Pabay*, priest's isle ;
Rona, hraun-ey, rough isle ; *Stangraidh*, stangar-
ey, pole-isle ; *Flodday*, fljót-ey, float isle ;
Tannray, t-hafnar-ey, haven-isle, cf. Tanera ;
Vuya, G. Eilean Bhuidha, bú-ey, house isle ;
Valasay, ? hvalls-ey, whale isle.

Eyrr, a beach—*Eoropie*, G. Eòrrabaidh, eyrar-bœr,
beach-town ; *Earshader*, beach-settlement (saetr) ;
Eàrrabhig, eyrar-vík, beach bay ; *Eirera*, beach-
river.

Fit, meadowland by the seaside or by a river—
Fidi-gearraidh, Fitja-gerðr, the enclosed meadow
land ; *Fidi-geodha*, the cove of the pasture land.

---

[1] Gregory, *History of the Western Highlands*, p. 336.

Fjara, ebb-tide—*Feori-seadar* (Fjori-shader), fjoru-
setr, the shieling by the ebb-tide.

Fjall, a fell, a hill—terminal as *-val, -al, -bhal* ;
Hestaval, hesta-fjall, horse or stallion hill ;
Cleitshal, rocky hill, from klettr ; *Grinnabal*,
green hill ; *Mealasbhal,* ? Link-stead fell ; *Soval*,
sauᚦa-fjall, sheep-fell ; *Cracabhal*, kraku-fjall,
crow-fell ; *Ròineval*, hraun-fjall, rough-ground
fell ; *Suainebhal*, Sweyn's fell.

Fjörᚦr, a firth—*Loch Seaforth*, G. Loch Sìthphort,
sjà-fjörᚦr, sea-firth ; *Loch Hamasord*, G. Loch
Chamasort, hvamms-fjörᚦr, firth of the grassy
slope ; *Eilean Iubhard* or *Eu-ord*, ey-fjörᚦr, isle-
firth (transferred from the firth to the island).

Fors, a waterfall—*Abhainn an Fhorsa*, Fall river ;
Forsnaval, Fall fell ; *Forsnavat*, Fall loch, both
with suffixed article.

Gás, goose—Gais'a-murr or Gashamurr, goose rock ;
Gàs-cleite, Gasclete, goose-cliff ; *Gàs-sker*, goose-
skerry : *Gàsaval*, goose-fell or hill.

Gjá, a cleft—borrowed into Gaelic as geodha ; from
the genitive plural gjar we get *Gidhur-ol*, hill of
the rift or chasm.

Gljúfr, an abrupt descent in the bed of a river,
becomes *Globhur* ; *Loch a' Ghlobhuir* (O.S.M.
Loch a' Ghluair), loch of the abrupt descent. It
also appears to take the form gleadhar with a
Gaelic plural from Gleadhairean ; *Gleann Ghleadh-
arean*, in Carloway twice.

Gróf, a pit—Terminally *gro*, a very common stream
ending ; probably originally applied to streams

which cut their way through peat, cf. mó-gröf, a peat trench ; *Allagro*, eels' stream ; *Clisgro*, klifs-gro, stream of the cliff ; *Hallagro*, hallr, a slope, stream of the slope ; *Hundagro*, stream of the dogs ; *Molagro*, stream of the pebbly beach ; *Fidigro*, the stream of the meadow land ; *fit* means meadow land by the seaside or by a river ; *Allt Miagro*, narrow stream, allt being pleonastic.

Háls, neck, becomes in Gaelic *hàis*, *l* being dropped before *s* ; *Gob Hàis*, point of the neck, at North Tolsta, where there is a neck between a rock and the land.

Hlaða, to load—*Lathamur*, hlað-hamarr, loading rock, a projecting rock where ships could be loaded. It is also applied to steep rocks on the moor.

Holl, a hill—*Toll*, the hill, in Barvas and elsewhere ; *Tollar*, a ridge at Laimishader, shows the plural hollar, the hills.

Holmr, a holm, islet, appears in Gaelic as Tolm, whence Duntuilm, in Skye ; terminally it shrinks to *(a)m*. *Craigeam*, kraku-holmr, crow-isle ; *Greinam*, green isle ; *Lingam*, heather-isle.

Holt, rough hill ground — *Erisolt*, Erik's rough pasture or outrun ; *Neidalt*, neyt-holt, the rough cattle outrun ; *Sgianailt*, skjóna-holt, the holt of the dappled horse.

Hross, a horse—*Rossay*, hross-ey, horse-island, cf. Eilean nan Each ; *Rosnish*, horse point, both at Marvig ; *Rossol*, hross-holl, horse-hill, at Gress ; *Rosnavat*, loch of the horses, on Laxdale Moor, with the article suffixed ; *Rosmul*, hrossa-múli,

the ridge of the horses ; *Rosgil*, at back of Cross-
bost, the gulley of the horse.

Klettr, a rock, cliff—*Loch Rahacleit*, rauδr-klettr,
red-cliff ; *Breacleit*, from breiδr, broad-cliff ;
Breasclete, breiδ-áss-klettr, broad-ridge cliff ;
Enaclete, enni-klettr, brow-cliff ; *Loch Mheatha-
cleit*, mjó-klettr, narrow-cliff ; *Sgiobacleit*, skipa-
klettr, ship-cliff ; *Eacleit*, ey-klettr, island cliff ;
Haclete and *Taclete*, há-klettr, high-cliff.

Kuml, a mound, burial place (Lat. cumulus)—
Tràigh Chumil, beach of the cairn.

Mjó, from mjór, narrow—*Miagro*, G. Meathagro,
narrow stream ; *Meathadal*, or Miadal, the narrow
dale ; *Meathanish*, or Mianish, the narrow ness ;
Meathacleit, the narrow cliff ; *Miasaid*, at Loch
Langavat and Loch Skibacleit, is for mjó-sund,
narrow sound ; also Cnoc a' Mhiasaid at Raanish.

Myrk, dark—*Mircavat*, dark loch, cf. Gael. Dubh-
loch ; *Mircol*, dark hill, at Valtos ; Uamha
Mhircol, cave of the dark hill, at Uig.

Nes, a ness, cape—*Shilldinish*, sílda-nes, herring-
point ; *Steinish*, stone-point ; *Roishnish*, hross-
nes, horse-point ; *Aignish*, egg-nes, ridge or
edge point ; *Stathanis*, stödvar-nes, harbour-
point ; *Callanish* or *Callernish*, derived by Captain
Thomas from kjalar-nes, keel-ness ; but as there
is no trace of the *kj* sound in the Gaelic pronoun-
ciation, this must be regarded doubtful ; *Aird
Thoranish*, Thori's point ; *Dùn Bhorranish*.
from Borgar-nes, fort-promontory ; *Breidhnis*,
broad ness ; *Ranish*, roe ness ; *Linish*, flax ness ;
Phenish, fé-nes, sheep-ness ; *Griamanais*, Grim's

ness; *Arnish*, eagle-ness; *Drobhinish*, from dröfn, spotted ness; *Bratanish*, from brattr, steep ness; *Altanish*, from alft, swan, swan-ness; *Rudha Robhanish* (the Butt of Lewis), from rof, an opening, Hole-ness—with reference to the "Eye of the Butt."

Neyti, from naut, cattle—*Neidelan*, neyti-land, cattle land, at Shader, Barvas, and Mealista; *Neadavat*, neyti-vatn, cattle loch; *Naidaval*, cattle hill; *Neadaclif*, the cattle's cliff; *Neidal*, at North Tolsta, cattle dale.

Papi, priest—*Pabbay*, priest's isle; *Bayble*, priest's town.

Sandr, sand—*Sandwick*, G. Sandabhaig, sandy bay; Sandavat, sandy loch.

Sauðr, a sheep—*Soval*, sauða-fjall, sheep-hill, thrice in Lochs; (Gearraidh) *Shoais*, sauða-áss, ridge of the sheep; *Soray*, one of the Flannan isles, sauðar-ey, sheep isle.

Setr, a residence, mountain pasture, dairyland—*Shader*, G. Siadair; *Sheshader*, sjá-setr, sea-stead; *Cuidha-seadar*, kvía-setr, fold stead; *Laimishader*, lamb-stead; *Linshader*, G. Lìseadair (*i* nasal), flax-stead, cf. Linside, G. Lionasaid, in Sutherland; *Kershader*, kjörr-setr, copse-stead; *Ungashader*, Ung's stead; *Carishader*, Kari's stead; *Grimshader*, Grim's-stead; *Hamarshader*, hammer stead; hamarr means a hammer-shaped crag, or a crag standing out like an anvil; *Sulishader*, pillar stead, or solan-geese stead; *Earshader*, G. Iar-seadair, ? beach-stead; *Horshader*, Thori's stead.

Síld, a herring—*Shildinish*, herring point ; *Sildam*, síld-holm, herring-isle.

Skáli, a shieling, plural skálar — *Scàilleir*, the shielings, two hills south of Valtos, Uig.

Sker, a skerry or rock—*Vatisker*, vatns-sker, water-skerry, covered at high tide ; *Màs-sgeir*, sea mew skerry ; *Sgarbh-sgeir*, Skarfs-sker, Cormorant skerry ; *Hùnisgeir*, húna-sker, young bear skerry ; but Húnn may be a proper name ; *Cleibisgeir*, ?from kleppr, a plummet, lump ; *Cobha-sgeir*, kofa sker, young puffin skerry.

Skip, a ship—*Sgiobadal*, ship dale ; *Sgioba-geodha* in Rona, ship cove.

Staðr, a farm, stead, appears terminally as *-sta*. *Tolsta*, Tollosta (Blaeu), Toli's stead ; *Mealasta*, Link's stead, from melr ; *Scàrasta*, Skára-staðr, from skári, a young sea-mew ; *Eirasta*, beach-stead ; *Grimersta*, Grim's stead ; *Sgiogarsta*, Skeggi's stead ; *Mangarsta*, múnka-staðr, Monks' stead ; *Torastaigh*, Thori's stead ; *Cabharstaigh*, ? kafa-staðr, diving-stead.

Stöð, a harbour—*Stathanis*, near the Butt ; *Port a' Stoth*, south of it. a tautology.

Sund, a sound—*Miasaid*, a name recurring several times, mjó-sund, narrow sound.

Tjörn, a small lake, tarn—(Loch an) *Tighearna* in Bernera.

Urð, a heap of stones on the sea beach, or from a landslip—*Urranan*, at Barvas Moor, with Gaelic plural ; *Loch Urradhag* or Ourahag, urð-vík, the bay of the heap of stones, near Arnol ; another place of the same name is at the Carloway shore.

Vágr, a creek, bay, appears as -*way*, -*ay*, ; Gael.
-*bhaidh*, -*aidh*.   *Carloway*, Karl's bay ; *Storno-*
way, G. Steòrnabhadh, stjórnar-vagr, steerage
bay or rudder bay ; cf. Loch Steornua in Argyle ;
Loch Thealasbhaigh, hellis-vágr, cave-bay ; *Leir-*
avay, G. Lèurabhaigh, muddy bay ; leir, mud ;
Loch Thamnabhaigh, hafnar-vágr, harbour-bay ;
cf. Hamnavoe and Hamnadale in Shetland ;
Tarravay, Thara-vágr, seaweed bay.

Vatn, water, a lake, appears terminally as -*vat*,
Gael. -*bhat*.   *Grinnavat*, green loch ; *Sandavat*,
sandy loch ; *Ullavat*, Ulli's loch ; *Langavat*, long
loch ; *Baccavat*, ridge loch ; *Tarstavat*, t-hjarta-
vatn, stag loch ; *Lingavat*, heather loch ; *Gros-*
avat, grassy loch ; *Allavat*, eels' loch ; *Raoinavat*,
reyni-vatn, rowan loch ; *Scaravat*, young sea-mew
loch ; *Breivat*, broad loch ; *Maravat*, gull loch ;
Drollavat, from troll, haunted loch ; *Laxavat*,
salmon river loch ; *Tungavat*, tongue-shaped loch ;
Seavat, sjá-vatn, sea loch ; *Strandavat*, strand
loch ; *Loch Mhileavat* (from milli, between),
between (the) lochs ; *Stacsavat*, stakks-á-vatn,
stack-river loch.

Vík, bay, appears terminally as -*uig*, -*bhic* ; hence
the parish of Uig.   *Miavaig*, mjó-vík, narrow
bay ; *Kiriwick*, from kyrr, quiet bay ; *Seilibhig*,
seal bay ; *Breivig*, broad bay ; *Earavick*, G. Iara-
bhaig, beach bay ; *Fivig*, G. Fiabhaig, fjár-vik,
sheep bay ; *Smiuig*, Cave bay ; *Brataig*, steep
bay ; *Maravaig*, sea-gull bay ; *Nasabhig*, nose
bay ; *Glumaig*, Glumr's bay ; *Islivig*, ís-hlið-vík,
ice-slope bay.

ADDITIONS AND CORRECTIONS.

Gleann a' Ghràig, between Strathcarron and Carn Bhren. The large flat rock where tinkers camp by the roadside between Ardgay and Fearn is *Leac a' Ghràig.*

Eileag Bada Challaidh (also éileag Bad-cailidh), the Eileag of the Hazel Clump (near Amat). For *eileag* see *Sian na h-Eileig.* With *callaidh* cf. *Bealach Collaidh.* There used to be a saying in Kincardine that the people of old could never be starved into submission so long as they held Eileag Bada Challaidh and *Cairidh Cinn-chàrdain,* the weir of Kincardine. This famous salmon weir was near the Parish Church, and its name survives in *Eilean na Cairidh,* Isle of the Weir, now a nice field reclaimed from the sea.

Leac a' Chlamhain — Flagstone of the Kite, is a flat stone near the U.F.C. Manse ; cf. Gledfield.

P. 4. *Alltan nam Fuath* — Burnlet of the Spectres, comes through the *Gearrchoill,* Short Wood, not Garbh Choille.

Conachreig — Combination of rocks ; cf. Cona Glen, G. *Conaghleann,* etc.

Allt a' Bhramain — the Devil's Burn, flows through Ard-chronie.

Caoilisidh — the Place of the Narrow.

An Claigionn — the Skull, is a hillock near Caolaig Bridge. Also, *Ach-a-Chlaiginn,* Field of the Skull ; *An Cragan Soilleir,* the bright little rock ; *Poll nan Gobhar,* Goats' Slack ; *Creag Ghlas,* Gray Rock.

P. 5. *Clais a' Bhaid-choill* — Hazel Clump Dell.

P. 6. *Crianbhad* — Small Clump or Withered Clump, not Grian-bhad of O.S.M.

18

P. 7. *Coylum,* better from *cuing-leum ;* same meaning.

P. 9. *Bàrd,* common in the Reay Country, and derived from English *ward ;* not Norse.   *Asaireadh* or *asaradh* is elsewhere *fasanadh,* good hill pasture.

P. 11. *Meall na h-ùgaig,* not Meall na Cuachaige.   The latter is the O.S.M. form, which I was wrongly informed to be correct.   ? cf. Sròn 'n ùgaidh.

P. 11. *Coire Bhenneit*—Near Meall Bhenneit.

P. 12. *Creag(a) Raoiridh* means Ryrie's Rock; cf. *Leac Roithridh.*

P. 15. *Loch Struaban.*   The MS. referred to is in the Advocates' Library, Edinburgh.

P. 15. On last line read *dheirg.*

P. 16. Abhainn dubhach—Unverified and doubtful.

„   *Allt Coire Ruchain,* not Allt coir an Rùchain (O.S.M.).

P. 17. *Allt Eileag*—Doubtless means Burn of Eileag's ; for *eileag, v.* p. 237, and cf. Eileag Bada-Challaidh.

„   Oykell, G. Oiceil.

P. 20. Achnagart—read *enclosures.*

EDDERTON.

Altnamain—the Inn is called *Tigh a' Mhonaidh,* Moor House ; also often " the Half-way House."

Cnoc a' Chlaiginn—Skull Hill, a little to the south of Easter Fearn ; otherwise called

Cnoc Dubh eadar dà Allt a' Chlaiginn—Black Hill between two burns of the Skull.   Here tradition locates a Scandinavian treasure.

P. 25. *Baile na' Foitheachan* means Stead of the places of lawns or greens ; *faithche* has come to be sounded foi' ; cf. Foy Lodge.

P. 26. *Pollagharry*—Pool of the Cutting; a thunderbolt once fell here, and made a cutting in the soil.   Gearraidh in the other sense, N. gerði, is not found on the Mainland.

P. 27. 1. 8, for " *seems to be* " read " *is.*"

„   *Daan,* cf. Introduction, p. 1.

P. 28. Cnocan na Goibhnidh should probably be *Cnocan na' Gaimhne,* Hillock of the Stirks.

P. 29. Allt na Corrach read *Allt na' Coireach.*

P. 30. Cnoc Thorcaill (O.S.M.), read *Cnoc Chorcaill;* also *Coire Chorcaill.*

„ *Cnoc a' Chlachain:* the clachan in question was rather the old church of Kincardine.

P. 31. *Dùn Alaisgaig* means the Fort of Ali's Strip, N. Ali-skiki.

TAIN.

P. 32. Baile-Dhubhthaich bòidheach, Dornoch na goirt,
Sclobul nan ùbhlan, 's Bil an arain choirc ;
Eiribul nan coileagan, Dùn-Robain a' chàil,
Goillspidh nan sligean dubh, 's Drum-muigh a' bhàrr.

This, one of our best known topographical rimes, characterises Tain, Dornoch, Skibo, Bil, Embo, Dunrobin, Drummuie. Translation spoils it.

P. 35. *Cnoc nan Aingeal* is the small hill, now cut through by the railway, north-west of the old chapel; the road to the cemetery crosses the cutting by a bridge.

„ Cnocanmealbhain : read *Cnocan Mealbhain,* Hillock of the best grass.

P. 36. *An aideal* cannot come from N. vaðill ; Norse ð would here disappear in Gaelic.

P. 37. l. 3, *drochaid an obh*: *bh* is here sounded long; pronounced *ow,* with a lingering emphasis on *w.*

P. 38. Muileann and Allt Luaidh : better *Luathaidh.*

P. 40. l. 14, read *dhuibh.*

FEARN.

P. 41. *Balmuchy:* muchaidh may be Pictish, cf. Welsh *mochyn,* a pig. If so the old form would have been Pitmuchy, with which cf. Pitmachie in Strathbogie.

P. 43. *Allan:* Clay of Allan is in G. *Criadhach Alain Mhóir,* Clayey Place of Meikle Allan. The *criadhach* is a Gaelic echo of Pictish *Allan,* meaning apparently " a swampy place." Cf. the Pictish Lovat, root *lov,* wash ; translated into Gaelic as *a' Mhor'oich,* the sea plain.

P. 45. l. 10, read *a' chailleach.*

l. 14, read Gòt ; so also in l. 16, and p. 48, l. 29.

P. 47. l. 8, read Rockfield.

NIGG.

P. 51. *Pitcalnie*, G. Baile-chailnidh : this difficult name may be
from the root seen in Gaulish, *călĕto-*, hard, representing
a primitive Călĕtoniācon.

P. 53. *Big Audle :* derivation possible but doubtful.   G. not found.

P. 54. Sul Bà, read Sùil Bà.

P. 56. l. 11, read dhuibh.

„ ll. 12, 13, for *an port* read *am port.*

P. 57. l. 20, read tòin.

LOGIE.

At Shandwick Farm is a tiny burn called *Dourag,* the
Little Water, from O.G., dobur ; cf. Aldourie, Dores, in
G. Dobhrag.

KILMUIR.

P. 63. l. 23, read Smiths'.

Apitauld : the first syllable is *àth,* a kiln.   There was of
old a kiln close to the site of the present smithy, and
the name applies only to that spot.   The old ford on the
Balnagown Water was lower down.

High up on the hill above Inchandown Farm is *Clach
Seipeil Odhair,* Stone of the Dun Chapel ; a large
granite boulder, which is now near the Newmore march,
and of old probably formed part of it.

P 68. *Strathrory : uar* in the Reay Country means a landslip, as
well as a torrent of rain ; near the Coag there are great
slides of boulder clay on the steep banks of the river.
Cf. *Allt Uaraidh,* behind Abriachan, Inverness.

Plubag, the little " plumping " place ; from a tiny gurgling
burn ; cf. an Uidh Phlubach.

ROSSKEEN.

P. 70. Invergordon : in G. *an Rudha,* the Point ; " I was in
Invergordon," bha mi air an Rudha.   I have also heard
Rudha Nach-breacaidh.   Port Nach-breacaidh, Invergor-
don Ferry.

P. 71. *Achnacloich :* G. Ach' na Cloi', Field of the Stone.   There
must have been *one* stone in some way remarkable.   In
point of fact, there are some very large travelled
boulders of granite in the place.

P. 72. Above Cuillich is *Bail' a' Mhullaich*, Summit Stead. Cuillich itself, G., Cuinglich, is better taken as *cuing-laich*, from cuinge, narrowness. The meaning is in any case the same.

„ Coire-ghoibhnidh : better *Coire Ghaimhne*, Stirk Corry.

P. 73. 1. 2. *Mylne-chaggane* of the record is still remembered as *Muileann a' Chlagain*, Mill of the Clapper. It was on the Strathrusdale river (or Black River), about 200 yards from its junction with the Averon. The straight, steep road, a quarter of a mile west of Tolly Farm, between the public road and the White Bridge on Averon was of old, " before it was made," called *Cadha Fionntain*, Finntan's Path, obviously an ancient name.

Nearly a mile east of Dalnacloich Farm, in the march between Newmore and Ardross, and close to the south side of the public road, is a big granite block called now *Clach Ceann-a-mheòir*, as if Stone of the Finger-tip. The story goes that here a lad's finger point was cut off to ensure his recollecting the position of the march. In 1571 it appears in an account of the marches of Newmore as " the marchstone called Clachinnumoir," which suggests the real name to be *Clach an Neo' Mhòir*, Stone of Newmore, of which the modern form is a corruption.

ALNESS.

P. 75. *Alness :* cf. also Alauna, Alaunos, and Alaunium in Gaul (Holder: *Alt-Celtischer Sprachshatz*).

P. 76. *Balnacraig :* parts of Balnacraig Farm, north of the public road, are called *Caoilisidh*, the narrow place or stripe ; and the *Siab ;* cf. siaban, a sand drift.

Dalgheal is locally pronounced in G. Dail-ghil, a locative form meaning " at the white dale." In English it is pronounced Dal-yil, thus proving its identity with the common Dalziel.

P. 77 *Fyrish :* the spelling *Foireis* is inadequate: rather Faoighris. I fear that the name is Pictish.

P. 78. *An Lainn :* also called *Lainn a' Choirc,* the Oat-flat or
enclosure.   The Blàr Borraich is a somewhat extensive
moor, and covers more than is contained in Lainn.   The
narrow spit of land between Allt nan Caorach and the
Allt Granda at their junction is *an t-Eilean Dubh,* the
Black Isle—a peninsula.

„   *Meall an Tuirc :* from some points near Glenglass School
this hill is the perfect picture of a colossal boar.

P. 79. Cnoc Coille Bhrianain I have now got as *Cnoc Gille Mo-
Bhrianaig,* Hill of the follower of St Brendan.   This is
doubtless the genuine form.   On *Cnocan,* the Hillock, in
Glenglass, are *Blàr nan Ceann* and *Fuaran Blàr nan
Ceann,* Moor of the Heads and Well of the Moor of the
Heads, with legend of a combat.   At Tigh na Creige
moss is *Fuaran Bod-muice.   Fuaran Dhruim Dhuibh
Ruigh Bhannaich,* Well of the Black Ridge of the
Bannock-slope, is behind *Cnoc na Mòine,* Moss-Hill, in
Glenglass.   *Fuaran Seachd-goil,* Well of seven Boilings,
is at *Ruigh 'n Fhuarain,* Well-slope, between Boath and
Glenglass.   It is said to bubble up through the sand in
seven distinct jets.   *Tòrr a' Bholcain* is a knoll near the
path between B. and G. as one comes in sight of
Swordale.   *Torran Dubh Gob na Coille,* Black knoll (at
the) Point of the Wood, is near the same path where the
burn bends at right angles near the Boath peat-mosses.
There is not a vestige of wood anywhere near it.

Clach nam Ban, The Women's Stone, is north of Kildermorie ; so called from some women having perished
there in a snowstorm while crossing from Strathcarron.

A' Chlach Goil, the Boiling Stone, is on the drove road
between Strathrusdale and Ardgay.   Those who used
the road boiled water there.

P. 83. *Multovy,* better Pictish *Moltomagos,* wedder plain.   The
original Multovy was the level part ; west of it, now part
of the farm, was *Baile nan Seobhag,* Hawks' Stead.   The
long *Clais* at the back was reclaimed within the last
thirty years or so.

P. 83. *Céislein* : there are two, viz., *Céislein a' Choire Dhuibh* and *Céislein a' Choire Bhreac* (sic). For meaning cf. *Céis Coraind*, Sow of Corann, the name of a hill in Ireland.

„ *Averon* : the termination *-on* more probably represents primitive *-ona* ; Pictish. On the Averon below the intake to Dalmore is *Poll a' Charrachaidh*.

KILTEARN.

South of Loch Glass is a rocky place called *an Fhiaclaich*, the Place of Teeth (O.S.M. Feachdach) ; also *Beul na Fiaclaich*, Mouth of the Tooth-place, and *Coire Granda na Fiaclaich*, Ugly Corry of, etc. Near this is *Meall a' Chrimeig* (long *m*). At west end of Caoilisidh, above the Lodge, is *Meall-a-Bheithinnidh* (? *Mheithinnidh*)— close *ei* ; cf. Bealach Bheithinnidh. West of it is *an Toman Cóinnich*, the Mossy Knoll, and between the two is *Creag 'ic Gille Chéir*, Rock of the son of the Swarthy Lad.

P. 87. Balcony : the narrow flat between the Allt Granda and Allt-na-Sgiach to the south of the public road is known in Gaelic as *Innis a' Choltair*, Coulter Mead. There is also *Sgorr a' Choltair*, Point of the Coulter, in Glenglass. *Coltar* is an early Irish loan from Lat. *culter*, and seems to have been applied to places from their shape, as it was to the razorbill (*coltraich*), from the form of his bill. Cf. Portincoulter, the old name for the Meikle Ferry, where there is a coulter-shaped point on the Ross side. The various Culters and Coulters, popularly derived from *cùl-tìr*, back land—a rather harsh and doubtful formation —may be compared. They are now pronounced Couter, in early spelling Cultyr, which phonetically represents the Scottish pronunciation before *l* became silent.

P. 91. *Claon Uachdarach*, Upper Clyne, is now Woodlands.

P. 92. On Allt na Làthaid is *Drochaid na Làthaid*, otherwise *Drochaid Chrabart*. *Fèith Dhubh 'ic Gillandrais*, Gillanders' Black Hag, is said to be on the march between Tulloch, Kildermorie, and Dianaich.

P. 93. *Bealach Collaidh* is the gap between Inchbae and Coire-bhacaidh. Near it is *Bealach nam Bròg*, Gap of the Brogues, the scene of a famous fight between the Munros and the Mackenzies.

KILLEARNAN.

P. 146. l. 8, read fàilligh.

l. 12, for " of " read " cf."

CONTIN.

Clach Und(a)rain (possibly Chund(a)rain) is at the head of Strathconon. ? Cf. Coire Chundrain.

P. 154. *Main*, G. Mèinn, is at the present day understood to denote the district of which Porin is part. This is about three miles east of Invermany. In view of its being a district name it is difficult to connect with G. mèinn, ore ; more probably Pictish ; ? root seen in G. mèith, sappy ; Welsh mwydo, soften.

Conon Bridge is in G. *Drochaid Sguideil*.

KINTAIL.

P. 179. *Inverinate*. For the dropping of *dh* in Inbhir-dhuinnid, cf. Inver-uglas for *Inbhir-dhubhghlais* ; Aberdeen, G. Obair-eathain for Obair-dheathain. The possibility of this dropping of *dh* is always worth considering in cases where Inver or Aber is immediately followed by a vowel in Gaelic pronunciation, *e.g.*, Abriachan, G. Ob'r-itheachan.

LOCHCARRON.

P. 199. Coire Fionnaraich—*fionnar*, cool is from *fionn-* or *ionn-* to, against, and *fuar* ; M. Ir. indfhuar.

APPLECROSS.

About a mile west of *Airigh-Dhriseach*, Bramble Shieling, is *Draoraig*, N. dreyr-vík, Blood Bay.

GAIRLOCH.

P. 221. l. 4, *faithir* is probably *fo-thìr*, under-land ; it can hardly be the Irish *fachair*.

P. 229. Rudha an t-Sàsain : the *Sàsan* is a rock on the lee side of which boats ride by the painter, which affords the most satisfactory explanation of the name.

P. 239. Loch na Fideil : the Fideal, whose haunt was in this loch, was at last encountered by a strong man named Eòghainn. " Bha còmhrag eadar Eòghainn agus an Fhideal. ' Ceum air do cheum, Eòghainn,' ars' an Fhideal, 's i teannadh air an duine. ' Ceum air do cheum, a Fhideil,' ars' Eòghainn, 's e teannadh air an Fhideil a rithist. Mharbh Eòghainn an Fhideal, agus mharbh an Fhideal Eòghainn." There was a combat between Ewen and the Fideal. " A step on your step, Ewen." said the Fideal, pressing on the man. "A step on your step, Fideal," said Ewen, pressing hard in turn. Ewen killed the Fideal, and the Fideal killed Ewen. (It is worth noting that the Fideal is feminine.)

LOCHBROOM.

P. 255. Glutan, G. *Glotan.*

Bad-a-Chrònaidh and *Clais Bad-a-Chrònaidh* are at Bad-rallach ; cf. Ardchronie.

INDEX.

INDEX.